A Parent's Guide® to
Toronto

Ilona Biro

parent's
guide
press
Los Angeles, CA
www.pgpress.com

A Parent's Guide® to
Toronto

Text and Maps © Mars Publishing 2002

All photos courtesy of Ontario Tourism

ISBN: 1-931199-17-5

This book, and all titles in the Parent's Guide series, are available for purposes of fund raising and educational sales to charity drives, fund raisers, parent or teacher organizations, schools, government agencies and corporations at a discount for purchases of more than 10 copies. Persons or organizations wishing to inquire should call Mars Publishing at 1-800-549-6646 or write to us at *sales@marspub.com*.

At the time of publication of this book, all of the information contained within was correct to the best of our knowledge. If you find information in this book that has changed, please contact us. Even better, if you have additional places to recommend, please let us know. Any included submissions to the new edition of this book will get the submitter a by-line in the book and a free copy of any Mars publication.

Please contact us at *parentsguides@marspub.com*

parent's guide press

Edwin E. Steussy, CEO and Publisher
Lars X. Peterson, Project Editor
Michael P. Duggan, Graphic Artist

PO Box 461730
Los Angeles CA 90046

contents

contents

acknowledgements

I'm thrilled to have written a guide to Toronto, a city that holds countless surprises for those who live here and those who visit. But I never could have managed it without the help and encouragement of my wonderful husband, Jeff Silverstein, and my dear mom, Melanie Biro. Both of them happily baby-sat, cooked meals, read drafts and kept the home fires burning while I went about visiting and gathering information.

More thanks of a different kind go to my terrific kids, Max and Maya, who enabled me to see things from their perspective, which, after all, is what this book is all about. They also did one of the hardest things a kid can do while I researched this book: they showed great patience while I took notes, did impromptu interviews and otherwise made them wait, and wait and wait!

For very practical help, I thank Rey Stephens of Tourism Ontario and Ellen Flowers at Tourism Toronto, who assisted me with mounds of information and access to Toronto's best-known places. I also owe a huge debt of gratitude to Brenda McGowan and Heather Dunsmuir of York Region Tourism, and Patti Watson of Durham Tourism who showed me the way – quite literally – around the highways and byways of their beautiful regions. Now I know where to go, and when, to experience some of the best attractions in the Toronto area.

The staff at Parent's Guide Press were helpful, patient and enthusiastic, and gave me tremendous support during the writing of this book. Thanks also to the countless parents I spoke with who went and saw and told me about great places to visit and include.

And last but not least, I have to thank Bruce Bishop for all his support, which was much appreciated!

— Ilona Biro, October 2002

Introduction

For many years, a series of well-meaning slogans – Toronto the Good, The City That Works, New York Run by the Swiss – helped to perpetuate the notion that Toronto was a safe, well-run, but quiet sort of place. That reputation was largely due to the 1911 Lord's Day Act, which forbade all public activity except churchgoing on Sundays. 'Toronto the Good' prevailed until the Forties, when, ever so slowly, the city began to loosen its grip on its citizens. Cocktail lounges were approved in 1947, followed by Sunday sporting events in 1950. Yet until 1960, no movies were screened on Sundays, and a ban on Sunday shopping remained in force until the early 1990s, (though the law was widely ignored by then).

It all sounds a bit dull now, and completely unlike the vibrant city I've grown to love. Yes, Toronto functions marvelously well, but it's also pulled off an extraordinary trick: it's managed to combine efficiency with daring, and has become the kind of rare big city that appeals to sophisticated singles and families alike.

I give a lot of credit for this transformation to the many waves of immigrants, who continue to give Toronto a giant dose of the *joie de vivre* it was lacking. For my money, it's these newcomers who've turned Toronto the Good into Toronto the Great. But Toronto's success must also be shared with those citizens who regularly rally to its defense whenever a major development threatens to destroy something they hold dear. When downtown neighborhoods were jeopardized by an expressway, activists banded together to stop its construction, and won. When the city wanted to "clean up" Kensington market, local residents refused, knowing it would destroy all the qualities that make the market as colourful as it is. Again and again, Torontonians have stood up for their neighborhoods, making them – and the larger city – a healthier and more viable place to be. It's their visions, as diverse as the population itself, that have all worked their magic in some small way.

Introduction

While I will sing the praises of Toronto in every season, from June until October, it's one long party, with festivals and special events happening virtually every day of the week. And every attraction, no matter how small or large, caters to the youngest of participants, making it hard for families to know where to begin. Depending on the month, you might find us samba-ing alongside the Carnival parade, splashing down at a space-age water park on the lakeshore, or milking cows at Toronto's inner-city farm. In winter months, museums and galleries welcome families with top-notch programs and entertainment, while athletic types hit the cross-country ski trails and lively community ice rinks.

While Torontonians (in true Canadian fashion) continue to downplay their city's successes, word is getting out. 'The city that works' has ranked at or near the top of any international quality of life study you care to mention, and has garnered praise from *Forbes* magazine, the United Nations, and the many millions who come to experience it themselves each year.

For my husband and I, Toronto seemed the natural place to return to, after five years spent working abroad. We worried that Toronto would somehow transform us into over-worked office types. How wrong we were. Ten years later with two small children in tow, we can't think of a place we'd rather be. Come, bring your family, and see exactly what I mean.

Courtesy Ontario Tourism

What a beautiful city!

Introduction

How to Use This Book

The rest of this chapter will help you learn about the city's past, present, and future. In Chapter One you'll find lots of information to help you get the most out of a visit to Toronto, and I'll offer tips on how to get around this sprawling metropolis. The nuts and bolts of traveling to Toronto are in Chapter One too – important phone numbers, family-oriented accommodations, and a bit about Toronto weather, which it pays to prepare for. Also, remember that prices, hours, and other information were accurate when this book went to print, but all of those things are subject to change. It's always best to call ahead and confirm the details.

All kinds of fun stuff!

Courtesy Ontario Tourism

If you're here for only a day or two, consult the Top Ten lists in Chapter Two. I usually balk at listing favourites, but I think it makes sense to cut to the chase when kids are involved. And there's nothing that pleases kids of all ages more than festivals, so along with the Top Tens, see the Appendix – A Kid's Calendar of Festivals and Events, listing the best kid's entertainment month by month. Seasonal favourites like the Santa Claus Parade – a tradition since 1904 – and the Canadian National Exhibition number among them. But it's always good to check local media for new festivals and events – they seem to spring up every year.

The rest of the chapters are organized geographically, so you'll know what activities you can comfortably combine without getting caught up in traffic. Chapter Three starts with the Lakeshore, and subsequent chapters radiate outwards to Downtown, Midtown, the 'burbs' and daytrips. Finally, Chapter Eight is devoted to Niagara Falls, since so many visitors to Toronto combine their trips with a day or two at the Falls.

So let's begin your quick tour of Toronto with a little history – just enough to keep the kids interested during the drive in from the airport.

Introduction

A Brief History of Toronto

It was a French explorer, Etienne Brûlé, who first came to the area where Toronto was founded in 1615. He found a stretch of the lakeshore where several rivers ran down to the lake, where navigating was easy, and the hunting and fishing plentiful. One hundred years later, in 1720, France established a trading post at Toronto, and followed that 30 years later with Fort Rouillé. In 1759, Fort Rouille burned during the British conquest, and the Treaty of Paris in 1763 effectively ended French rule in Canada. From then on, the area was steadfastly British. In 1787, Lord Dorchester, British governor of Quebec, purchased land stretching from Scarborough in the East to Etobicoke in the West from the Mississauga tribe. This parcel of land effectively encompasses the Toronto of today, while Mississauga, Canada's sixth largest city, remains independent, flanking Toronto's west end.

Toronto was founded as the Town of York in 1793 by John Graves Simcoe, the first Governor of Upper Canada, who described the city's site as "better calculated for a frog pond or beaver meadow than for the residence of human beings." (One of Toronto's earliest nicknames was Muddy York.) Despite that discouraging assessment, it was undeniably desirable territory, and the Americans captured York in the War of 1812, burning down its Parliament Building in the process.

In 1834, York was renamed Toronto, and the first City Council was established, replacing the appointed magistrates. A firebrand politician, William Lyon Mackenzie, became Toronto's first mayor and, a few years later, led a rebellion against the so-called Family Compact – a circle of influential families that effectively ruled the colony. While it did not succeed in ousting the British, (in some ways Canada still hasn't managed that!) it made them sit up and take notice.

The second half of the 19th century was a time of monumental growth. From 1851 to 1901, the population grew from 30,000 to 208,000. During that same period, Toronto opened a stock exchange and inaugurated the Grand Trunk Railway, linking Toronto, Montreal, Quebec City, and Sarnia. By 1861, a horse-powered streetcar was running along Yonge Street to Yorkville, an unabashedly modern development. And a few years later, two key downtown landmarks – Old City Hall and St. James Cathedral – were completed, and Toronto gained stature as one of North America's leading cities.

The Canadian Confederation in 1867 also created the new province of Ontario and made Toronto its capital. Its excellent geographic location made it the hub of economic activity in central Canada and ensured it would be the main link with the huge American market from its earliest days. Cultural life was heady too, with literary gatherings and concerts a regular feature of life in Toronto. The sporting life was lived to the fullest as well, with rowing and yacht clubs active on the lake, and hockey's first Stanley Cup championship held here in 1893.

Introduction

The year 1914 was a pivotal one, when Toronto opened both the Royal Ontario Museum and Union Station. Its beloved hockey team won the coveted Stanley Cup that year and baseball's Babe Ruth hit his first professional home run in a stadium on the Toronto Islands. Word spread fast, and immigrants doubled the population to more than half a million by 1921. Even a globetrotting Ernest Hemingway decided to live in Toronto for a time, finding work as a reporter for the *Toronto Star*.

Like other cities, Toronto limped through the Depression, with thousands of people on relief. But the Second World War brought prosperity, as the city became a training hub and major supplier to the Allied war effort. After the war, model suburbs like Don Mills sprouted up and major industries grew, establishing Toronto as Canada's banking and manufacturing center.

That era of growth and optimism continued through the 1960s and 1970s, when the public purse opened wide to fund major urban projects like the Toronto Zoo, the CN Tower, and Ontario Place. The doors to the country also opened wide, and Toronto became Canada's major beneficiary of immigration. The numbers are staggering: in 1951, the population was 31 percent foreign born, but in 10 short years, it was up to 42 percent. Today the number of foreign-born residents is closer to 50 percent, and the city is a far more interesting place as a result.

By the city's 150th anniversary in 1981, the population was almost four million, and Torontonians wanted an athletics stadium that proved they had arrived. In 1989, they got Skydome, an awesome architectural feat with its then-revolutionary retractable dome. While critics lashed out at its $570 million (US $388 million) cost, the hullabaloo was forgotten a few years later when the Blue Jays won back-to-back World Series championships in 1992 and 1993.

By the mid-1990s, Toronto was hitting its stride, celebrated in a 1996 *Fortune* magazine article proclaiming it the best city in the world in which to work and live. Not long after, the province and the city began sparring over funding of transit, affordable housing, and education. The turbulent period continued when the provincial government decided to amalgamate Toronto and the six cities that surrounded it in a bid to cut costs. Despite vigorous protest from citizens, who felt the strength of the city lay in its decentralized municipalities, the new megacity was born in 1998. Though the worst fears of critics have not materialized, residents are still waiting for the promised benefits of the megacity to appear.

But all that's history now. Today, the confidence people have in the future of Toronto is reflected in the glass towers being erected down by the lakeshore, in the city's recent bid for the 2008 Olympic Games, and most prominently, in the massive 12 billion dollar revitalization project planned for Toronto's waterfront. Once again, Toronto seems to be on the cusp of yet another era of optimism and growth.

Introduction

Toronto Today

Toronto is named after a Huron word meaning 'meeting place,' and there's no more fitting name for a city that the United Nations declared the most multicultural in the world. Home to 4.5 million people from more than 100 countries, Toronto's rich ethnic mix gives the city an energy evident in its bustling neighborhoods. The city's slogan, "Toronto: The World in a City," rings true whenever you sit on a bus or listen to the radio or television. More than 80 languages are spoken widely, and two multicultural television channels broadcast in 50 languages around the clock. The city's 7,000 restaurants include cuisines as exotic as Afghani, Tibetan, and Somali, and city notices are routinely translated into about a dozen languages. Call up Toronto's transit information line and you can get help in 18 languages, from Korean to Farsi to Somali.

So Toronto isn't just a meeting place, but a place of welcoming, where so many groups have found a place to call home. And that carries over into its reputation for safety too. Despite its size, Toronto is actually safer than Montreal or Vancouver, and a good deal safer than most U.S. cities.

Finally, I can't write about Toronto without mentioning its world-class cultural scene. It's the third-largest theatre centre in the world after New York and London, drawing tourists to North American premieres and long-running family shows such as *The Lion King* and *Mamma Mia*. Its annual Festival of Authors draws international writers, and a full slate of ethnic cultural festivals regularly shake up the city with sounds of the global village. Its film festival is legion, and its popularity as a film location has given it the nickname Hollywood North. Walking downtown, you're almost certain to see a film crew transforming Toronto into London or New York – with the help of a few checker cabs or a Union Jack flapping in the wind.

Today, there's renewed energy and commitment to making Toronto an even better place to live. Current plans to revitalize the waterfront have the ambitious goal of improving its entire 46 kilometre (27 mile) length. And citizens are pushing for the development of a local source of renewable energy, likely to take the shape of a wind turbine farm fuelled by the fresh breezes coming off Lake Ontario. With the population projected to grow rapidly in the coming decades, Toronto's challenge will be to manage growth and improve the quality of city life at the same time. So far it's managed that very well.

Chapter One

Toronto Basics

Getting Around

Toronto is easy to navigate, with the CN Tower and the lake as your southern landmarks. British surveyors laid out streets in a grid running north-south or east-west with few exceptions. A good map and this book should be all you'll need to find your way around whether you decide to see it on foot, by car or taxi, or by public transit. The city boasts one of the safest public transit systems in North America, and kids get an extra kick from riding the Red Rockets – Toronto's street-

cars. You can get to distant places like the zoo by bus, and even attractions in the suburbs like Canada's Wonderland and Wild Water Kingdom can be reached via transit.

Courtesy Ontario Tourism

Chapter One

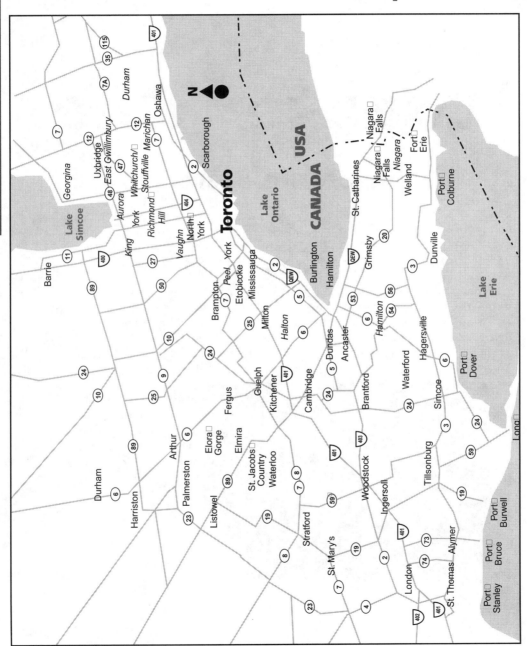

Toronto Basics

Driving In and Around Toronto

If you're determined to see Toronto from the seat of your car, you can count on plenty of parking. In fact, a recent convention of parking experts that met in Toronto declared it one of the best cities for parking, based on number of spaces and cost. Traffic is another story – avoid driving during the afternoon rush hour when things can slow to a crawl on most major streets and highways.

The main east/west arteries are the Gardiner Expressway that runs along the lakeshore, and much farther north, Highway 401. In between there are major streets and avenues starting with King and Queen downtown, then Dundas, College, Bloor, St. Clair, Eglinton, and Lawrence as you head north. The main north-south arteries are the Don Valley Parkway, which runs alongside Toronto's downtown right down to the lake, and on the other side of town, Bathurst Street. The most famous street in Toronto, Yonge Street, is right in the middle and is the world's longest – running 1,896 kilometres (1,178 miles) from Toronto's lakefront up to the town of Rainy River in northern Ontario. The downtown streets you'll be getting most familiar with are Queen, King, Front, Bloor and Dundas.

If you're combining a visit to Toronto with Niagara Falls, the highway that leads west, wrapping around Lake Ontario to Niagara and the U.S. border, is the Queen Elizabeth Way, or QEW.

Taking Transit

The Toronto Transit Commission (known locally as TTC) is a well-run system that encompasses two subway lines, numerous streetcar lines, and hundreds of buses. It's the best option for visitors to Toronto, since you can get everywhere listed in this book (with the exception of the Daytrips chapter and Niagara Falls) by TTC. Pick up a copy of the transit map and keep this number handy: (416) 393-INFO. The transit information line is available in 18 languages, 24 hours a day. TTC fares are $2.25 for adults, $1.50 for students with ID, 50 cents for kids 2 to 12. A day pass is available for $7.50, weekdays after morning rush hour, weekends and holidays all day. On Sundays and holidays, a family pass is just $7.50 and includes up to six people with a maximum of two adults. Strollers and bicycles are welcome on all transit vehicles, outside of morning and afternoon rush hours.

Chapter One

Bicycling

In 1995, Toronto was chosen the best city for cycling in North America by *Bicycling* magazine. There are bike lanes on certain major thoroughfares (you can obtain a cycling map from City Hall), but I wouldn't suggest cycling as a family unless your kids are skilled urban riders. (Getting wheels stuck in streetcar tracks is a common hazard.) You can combine cycling with public transit since bicycles are permitted inside all city buses, streetcars, and subway trains, except during morning and evening rush hours.

A popular place to cycle is car-free Tommy Thompson Park, better known as Leslie Spit, where the wildlife attracts birders from all over the city. Another choice spot would be High Park, which is car-free on Sundays, and for a full day of cycling, you can go from Leslie Spit to High Park along the Martin Goodman Trail, stopping at scenic points along the lakeshore (see page 39 for details.) For families with younger kids, I'd suggest renting bikes and a trailer on the (always car-free!) Toronto Islands, where a lot of Toronto kids get their first bike lessons. Bicycle rentals are available on Ward Island.

Taxis

Taxis in Toronto are clean, safe, and reasonable for short jaunts. It's usually easy to flag one if you're downtown, midtown, or near Harbourfront.
- Beck Taxi – (416) 449-6911
- Co-op Cabs – (416) 504-2667
- Diamond Taxis – (416) 366-6868

Useful Facts

Telephone Codes

Telephone area codes are not optional in Toronto. Every time you dial you must make sure to include them, even if you're dialing locally. Numbers in central Toronto start with 416, while most of the suburban places listed in this guide start with 905.

Weather

Tales of igloos notwithstanding, Toronto has one of Canada's mildest climates. In fact, it's on the same latitude as Cannes, and just one degree north of Boston. Generally speaking, spring and summer temperatures range from 15C (60F) to 25C (80F). During winter months, the average daytime temperature, with the exception of January, the coldest month, hovers just slightly below freezing and a snowfall of more than 10 cm (four inches) is unusual.

Toronto Basics

Holidays

Visitors to Toronto should be aware of these national and provincial holidays:

- **Jan 1** – New Year's Day
- **March/April** – Good Friday, Easter Sunday, and Easter Monday
- **May** – Victoria Day (the Monday on or preceding May 24)
- **July 1** – Canada Day
- **1st Monday in August** – Simcoe Day
- **1st Monday in September** – Labour Day
- **2nd Monday in October** – Thanksgiving Day
- **November 11** – Remembrance Day
- **December 25** – Christmas Day
- **December 26** – Boxing Day

Many seasonal attractions open on Victoria Day, and close either on Labour Day or on Canadian Thanksgivings Day.

Local Media

Any trip to Toronto can start with a quick tour of its four daily newspapers' Internet sites. Another good source of information on current events is Toronto.com and *Today's Parent* magazine website which has a Toronto section.

Major Daily Newspapers

- *The Globe and Mail* (Check weekend edition for events.)
- *Toronto Star* (Thursday listings for weekend events.)
- *Toronto Sun*
- *National Post*

Alternative Weeklies

- *NOW* magazine (Check Seven Days listings of events.)
- *Eye* magazine

Family-oriented Publications

- *City Parent* (Free)
- *Today's Parent* (Available on newsstands.)

Chapter One

Local Television

- CITY TV
- CFMT (multicultural, fun to check out)
- CBC (national broadcaster)
- CFTO – CTV affiliate
- TVO (provincial educational broadcaster)

Selected Radio Stations

- CBC 1 (99.1 FM) – News and information
- CBC 2 (94.1 FM) – Classical music
- CJRT (91.1 FM) – Jazz music
- TALK 640 (AM) – As it sounds
- EZ Rock (99.9 FM) – Easy listening
- CFNY (102.2 FM) – Alternative rock

Numbers to Know

- Emergencies (fire, police, ambulance): 911
- Hospital for Sick Children: (416) 813-1500
- Telehealth Ontario offers free telephone access to registered nurses, 24/7, at 1-866-797-0000
- Access Toronto: (416) 338-0338
- Toronto Public Library's Dial-a-Story line: (416) 395-5400
- Tourism Toronto: (416) 203-2500; 1-800-363-1900
- Tourism Toronto Travel Consultants: 1-800-499-2514
- Traveler's Aid: Union Station: (416) 366-7788, Toronto Coach Terminal: (416) 596-8467, Pearson International Airport: (905) 676-2868
- Road 24-hour closures hotline: (416) 599-9090
- Road 24-hour emergencies hotline: (416) 392-5555
- Road information Toronto: (416) 235-4686; 1-800-268-4686
- Toronto Transit Commission information: (416) 393-INFO
- Airport information: (416) 247-7678
- Toronto Island Ferries: (416) 392-8193
- Toronto Beach hotline: (416) 392-7161

Toronto Basics

Staying in Toronto

Toronto hotels run the gamut from Four Seasons-style luxury to hostel-style modest. Here is an admittedly biased list of some of Toronto's best hotels for families, starting at the top of the scale and ending with the least expensive options.

One of the best ways to save on hotels is to book through Tourism Toronto. They have special packages and some of the best deals going with all the major hotels; they also know what rooms are available at the last minute. Call 1-800-499-2514 to speak with a Tourism Toronto travel consultant.

Once you've checked in for the night, why not call the Toronto Public Library's Dial-a-Story line, (416) 395-5400, where kids of any age can hear stories read in English, French, Italian, Spanish, Portuguese, or Cantonese? Your kids can choose between stories for kids 7 and under, and for older kids up to 12.

Royal York Hotel

100 Front Street West
Toronto, ON, M5J 1E3
(416) 368-2511; 1-800-441-1414
www.fairmont.com

Since opening in 1929, the grand old Royal York has starred in movies and commercials, and has hosted stars of stage and screen as well as three generations of royalty. It also has the largest kitchen in Canada, with 110 chefs capable of preparing a meal for 10,000 people at one sitting! The elegant wedding cake-like building sprawls along Front Street, close to all the downtown action. The Royal York is fond of families – call to find out what packages are on offer.

Royal York facade with doorman

Chapter One

Westin Harbourcastle

One Harbour Square
Toronto, ON, M5J 1A6
(416) 869-1600; 1-800-228-3000
www.westin.com

This hotel is a short walk from Harbourfront, and is adjacent to the Toronto Island Ferries dock. It has excellent family amenities including a Kids Club, playroom, cribs/cots, restaurant and room service with children's meals, bed rails, booster seats, high chairs, and jogger strollers. Kids get a welcome package upon checking in and can dial up bedtime stories on the in-room telephone. The Harbourcastle offers a changing slate of Family Fun packages; call for details.

Delta Chelsea

33 Gerrard Street West
Toronto, ON, M5G 1Z4
(416) 595-1975; 1-800-CHELSEA
www.deltachelsea.com

The Chelsea is right next to Eaton Centre, close to the theatre district and the Yonge subway line. Family Fun suites include kid-friendly items such as bubble bath, kids' bathrobes, step-up stools, children's chairs, cookie jars, alphabet fridge magnets, bunk-beds, and take-home gifts. A special 'Kids Koncierge' and check-in allow kids to take an active role in their stay. Plus, the hotel has a separate pool and hot tub specifically for families with children, and a Children's Creative Centre that provides children with complimentary activities such as arts and crafts, painting, video games, co-operative group play, movie nights, and themed weekends. Older kids can chill in the Starcade Games Room, with video games, a pool table, and air hockey too. The Centre also offers a babysitting service for children aged 3 to 12 years for a nominal fee.

Comfort Suites City Centre

200 Dundas Street East
Toronto, ON, M5A 4R6
(416) 362-7700
www.choicehotels.ca

This one's a favourite with families with its selection of junior, one-bedroom, and two-bedroom suites, many with whirlpools. Nintendo in the rooms, plus a heated indoor pool and whirlpool make this a winner with kids. For parents mixing business with pleasure, this hotel has all the business amenities needed (work desks, ergonomic chairs, track lighting, data ports, fax service). Located a short walk from the Eaton Centre.

Toronto Basics

The Quality Hotel Midtown

280 Bloor Street West
Toronto, ON, M5S 1V8
(416) 968-0010
www.choicehotels.ca

This hotel has a prime location with Yorkville, ROM, and the Gardiner Museum within walking distance and many more accessible via the TTC, which is just steps from the hotel (St. George Station). Pets are welcome at the hotel.

The Quality Suites Airport

265 Carlingview Drive
Toronto, ON, M9W 5G1
(416) 674-8442
www.choicehotels.ca

Ideal for families arriving by plane, and a good location for those traveling to Niagara Falls and for visiting Ontario Science Centre and the Zoo. At the on-site restaurant, Graffiti's Italian Eatery & Saloon, favorites include a huge selection of pizzas and gourmet desserts. Pets are welcome.

Neill-Wycik Summer Hotel

96 Gerrard Street East
Toronto, ON, M5B 1G7
(461) 977-2320; 1-800-268-4358
www.neill-wycik.com/nwh1.htm

A great alternative to a hotel, the Neill-Wycik is open each year from early May to late August. Recently renovated, the hotel features in-room telephones, a breakfast café, laundry and kitchen facilities, daily housekeeping, front desk and concierge service. Located in the heart of downtown Toronto, five minutes from the subway and on bus routes. Rates for 2002 were $62.50 for a quad/family room, which sleeps four.

Toronto International Hostel

76 Church Street East at Adelaide, one street east of Yonge Street
Toronto, ON, M5C 2G1
(416) 971-4440; (877) 848-8737
www.hostellingint-gl.on.ca/toronto

Family rooms are available at Toronto's newly renovated hostel. Inexpensive (about $25 per person, per night), and nicely appointed and convenient to attractions downtown.

Chapter One

Restaurants

Toronto is a veritable feast for foodies with over 7,000 restaurants from Afghani to Italian, plus some marvelous markets for grazing. The eateries I've listed feature the kind of food, the speedy service, and the atmosphere that make them family-friendly. Suffice it to say there are no five star, Michelin guide restaurants included here. But if your family is made up of epicureans who prefer their food fancy, then I suggest checking out the Toronto Life restaurant guide, online at www.torontolife.com. Another guide that lists more reasonable fare can be found on *NOW* magazine's web site at www.nowtoronto.com/minisites/restaurant.

Ways to Save Money

There are all kinds of ways families can save money while exploring Toronto. Many of the attractions have family admission tickets, which can be a big saver. Toronto transit family passes are available on Sundays and holidays for families with up to six members for just $7.50. Many major attractions offer after-hours deals. For instance, you can save $10 at Wild Water Kingdom by going after 4 pm. And grounds admission at Ontario Place is free after 5 pm, a savings of $10 per person.

Last-minute half-price theatre tickets can be had at TOTix, and if you can attend a preview performance or a pay-what-you-can show which many Toronto theatres offer, you can save enough money for a nice dinner out.

If you are planning to see the Falls, make sure to get a one- or two-day Niagara Parks pass. They provide admission into most Parks attractions plus all day passes for the People Mover buses, which are essential for moving easily and cheaply among all the sights along the Niagara Parkway.

Tourism Toronto is an indispensable source for special family packages and deals offered by hotels and entertainment venues. Especially popular are theatre/hotel packages. Their Museums pass includes the Royal Ontario Museum (ROM), Fort York, the birthplace of modern Toronto, and seven other fascinating museums that showcase Toronto's heritage. It's a great value at $25 for adults and $15 for kids 5 to 18 years of age.

Finally, an organization called Attractions Ontario has a passport with coupons that can save you up to $500 on reduced admission rates to many major attractions. If you'd like the Passport Magazine mailed to you, there's a cost of $5. But visit the Attractions Ontario website and you can download and print any or all of the 48 e-coupons, which saves you at places such as Casa Loma or Black Creek Pioneer Village. You can also pick up the Passport Magazine free of charge at any Ontario Tourist Information Centre and through tourism information booths, chambers of commerce, convention bureaus, car rental facilities, and hotels throughout Ontario. Write to them at:

Toronto Basics

Attractions Ontario
133 Richmond Street West, Suite 300
Toronto ON M6C 3M8
(416) 868-4386; 1-877-557-3386
www.attractionsontario.ca

Theatre and Live Entertainment for Families

Toronto has a number of excellent theatre companies catering to children, along with productions such as Disney's *Lion King*, which has been playing at the Princess of Wales theatre in Toronto for several years with no sign of closing.

My family always looks forward to seeing the annual play produced by Cliffhanger Productions, presented outdoors at the Guild Inn in Scarborough. What could be more magical than seeing *The Odyssey* presented among the marble capitals, arches, and columns of the Inn's Greek Theatre stage? Or seeing a French Canadian folk tale played out under the majestic maples in a real forest?

Two children's theatres offering full seasons are Lorraine Kimsa Theatre for Young People and Solar Stage Theatre. There's also Harbourfront's popular series of Cushion Concerts, for kids 5 to 12, on selected Sundays from September to May.

Pack your picnic basket and head to High Park to see the Dream in High Park, Canadian Stage Company's annual Shakespeare play staged on the amphitheatre. Or take in a production at Famous People Players, a world-famous theatre group made up of disabled performers whose marriage of large-scale puppetry with the magic of black light, has astounded audiences around the world. And don't forget to check if the Puppetmongers Powell are presenting a show while you're here. Their annual Christmas show is always a gem, and their school of puppetry offers classes year round.

You can save on ticket prices if you see a preview production or a pay-what-you-can show. Another option is calling up T.O. Tix for same-day half-price tickets to a wide variety of theatre, dance, comedy, opera, and music events. Call (416) 536-6468, ext 40 for availability; tickets must be purchased in person at the T.O. Tix booth, located on level two of the Eaton Centre. Hours are Tues-Sat, noon to 7:30 pm. Tickets for Sunday and Monday performances are sold on Saturdays.

Chapter One

Lorraine Kimsa Theatre for Young People

165 Front Street East
Toronto, ON, M5A 3Z4
(416) 862-2222
www.lktyp.ca

Solar Stage

4950 Yonge Street, lower
level of the Madison Centre
Toronto, ON, M2N 6K1
(416) 368-8031
www.solarstage.on.ca

Harbourfront Cushion Concerts

235 Queen's Quay West
Toronto, ON, M5J 2G8
(416) 973-4000
www.harbourfront.on.ca

Hummingbird Centre

1 Front Street East
Toronto, ON, M5E 1B2
(416) 393-7469
www.hummingbirdcentre.com

Living Arts Centre

4141 Living Arts Drive
Mississauga, ON L5B 5B8
(905) 306-6000
www.livingarts.on.ca

Royal Alexandra Theatre

260 King Street West
Toronto, ON, M5V 1H9
(416) 872-1212
www.mirvish.com

Princess of Wales Theatre

300 King Street West
Toronto, ON, M5V 1J2
(416) 872-1212
www.mirvish.com

Dream in High Park

High Park Amphitheatre
Toronto, ON, M5H 2N2
(416) 367-1652, ext 500
www.canstage.com

Cliffhanger Productions

2369 Kingston Rd, Box 28004
Scarborough, ON M1N 4E7
(416) 264-5869
www.cliffhangerproductions.ca

Famous People Players

110 Sudbury Street
Toronto, ON, M6J 3S6
(416) 532-1137; 1-888-453-3385
www.fpp.org

Puppetmongers Powell

101 Spruce Hill Rd
Toronto, ON, M4E 3G5
(416) 691-0806
www.puppetmongers.com

Toronto Basics

Summer and March Break Camps

Kids in Toronto are treated to an astounding variety of camps, from comic book camp to digital animation camp. I thought it would be useful to list some of the camps that my kids have experienced or those I've heard good things about. While the list below is for summer camps, most of the institutions listed below offer March Break programming. Call for details. Overnight camps are too numerous to include, but start at the Ontario Camping Association to get a list of accredited camps that fulfill their requirements. Contact them at (416) 485-0425 or go to their website at www.ontcamp.on.ca.

Alliance Française

12 Bannockburn Avenue
North York, ON, M5M 2M8
(416) 922-2014
Burnhamthorpe Road W, Suite 111
Mississauga, ON, L5C 4E9,
(905) 272-4444
1 Elmhurst Avenue
North York, ON, M2N 1R3
(416) 221-4684
www.alliance-francaise.com

Bilingual summer camp for three to 10-year-olds in collaboration with the Children's Montessori Independent School. Performing arts... en Français, creative arts, French cuisine, computers, gymnastics, swimming, travel excursions.

Art Gallery of Ontario

317 Dundas Street West
Toronto, ON, M5T 1G4
(416) 979-6608
www.ago.net/www/services/ago_smart

Two-week art camp sessions for kids ages 6 to 14. The gallery's one-of-a-kind programs include painting, sculpting, drawing, printing, multimedia, video and digital art with professional instructors in a spacious, light-filled studio. Sample camps include Cartooning, Motion Commotion, and Culturequest.

Avenue Road Arts School

460 Avenue Road
Toronto, ON, M4V 2J1
(416) 961-1502
www.avenueroadartsschool.com

This camp is for 4- to 15-year-olds. Music, drama and visual arts projects in a theme-based integrated arts camp. Or choose from many specialized art classes for older children in pottery, painting, sculpture, cartooning, illustration, or drama.

Adventure Day Camp

Black Creek Pioneer Village
1000 Murray Ross Parkway
Toronto, ON, M3J 2P3
(416) 661-6600; (416) 736-1733, ext 5256
www.trca.on.ca

If your child is 8 to 14 and has a yen for make-believe or *Little House on the Prairie*, try the Adventure Day Camp at Black Creek Pioneer Village. Every day is an adventure in life in the 1860s! Campers will meet the villagers and the farm animals, explore the garden, play old-fashioned games, cook a meal on a pioneer stove, be part of a musical concert, go on a scavenger hunt, practice crafts, and be an apprentice to village artisans.

Chapter One

Camp Boulevard

1491 Lake Shore Boulevard West
Toronto, ON, M6K 3C2
(416) 532-3341, ext 134
www.boulevardclub.com/camp

This private club down on Lake Shore Boulevard opens its doors every summer to kids 4 to 16 who'd like to learn sailing and other water sports. Recent additions are a Dragon Boating camp and a beach volleyball court, in addition to their excellent badminton, rowing, junior sailing, tennis, land multisports, and water multisports camps. Early drop-off and after-hour supervision.

Canadian Children's Dance Theatre

509 Parliament Street
Toronto, ON, M4X 1P3
(416) 924-5657
www.ccdt.org

This Cabbagetown institution hosts serious dance students from 4 to 18 years in programs of dance (modern dance, ballet, and improvisation), music, and visual arts. They also have beginning classes for little dancers starting at age 4.

Children's Technology Workshop

Unit 7-105 Vanderhoof Avenue
Toronto, ON, M4G 2H7
(416) 306-6092; 1-866-566-4366
www.ctworkshop.com

Kids 7 to 14 can enjoy robotics, car and airplane prototyping, digital imaging and web design. Projects include simulation, animation, programming, and engineering.

City of Toronto Summer Camps

Throughout the area; call ahead.
www.city.toronto.on.ca

City camps fill up quickly so be sure to check in mid-March when camp registration generally starts. For programs offered in the North call (416) 395-7922; South, call (416) 392-1111; East, (416) 338-3278; and West, (416) 394-8510.

Gibson House Museum

5172 Yonge Street
Toronto, ON, M2N 5P6
(416) 395-7432
www.city.toronto.on.ca/culture/gibson_house

An arts and heritage camp lets kids live the life of a 19th century child and includes swimming at nearby Douglas Snow Aquatic Centre.

Greenwin Tennis Club

185 Balliol Street
Toronto, ON, M4S 1C2
(416) 487-1507
www.greenwintennis.com

Budding tennis stars from 5 to 15 are put through their paces with on-court and off-court drills and activities to enhance speed, strength, agility, sportsmanship, and cardiovascular fitness. A great staff works here! The location is central, between Mount Pleasant and Yonge Street, near Eglinton Avenue.

Toronto Basics

HarbourKids

235 Queens Quay West
Toronto, ON, M5J 2G8
(416) 973-4093
www.harbourfront.on.ca

My son loved his first summer camp experience here at Harbourfront. Close to a thousand kids take arts and crafts, drama, songs, canoeing, waterplay, dance, tennis, and sailing down at Harbourfront. From 4 to 17 yrs.

High Park Discovery Camp

Colborne Lodge
(416) 392-6916

School agers from 7 to 11 can spend summer in High Park. Activities take place at historic Colborne Lodge. Explorations, nature trails, crafts, cooking. Phone for more info.

Living Arts Centre, Mississauga

4141 Living Arts Drive
Mississauga, ON, L5B 4B8
(905) 306-6000
www.livingarts.on.ca

Kids from 6 to 14 can take one of a full slate of art and music camps, including a storytelling camp, a popular School of Wizardry camp, and a Movie Makers camp for kids 11 to 14, which takes aspiring film makers through all the steps, including storyboarding, scriptwriting, lighting, and shooting.

McMichael Gallery

10365 Islington Avenue
Kleinberg, ON, L0J 1C0
(905) 893-0344, ext 228
www.mcmichael.com

ArtVenture courses are designed for students from 6 to 14 years and offer participants the opportunity to be creative while experimenting with a wide variety of art materials and techniques in a unique environment of art and nature. Students spend time in the galleries, learning from the works on display. The classes are taught by experienced and professional artists/educators with assistants.

Ontario Place

955 Lake Shore Blvd
Toronto, ON, M6K 3B9
(416) 314-9900
www.ontarioplace.com

What could be better than camp at an amusement park? Kids 4 to 16 take sports, arts and crafts, play games, and enjoy water activities and IMAX films. But the bonus is playing in the Children's Village, on the Mini Bumper Boats, hydrofuge, waterslide, River Raft Ride, and more.

Ontario Science Centre Camp

770 Don Mills Road
North York, ON, M3C 1T3
(416) 696-3256
www.ontariosciencecentre.ca

Some of the best camps are run by the OSC. Starting at 5, kids can take themed camps like Science & Technology, Wild Discoveries in Nature, or the Human Body in Action. Demonstrations and workshops and lots of interactivity.

Chapter One

Royal Ontario Museum Summer Club

100 Queen's Park
Toronto, ON, M5S 2C6
(416) 586-5797
www.rom.on.ca

For decades the ROM has put together intriguing summer camps for kids. Recent offerings included Dungeons and Dragons, 5 and up. Courses include gym programs at the U of T athletic centre.

School of Toronto Dance Theatre

80 Winchester Street
Toronto, ON, M4X 1B2
(416) 967-6887
www.schooloftdt.org

This Cabbagetown arts school will put a spring in the step of your young Pavlova. From ages 3 to 16, boys and girls take part in mounting theatre productions, dance events, and international cultural festivals.

Seneca College Camps

1750 Finch Avenue East
North York, ON, M2J 2X5
(416) 491-5050
www.seneca.on.ca/home/kidstuff

The college offers a large selection of courses, including a computer animation course for teens. Strong emphasis on sciences, but includes arts and sports as well. From 4 to 14. On Newnham Campus, Don Mills & Finch.

Sunnybrook Stables

1132 Leslie Street
Toronto, ON, M3C 3L7
(416) 444-4044

At Sunnybrook, children can take riding lessons and learn about stable management and equestrian care. All levels of riders accepted, but only ages 9 and up.

Camp U of T

University of Toronto Athletic Centre
55 Harbord Street
Toronto, ON, M5S 2W6
(416) 978-3436
www.juniorblues.ca

U of T hosts sports camps for kids 4 to 16 in a great facility on the St. George campus. Kids choose from specific sports like baseball, volleyball, basketball, diving, or gymnastics. It also offers a mini-university camp, where kids take courses like engineering, law, business, computers, and sport medicine. It also hosts a unique Achieve Development Camp for girls.

Yamaha Summer Arts Camp

5075 Yonge Street North
North York, ON M2N 6C6
(416) 224-5590
www.yamaha.ca

Piano, keyboard, guitar, electone, singing, listening skills, reading music for 6- to 19-year-olds.

YMCA

Throughout the area; call ahead.
(416) 928-9622; 1-800-223-8024
www.ymcatoronto.org

The Toronto Y's offer a full slate of day camps for ages 4 to 17. They're always changing so check the web site for this year's offerings.

Zodiac Swim and Specialty Camp

2788 Bathurst Street Suite 301
North York, ON, M6B 3A3
(416) 789-1989
www.zodiaccamp.on.ca

Tots from 3 to 15 can better their swimming skills at Toronto's oldest swimming camp. In addition to swimming programs, there's snorkelling, synchro and competitive swimming, water polo, games, etc.

Toronto Basics

City Sports Facilities

Toronto sports by numbers: there are 281 pools, 833 playgrounds, 136 community centres, 1500 parks totaling 8,000 hectares in area, 2 alpine skiing centres, 642 sports fields, 5 golf courses, 121 indoor and outdoor arenas, and 756 tennis courts. Visit the city's website for more information: www.city.toronto.on.ca/parks/index.htm.

City Ski Centres

Most people living in Toronto probably don't even realize they have the uncommon privilege of having downhill skiing and snowboarding facilities right at their door. City ski centres are the ideal venue for the entire family to enjoy together, whether just learning or brushing up techniques that have gone rusty. Look into a Family Ski Pass and enjoy skiing day or night. There are rentals, lessons, hi-tech snowmaking, and snack bars on site to make your day on the slopes super!

North York Ski Centre

Earl Bales Park
4169 Bathurst Street
Toronto, ON, M3H 3P7
(416) 395-7934; (416) 33-TO-SKI

Centennial Park Ski Area

Centennial Park
256 Centennial Park Road
Etibicoke, ON M9C 5N3
(416) 394-8750; (416) 33-TO-SKI

City Golf Courses

Since golf is increasingly becoming a family activity, we're fortunate to have five excellent courses within city limits. They're affordable, easy to get to on public transit, and have high-calibre, well-maintained greens and quality instruction available. Clubs and carts can be rented at all of the courses, which also have fully licensed snack bars. So take the kids out to the golf course instead of the ball game and see what happens!

Don Valley

Enter at intersection of Yonge St and William Carson Crescent. William Carson Crescent is located between Wilson Ave and Hwy 401
(416) 392-2465

Humber Valley

Entrance is on Beatty Ave, east of Albion Rd
Etobicoke, ON
(416) 392-2488

Tam O'Shanter

Entrance is on Birchmont Rd, north of Shephard Ave East
(416) 392-2547

Dentonia

Entrance is on Victoria Park Ave, north of Danforth Ave
Toronto, ON
(416) 392-2558

Scarlett Woods

Entrance is on Eglington Ave West between Jane St and Scarlett Rd
Toronto, ON
(416) 392-2484

Chapter One

Community Centres

Toronto has a terrific network of city-run community centres, in every corner of the city. There are more than 500, so it's best to consult the City of Toronto website for a complete list (www.city.toronto.on.ca/parks/recreation_facilities/comcen/comcen_index).

Other community-run, public facilities include Toronto YMCAs and the Jewish Community Centres.

Toronto YMCA

Main information line:
(416) 928-9622; 1-800-223-8024
Metro-Central YMCA
20 Grosvenor Street (off Yonge Street, south of Wellesley)
Toronto, ON, M4Y 2V5
(416) 975-9622

Westend YMCA

931 College Street (at Dovercourt Street)
Toronto, ON, M6H 1A1
(416) 536-9622

North York YMCA

567 Sheppard Avenue East (at Bayview)
North York, ON, M2K 1B2
(416) 225-9622

Scarborough YMCA

2390 Town Centre Court
(just off McCowan and 401 East)
Scarborough, ON, M1P 4Y7
(416) 296-9622

Jewish Community Centres

Miles Nadal JCC

750 Spadina Avenue
Toronto, ON, M5S 2J2
(416) 924-6211

Bathurst JCC

4588 Bathurst Street
Toronto, ON, M2R 1W2
(416) 636-1880

Chapter Two

Toronto Favourites

Normally I shy from making Top Ten lists of anything, but it makes sense to feature the major events and attractions that Toronto is known for. These are the places that families buy memberships to, so they can return again and again. And these are the events that no family wants to miss.

Toronto's Top Ten Kids' Attractions

African Lion Safari

If a family vacation in Africa is out of the question, the next best thing may be a drive through this park's game reserves. With doors locked and windows up, a one-hour drive through the reserve takes families past grazing giraffes, playful monkeys, exotic birds, and majestic lions and tigers. A spectacular daytrip that families never forget. (See page 150 for details.)

Courtesy Ontario Tourism

Elephant riding at the African Lion Safari

Chapter Two

CN Tower

What is it about verticality and cities? Ever since Eiffel built his famous *tour*, it seems that a tower is an essential part of a city's skyline. Toronto's tower is called the CN Tower after its original owners, the Canadian National Railway, and it is, ahem, the tallest free-standing structure in the world. Zipping up the side in a glass elevator at 20 feet per second is almost as thrilling as standing on the glass floor and looking between your feet at the ground some 1,122 feet below. Go even higher to the Skypod level and you almost feel airborne. (See page 63 for details.)

The CN Tower

Ontario Place

Ontario Place

Ontario Place is a futuristic family playground set on Lake Ontario, with stark white pods elevated on stilts over the water, all of it joined together by a network of long ramps and pontoons. People paddle around its waterways, imagining they're in the Jetsons' own backyard and gazing up at the enormous geodesic dome (where IMAX films are shown year-round). As Toronto's only downtown water park with rides and live entertainment, Ontario Place is the place to be on summer weekends. (See page 43 for details.)

Harbourfront

You'll never know what you'll find on a typical day at Harbourfront. A free concert by a pop group from Madagascar, a hot and spicy food festival featuring top Toronto chefs, or perhaps a cushion concert for kids. Toronto's most popular entertainment venue, Harbourfront programs a full summer of concerts and events, many of them free. (See page 48 for details.)

Canada's Wonderland

Since 1981, Canada's Wonderland has drawn Torontonians to its enormous offering of rides, midway games, and concerts. Most notable is North America's largest collection of roller coasters, including Top Gun, Canada's only inverted, looping jet coaster, and SkyRider, a stand-up version. For wee tikes, there's Hanna-Barbara Land, where carousels and other gentle rides await and Paramount pals like Yogi Bear and Scooby Doo wander about, stopping for photos and bear hugs. On hot days head to Splashworks, an enormous water park, or take in one of the many ongoing performances. (See page 127 for details.)

Toronto Favourites

Casa Loma

Folly is the word for Sir Henry Pellatt's castle on the hill, built at an enormous cost and then repossessed because of unpaid taxes. Today it's a tourist spot, a film location, and a popular backdrop for wedding photos. Come see its beautiful gardens, find its secret passageways, and climb up its turreted towers. (See page 90 for details.)

Casa Loma

Ontario Science Centre

If your kids think science is for eggheads, the Science Centre will change their minds in a millisecond. Revolutionary in its time, the OSC's 800+ exhibits, most of them interactive, thrill kids from about 6 and up. Pick a hall focused on space, food, sport, Earth, transportation, communication, chemistry, or the body and start interacting. See the latest traveling exhibits or an IMAX movie as well. (See page 108 for details.)

Toronto Zoo

Toronto's Zoo features miles of walkways, five indoor pavilions, and underwater exhibits showcasing 5,000 animals. So bring your walking shoes! Strollers and wagons can be rented, or take the Zoomobile to get a tour and hop-on, hop-off service around the park. The zoo's main attraction these days is the newly-renovated Gorilla Rainforest, North America's largest. Catch one of the daily Meet the Keeper sessions where you'll be able to ask questions and watch a feeding. (See page 133 for details.)

Toronto Islands

The Islands are Toronto's largest playground and a car-free paradise in the summer, with an amusement park perfect for tiny tots to pre-teens, a farm, swimming beaches, boating competitions, festivals, and all the walking and exploring you can do in a day. Best way to see them is to rent one of the family-style bicycles and go from one end of the Islands to the other. (See page 52 for details.)

Royal Ontario Museum

The ROM is Ontario's most prestigious museum with the dual mandate of documenting both cultural and natural history. In addition to world-class Chinese and European antiquities, a bat cave, dinosaur hall, and an exploding volcano, the ROM has an ingenious Discovery Gallery for kids, plus Franklin the turtle's house and play area for toddlers. (See page 86 for details.)

Chapter Two

Toronto's Top Ten Kids' Events

See the Appendix (page 177) for more Toronto area festivals and events.

Canadian National Exhibition

Exhibition Place
Lake Shore Boulevard, between Strachen Ave and Dufferin St
(416) 263-3800
www.theex.com

Canadian National Exhibition
When: The last two weeks of August until Labour Day. Daily, 10 am - midnight.
Cost: Adults, $9; 6 and under, $6; Babes in arms, free.

The Ex, as it's known to Torontonians, is a tradition that dates back more than a century. Over the years it's grown to the point that it now ranks as North America's largest annual fair, featuring food, agricultural and technological displays and demonstrations, big-name entertainers, and a giant midway. We like the fact that it is all things to all people – grandmas, teenage boys, and tiny girls are all rewarded by some element of the show. Families should head for the Kids Midway, where smaller rides for shorties 42 inches and less rule. There's Kidscience where you can make giant bubbles and see interactive displays, a reptile show, the Kids playhouse theatre, Weird on Wheels by kids broadcaster YTV, a backyard circus where everyone's a clown, and Inferno – a nightly extravaganza of fire, lasers, and pyrotechnics featuring acrobats, stiltwalkers, and more.

Another big draw for families is the International Airshow, which can be watched from any location that offers a view of the section of Lake Ontario, slightly west of Ontario Place. The best viewing area is the water-skiing area inside the CNE.

Courtesy Ontario Tourism

Girl at the Canadian National Exhibition

Plan on spending the entire day and ending it with the fireworks display. Don't even try to park; take the southbound Bathurst streetcar from Bathurst station, which will take you right to the gates.

Toronto Favourites

Royal Agricultural Winter Fair

Exhibition Place
(416) 263-3400
www.royalfair.org

Every year in early November, the largest indoor agricultural, horticultural, and equestrian exhibition in the world opens in Toronto. For ten days, the Royal brings the country to the city in a big, bold way. For my family, there's no better place to be when the first cool days of winter kick in and the smell of hay and, well, other farm smells, beckon us city folk to the exhibition grounds once again.

It's impossible to say what the best part of this huge spectacle is. We adore the best breeds competitions, where exotic and heritage breeds of geese, rabbits, ducks, and chickens vie for blue ribbons. The dog show is a stand-out, with breeders, trainers, police dogs, and other working dogs all on hand to showcase Canadian's favourite pets. The main ring also heralds the return of the highly entertaining Canadian Disc Dogs whose daily performances involve routines with Frisbees set to music. Then there are the endless rows of showcase livestock, the pens full of freshly shampooed sheep, and the bustling petting farm where goats, chickens, sheep, and donkeys roam a farmyard, getting up-close-and-personal with breathless preschoolers.

Royal Agricultural Winter Fair
When: Early November. Daily 9 am - 8 or 9 pm, depending on the day.
Cost: Adults, $15; Kids 5 to 14, $9; Under 4, free. Family pass $34 (admits two adults and two kids). Two for one admission M-F 5 p.m.

The Royal Agricultural Winter Fair

Courtesy Ontario Tourism

During the Cavalcade of Horses, visitors are introduced to breeds ranging from the giant Shires and flashy Rocky Mountain Horses to the Newfoundland Pony. Daily demonstrations of equine sporting events include reining, vaulting, therapeutic riding, and dressage, and a prestigious equestrian competition draws teams from around the world.

My son Max likes nothing better than to watch the farm boys and girls patiently blow drying the silky coats of their prize-winning calves. Or sometimes we hang out in the Horse Palace stables watching the horsey folk enjoy cocktail hour in front of their stalls. When we get hungry, we buzz along the food stalls grabbing samples until we finally settle on something. We always have a peek at the giant vegetables; the pumpkins as big as our refrigerator and corn stalks as tall as our house always amaze.

The Food Hall is where you'll find displays of award-winning produce and preserves and endless rows of food stalls. Try a homegrown snack like delicious Mapleton organic ice cream, or a fresh Ontario candy apple. Max has made a tradition of attending 'classes' at the Pizza Nova pizza school, where you get to eat your handiwork after 'school' lets out.

Chapter Two

Milk International Children's Festival

At Harbourfront Centre
235 Queen's Quay West
(416) 973-4000
www.harbourfront.on.ca/milk

Milk International Children's Festival
When: May. Weekends, noon - 5 pm; Weekdays, 10 am - 3 pm.
Cost: Wristbands $6 in advance, $7.50 on the day. One show: $10 in advance, $12 on the day; two shows $12 in advance, $15 on the day.

It's always a treat to receive the Milk International Children's Festival brochure in the mail – a sure sign of spring that usually arrives on a blustery February day. The festival brings together innovative performers from literally every corner of the world along with local talents and intriguing crafts and hands-on activities. A typical year might include musical and theatre groups from Italy, Denmark, Australia, and Switzerland. It runs for a week every May and can be packed on weekends, so buy your tickets in advance and try to attend during the week if possible.

Some of our favourite moments have been spent behind tent flaps at the Five Minute Marvels. We spied a juggler who showed us his moves and then taught us a few; we listened to an Australian didgeridoo player and watched a darling puppet show by a Hungarian group called Mikropodium. Though we couldn't see it all (you never can), more of the marvels included an opera rehearsal, a quilting bee, and a pretend movie house all ready for exploring and experiencing. These up-close-and-personal opportunities to mingle with artists gave us plenty to marvel at, if only for a moment.

Crafts tables will tempt pint-sized Picassos with "make and take" projects from around the world. One year, kids made Peruvian dance capes, African lion masks, and cosmic hats, inspired by Harry Potter. For crafty kids, hands-on activities with glass, metal, ceramics, and textiles are led by the talented artists who work in the Harbourfront art studios.

Excitement was provided by a hip hop dancer who taught kids the latest moves, along with a hands-on (and feet-on) climbing wall, and an awesome demonstration by professional bicycle stuntmen. There's even a showcase for young local performers called Kidzone and games on the grass that had kids running obstacle races and rolling a giant earth ball around. The festival's Fenetre Francophone is a special day at the festival, with dazzling acts from Quebec and other French-speaking countries. A lot of these shows can be enjoyed by kids who don't speak French, and some parents use them as a way to gauge their kids' interest in learning other languages.

Toronto Favourites

Kidsummer

Throughout the area; call ahead or check website for details.
(866) 363-KIDS
www.todaysparent.com

For kids not enrolled in daycamps, Kidsummer is a real boredom buster. For their parents, it can be a lifesaver! One of Toronto's greatest summer-time pleasures, this is two solid months of daily outings and events, co-sponsored by Kellogg's and *Today's Parent* magazine.

The best way to find out what's going on is to head to the *Today's Parent* website (www.todaysparent.com). Events run the gamut from ice cream factory tours to free concerts by kids' performers like Sharon, Lois and Bram, or Raffi. Some activities are restricted to a certain number of participants and require advance booking and/or a small fee, but the majority are free and open to all comers. The website is usually up by mid-June, and then the race to sign up for favourite events is on.

Santa Claus Parade

(416) 599-9090, ext 500
www.thesantaclausparade.org

Courtesy Ontario Tourism

Santa waving to the crowd!

The Parade begins at 1 pm, but by then many families have been on the road for hours. They want to arrive in plenty of time to get their favourite spot – usually the same one they've occupied for years. The parade began in 1904, and many family traditions have grown up alongside it. We're fairly new to it, and usually manage to get seats at the last minute by squatting down in front of people standing. The only thing that's essential to remember is a thick blanket to sit on! If you're running late that day, no worries; just head toward the end of the route to make sure you don't miss anything. The parade lasts about an hour or so, with Santa's float coming last, but it doesn't get down to Front Street until about 4 pm.

The entire spectacle is created by about 1,000 volunteers with more than 25 floats and two dozen marching bands from Canada and the U.S. It is truly an amazing site to see, for kids of all ages. My son loves spotting characters he recognizes on the floats, like Budgie the Helicopter and Coca Cola's polar bear mascot. (This irked me the first time we went to the parade – can't they stop marketing to kids for even one day, I wondered?) But they

Chapter Two

are entertaining, and without them I'm sure there'd be little left to see. One year, a float with a towering yellow dinosaur proved a little too entertaining, scaring more than a few preschoolers. But not enough to make them surrender their spots on the sidewalk before the jolly old man appeared.

And when Santa finally does appear, kids rush the float, handing their letters up to Santa, in an age-old tradition that probably hasn't changed one bit since 1904.

Toronto Winterfest

Mel Lastman Square & Nathan Phillips Square
(416) 338-0338
www.city.toronto.on.ca/special_events/winterfest

> **Toronto Winterfest**
>
> **When:** February. Daily, 11:30 am - 8 pm.
>
> **Cost:** Some shows are ticketed; midway rides require tickets.
>
> **Directions:** Mel Lastman Square is just north of Yonge and Sheppard Streets in North York.

This annual mid-winter festival is split between Nathan Phillips Square downtown, devoted to teen and grown-up fun, and the North Pole venue, Mel Lastman Square, focusing on kid-friendly fare. This works well, though if your family is made up of both teens and kids, you may want to check out both squares during this weekend.

At the North Pole, the weekend kicks off with a family skate party on the rink where live music and celebrity entertainers keep the buzz going all weekend. There's a midway, a ticketed feature show, impromptu parades, face painting, musical acts, make-and-take crafts, and some of North America's top children's performers. Who wants to hibernate when you can celebrate the winter with thousands of other kids and Thomas the Tank Engine?

Downtown at the South Pole, there are rock and circus acts onstage most of the weekend along with routines by former Olympic skaters. Be awestruck by the antics of performing ice sculptors who produce breathtaking works of art to the sounds of pounding music and power tools.

Toronto Favourites

Mississauga International Children's Festival

Mississauga Civic Centre
Living Arts Drive, just north of Burnamthorpe Road West
(905) 306-6000
www.kidsfestival.org

For four days every June, a terrific children's festival takes over the civic center of Mississauga. We like it almost more than we like Toronto's famed Milk International Children's Festival since the acts are just as good, but tickets are easier to get and the crowds less daunting.

Between acts like Al Simmons, Dennis Lee, and Quebec's Dynamo Theatre, we played on the Tone Tubes, along with dozens of other kids. These were ingenious percussion instruments created by joining yards of PVC pipes together and attaching drums to the ends. It was great fun pounding away and sending sounds down the tubes on the giant post-industrial drum machine. There were loads of other hands-on activities, all free, including ingenious building toys that kids were using to construct enormous structures.

Families are welcome to pack a lunch and eat in the Purple Cow tent, which is filled with picnic tables and located on the front lawn of the Living Arts Centre.

There are food vendors on site, as well as two restaurants, one in the City Hall (Cafeteria) and one in the Living Arts Centre (more upscale). There is also the food court at Square One shopping center, but it is quite a trek across the parking lot. Call ahead for tickets – just in case.

> **Mississauga International Children's Festival**
>
> **When:** June. Daily 10 am - 4 pm.
>
> **Cost:** Most of the onsite activities are free. Performances $7 for the first show, $5 for additional shows. Weekend festival passes for two shows, $12.
>
> **Directions:** From the 401, 403, or 407, exit on Hurontario (Hwy10) and go south; turn right (west) on Rathburn Road West, then left (south) on Living Arts Drive. From the QEW, exit on Hurontario (Hwy 10), and go north. Turn left (west) on Burnhamthorpe Road West, turn right (north) on Living Arts Drive.

Chapter Two

Ontario Renaissance Festival

Milton
(800) 734-3779
www.rennfest.com

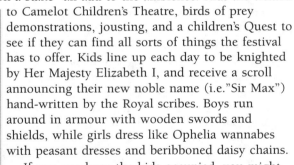

Ontario Renaissance Festival

When: Seven weekends: July 20 - September 2.

Cost: Adults, $16.95; Seniors, $15.50; Children 7-15, $8.95.

Directions: Fifteen minutes from Pearson airport, near the junction of Highway 401 and Trafalgar Road, south of Derry Road, north of Britannia Road, near Milton.

"Come lords and ladies for a day of feasting, fun, and frolic in the Royal Court of Elizabeth I." It sounded like fun, but we were completely unprepared for just how much fun it was! The Ontario Renaissance Festival is one of Toronto's more unique events, recreating a six-teenth century village called Trillingham. Characters that look as though they've stepped out of a Chaucerian tale strike up conversations with you at the mead bar, or involve you in an unfolding scene that takes some unwitting visi-tors aback – all for the further merriment of their guests. Kids love adopting the olde English vernacular of the day, and watching the live jousting tournaments down at the fields below.

Seven stages of hilarious performances (i.e. Theatre in the Ground), a giant crafts market, and food stalls selling "steak-on-a-stake" all add to the ambience. Kids are treated

Jester at Ontario Rennaissance Festival

to Camelot Children's Theatre, birds of prey demonstrations, jousting, and a children's Quest to see if they can find all sorts of things the festival has to offer. Kids line up each day to be knighted by Her Majesty Elizabeth I, and receive a scroll announcing their new noble name (i.e."Sir Max") hand-written by the Royal scribes. Boys run around in armour with wooden swords and shields, while girls dress like Ophelia wannabes with peasant dresses and beribboned daisy chains.

If you can keep the kids occupied, you might have time to slake your thirst with mead or tradi-tional ales from a local brewery in Burlington. If you plan ahead, you can catch a special children's weekend in July when lords and ladies under 11 get free admission.

A Parent's Guide to
Toronto

Toronto Favourites

First Night Toronto

Skydome
1 Blue Jays Way
(416) 362-3692
www.firstnighttoronto.com

First Night Toronto

When: December 26-30, 10 am - 5 pm;
Dec 31, 2 pm - midnight.

Cost: Dec. 29-30, Admission Passes, $10.
Dec 31, Admission Passes $15. All-Day
Unlimited Midway Ride Passes, $15;
Children 2 & under, free.

For an alcohol-free, family-oriented New Year's celebration, First Night is hard to beat. Held at the Skydome for six days leading up to Dec. 31st, expect face painters and magic makers, fireworks and fire eaters, plus hot kids performers like Jack Grunsky and the a cappella group Cadence. There are comedy acts, folk dancing, a petting zoo, and 13 family-oriented midway rides, too! Kids can transform themselves for the evening's festivities by making a headdress, mask, or costume. On New Year's Eve, there's a kids finale performance at 8:30 pm. And everywhere you look... magical, mystical surprises! Happy New Year!

Sugarbush Maple Syrup Festival

Kortright Centre
9550 Pine Valley Drive
Woodbridge, Ontario
(905) 832-2289
www.kortrightcentre.org
Bruce's Mill Conservation Area
Whitchurch-Stouffville
(416) 661-6600
www.trca.on.ca

Maple Syrup Festival

Courtesy Ontario Tourism

Sugarbush Maple Syrup Festival

When: End of February to early April.
Daily 10 am - 4 pm.

Cost: Adults, $6; Children, $4;
Under 4, free. Parking $2.

Kortright Centre

Directions: 2 km (1 mile) west of Hwy
400, south of Major Mackenzie Dr.

Bruce's Mill Conservation Area

Directions: Twenty minutes north
of Toronto; on Stouffville Road
east of Highway 404.

When the spring thaw starts, the sap starts to run and the maple syrup season begins in earnest. There are many regional festivals to choose from, but these two are closest to Toronto and run for about seven weeks. You can choose between Stouffville's Bruce Mill Conservation Centre or the Kortright Centre in Woodbridge, Canada's largest environmental education centre. Both host great festivals with demonstrations of how maple syrup was made in pioneer days as well as showcasing a modern operation. You can purchase a jug of syrup to take home, but try the sausage and pancakes with syrup right at the source. Horse-drawn wagons will take you on a bumpy tour around the sugar bush so you can see the intricate network of pipes that collect the sap and send it into the sugar shack for boiling down into syrup.

Chapter Two

Sprockets –
Toronto International Film Festival for Children

Famous Players Canada Square cinemas
2200 Yonge Street
Toronto, ON, M4S 2C6
(416) 968-FILM
www.e.bell.ca/filmfest/sprockets

A film festival just for kids makes sense in a movie-mad city that hosts the largest film festival in North America. And sure enough, the folks behind the film festival created Sprockets to bring animated and live action films from around the world to kids aged four to 18. Little ones from four to six get their own series called Reel Rascals. And their older siblings can take part in filmmaking and animation workshops that give them hands-on control over a short film. In 2002, they added more courses – one on special effects and another that took kids out to Bowmanville Zoo to meet animal actors.

> **Sprockets –**
> **Toronto International Film**
> **Festival for Children**
>
> **When:** April, 10 am - 9 pm.
>
> **Cost:** Adults, $10; Kids, $6.
> Get advance tickets as
> many films sell out.

The festival screens both contemporary films and classics, so kids can see movies that their parents – and even grandparents – might have enjoyed. The program guide has age recommendations and advisory notes for parents, warning of any scary or difficult parts present in each film. And they've gotten around the problem of subtitles by having a narrator read them out to the audience. The organizers deserve a hand – they seem to have done everything but pop the popcorn!

Chapter Three

Toronto's Lakeshore and Islands

Exploring Toronto's 46 km (28 mile) lakeshore and Islands could take a week on its own, but if you've only got a couple of days, spend at least one getting to know this vital part of the city. Where else can you find the largest drive-in movie screen in North America, an entertainment complex that showcases the world's best performing artists, and a playful 'music garden' inspired by Bach? Find it all right here, strung along the glorious 22 kilometre Martin Goodman Trail. Grab a bike or a pair of roller blades and enjoy the ride, stopping off at interesting places along the way. Take your bike on the Islands ferry and spend the day in a car-free paradise, picnicking on the beach, or enjoying family rides at Centreville Amusement Park. If it's a steamy day, you might want to stop at Ontario Place and take in an IMAX film, cool down in the amazing water park, or hop on the Wilderness Adventure Ride. Wherever you choose to stop, the lakeshore is definitely the place to be when the sun's shining.

Note: this chapter is organized as though you were traveling along the Martin Goodman Trail from the Humber River in the West to the Beaches in the East.

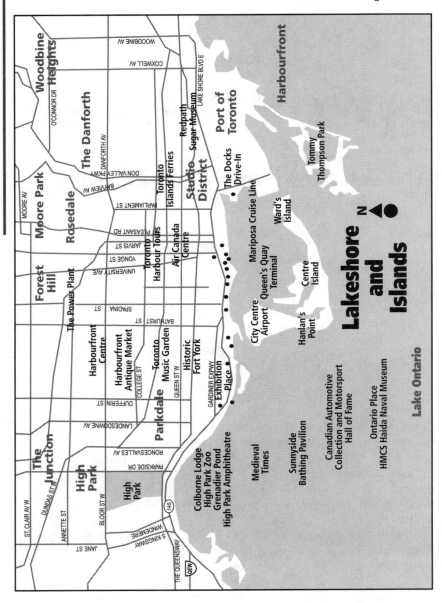

Toronto's Lakeshore and Islands
Things to Do

Martin Goodman Trail

www.ryerson.ca/vtoronto/wwwsite/themes/cultrec/html/goodmanw.htm

The Martin Goodman Trail is a 22 kilometre (13 mile) urban bike path extending from the Humber River in the West to the Beaches neighborhood in the East. While the Trail can be done in a day, I'd recommend starting out from Harbourfront and doing half the trail at a time. That will allow for stops along the way, which is vital if you're in a family group.

The trail begins at the **Humber River Pedway and Bicycle Bridge**, whose bright white arches can be seen from the elevated Gardiner Expressway. Up close you can admire the pair of thunderbirds that serve as braces and the carved turtles and serpents that adorn it. This is in homage to the Ojibway who used the mouth of the Humber as a meeting place for centuries. Interpretive plaques trace the prehistory of the region and commemorate explorer Etienne Brûlé who traveled down it (on behalf of Samuel Champlain) in 1615.

Farther along you come to **Sunnyside Bathing Pavilion**, a wonderful example of 20's art deco. Moving along this 10-kilometre stretch you pass by a dinosaur playground, innumerable beaches, boardwalks and picnic areas, finally reaching **Ontario Place** and the **Exhibition Grounds**. Continuing on, you reach the most developed area of the trail, which most people call **Queen's Quay**, after the street that runs along the lakeshore. Starting at the west end of Queen's Quay, you'll see the **Waterfront School**, a striking building that makes perfect use of its location. If school's in session, you can have a peek inside and see why it's so popular with students. Continue walking eastwards toward the **Toronto Music Garden**, where you can rent an audio guide narrated by cellist Yo-Yo Ma that explains the park's inspiration and intent. Next you'll pass the fireboat station, a huge hit with kids, and a couple of marinas and restaurants. Soon you're at **Harbourfront Centre**, where you're sure to find something going on, perhaps a free concert just beginning on the Ann Tindal Stage. See if the **Power Plant** (Toronto's contemporary art gallery) has a good exhibit on, or carry on to Queen's Quay Terminal shopping center for a little browsing or noshing.

Passing the Westin Bayshore hotel and the **Toronto Island Ferry docks**, you'll soon see a stretch of barren parking lot. Don't despair, as right after that is the **Redpath Sugar Factory**, the last industrial plant on the lakeshore, operating on clean steam-driven energy. Beyond Redpath, you enter a post-industrial landscape with the **Port of Toronto** looming on your right. This is where Toronto's 2008 Olympic Bid Committee planned to build the athlete's village, had it gotten the nod from the IOC. (For better or worse, Toronto lost the bid to China.)

Chapter Three

Do a loop through the Portlands to see where the narrow Great Lakes freighters dock, or to have a swim on one of the city's cleanest beaches, **Cherry Beach**. This is also where a couple of yachting and rowing clubs are based, and where windsurfers take to the waves. Once the trail reaches Cherry Beach, you'll enter a greenbelt that extends along the southern edge of the Portlands. Relatively unpolluted, this area is dotted with reminders of the area's industrial past, while hinting at what it could become, if the right mix of housing and parkland is allowed to take root here.

Turning north again the trail returns to the Lake Shore Boulevard and the Gardiner expressway until it enters the relatively pristine parklands of **Ashbridge's Bay** and **Woodbine Park**. Here a three-kilometre stretch of boardwalk leads into the **Beach**es neighbourhood with its village-like atmosphere and lively main street. If you've biked the Trail, this is a good spot for dinner – and you'll deserve it after all that exercise.

High Park

1873 Bloor Street W
Toronto, ON, M6P 3K7
(416) 392-1748
www.city.toronto.on.ca/parks/parks_gardens/highpark

High Park
Hours: Daily, dawn to dusk.
Cost: Free. Train tickets: Adults, $8; Children, $2.50.
Directions: Enter on Parkside Dr and Bloor St W, west of Parkside.

Courtesy Ontario Tourism

Autumn colors in High Park

High Park's 121 acres are crisscrossed with paths and nature trails, which are used as cross-country skiing trails in the winter, and biking and jogging paths the rest of the year. A very active committee is in the process of restoring the natural plants and trees to the park and holds informative walks during the summer months, which depart from the Grenadier Restaurant.

In summer, it's a pleasant place to hike, with rare flora, wildlife indigenous to the area, and a small zoo (see below). You might stumble upon the Nature Centre, which has Saturday morning drop-in programs for kids, or the Children's Garden where all kinds of activities are geared to getting kids excited about community gardening and growing their own food.

There's a swimming pool and tennis courts, and a nice collection of sculpture that dots the hills. Many families takes picnics to enjoy before seeing the Canadian Stage Company's annual Dream in High Park production on the amphitheatre. It's especially magical when they do *Midsummer Night's Dream*, but always well done no matter which Shakespearean play they tackle.

Toronto's Lakeshore and Islands

Colborne Lodge

On Colborne Lodge Dr in High Park
(416) 392-6916
www.city.toronto.on.ca/culture/colborne

If you're visiting High Park, why not pop into Colborne Lodge to see how John Howard, Toronto's first surveyor and a prominent architect, and his wife Jemima lived in the 1830s? The Howards are the original owners of High Park, and are buried in an elaborate grave just across the road from their house. Colborne Lodge is one of North America's oldest surviving buildings in the Regency Picturesque style, a cottagey affair popular among early landed gentry. It may look small from the outside, but step in and you'll find a surprisingly large home which still has many of its original furnishings intact.

> ### Colborne Lodge
>
> **Hours:** Tues-Fri, noon - 4pm; Sat-Sun, noon - 5pm. Closed Mondays, New Year's, Good Friday, Christmas, Boxing Day.
>
> **Cost:** Adults, $3.50; Youth (13-18), $2.75; Children 12 and under, $2.50. Christmas and Twelfth Night admission: Adults, $5; Youth, $4; Children 12 and under, $3.50.
>
> **Directions:** From Lake Shore Blvd, exit onto Coldborne Lodge Dr. From Parkside Dr, take High Park Blvd entrance, follow Centre Rd, turn left on Colburne Lodge Dr. From Bloor St West, stay on Colborne Lodge Dr.

Today the lodge serves as both an historical museum with guided tours available and a special-events venue throughout the year. Most days we've ventured over, there's been something going on, whether it's Easter egg dying using natural dyes, or a guided tour through the vegetable garden. We want to attend the Harvest Festival which features storytelling and music and the Twelfth Night Christmas event, when hot cider, shortbread cookies, and other holiday treats are served up piping hot from the Lodge's historic kitchen.

Animal Paddocks

High Park

Just under Colborne Lodge is the High Park Zoo, which is not really a zoo but a series of pens containing exotic breeds like yaks, bison, mouflon, llamas, highland cattle, and Barbary sheep. It lacks interpretation, and there's never been any staff around to ask questions of, but it's nevertheless an interesting spot for kids to see some impressive beasts.

Grenadier Pond

High Park

A lovely pond for strolling around in any season, especially in midwinter when it freezes over, and skaters appear. No music, just the sound of laughter and skates. A refreshment stand sells hot chocolate, impromptu crack-the-whip lines are formed, and the entire scene looks as though it came off a vintage Christmas card.

Chapter Three

Amphitheatre

High Park
www.canstage.com

The first time we saw the annual Shakespearean play produced outdoors on the amphitheatre in High Park, we were still without kids. But we did bring our surrogate child (a beagle named Sophie) along for some fresh air. Since an actor friend of ours had a part in the play, Sophie insisted on running up to the stage to greet her every time she came out for her lines. She had quite a large part, so my husband spent the first act trying to restrain Sophie until giving up and taking her away to a dog run nearby.

I tell you the story only because a night at the Dream in High Park, as it is known, is full of surprises – whether you're the one with the beagle or not. Children are positively enchanted by the goings-on – or not. And some wailing of infants is usually part of the evening. But do not be discouraged by this! It's a wonderful excuse for an evening picnic and a great night out if you have kids 10 or older.

Medieval Times

West end of Exhibition Place
Lake Shore Blvd, between Strachen Ave and Dufferin St
(416) 260-1234 or 1-800-563-1190
www.medievaltimes.com

Medieval Times
Hours: Wed & Thurs, 7 pm; Fri-Sat, 7:30 pm; Sun, 3:30 pm.
Cost: Adults, $54.95; Children 12 and under, $36.95. Royal Quest game: Adults, $12; Children 12 and under, $8.

It's expensive for sure, but if you're due for a treat it's worth splashing out just once. Eat a meal of finger foods (soup, chicken, ribs, and pastry) while watching jousting matches between knights in chain mail mounted on thundering live Andalusian horses. The show includes a performing falcon, the twirl of alabarda and bola (battle axe and spiked ball), and the romance of a costumed king, queen, and fair maidens (the serving wenches). Beware the unchivalrous gift shop where your offspring will be tempted by such alluring objects as toy swords and princess hats. Admission includes four-course dinner, two-hour show, beverages, and taxes. Give the kids a knight they'll remember (I couldn't resist).

Toronto's Lakeshore and Islands

Sunnyside Bathing Pavilion

1755 Lake Shore Boulevard
Toronto, ON M6S 5A3
(416) 392-6696

Sunnyside Amusement Park opened in 1922 as an entertainment facility for Toronto's overheated middle classes, who swarmed here on hot summer days. For a few decades, it was the place to go, with lockers for 7,700 bathers, two outdoor dressing room facilities, waterslides, a terrace restaurant, and live orchestral entertainment. But by 1956, the crowds had moved on. Most of the park was bulldozed in 1956 to widen Lake Shore Boulevard, and today all that remains is the bathing pavilion, the pool, and a rather scruffy dance hall called the Palais Royale, where the Rolling Stones recently played a spontaneous gig. The pavilion still retains a hint of its glamourous past, and is a magnet for filmmakers, wedding photographers, and fans of the vintage swimming pool era. The spectacular structure, with its colonnaded and arched façade overlooking Lake Ontario, is a delightful place to spend an afternoon. Kids can play on the expansive sand beach while mom and dad watch from the shaded comfort of the Sunnyside Café – an Italian joint that serves great pasta, coffee, and gelato. Sunnyside is located along the Martin Goodman Trail, so bring bikes or inline skates, and you can carry on exploring in either direction.

> **Sunnyside Bathing Pavilion**
>
> **Hours:** Courtyard: May-Oct, Mon-Sun, 9 am - dusk; Pool: Jun 8-Sep 2, M-F, noon - 6 pm; Sat-Sun, 9 am - 6 pm. (Extended Hours: Jun 30-Aug 25, Mon-Sun, 9 am - 4 pm, 5 pm - 7:45 pm); call for latest hours.
>
> **Cost:** Free, lockers cost 25 cents and are non-refundable.
>
> **Directions:** On Lake Shore Boulevard.

Ontario Place

955 Lake Shore Blvd W
Toronto, ON, M6K 3B9
(416) 314-9900
www.ontarioplace.com

After more than 30 years, Ontario Place is still a must-see for families. This futuristic entertainment complex on the waterfront of Lake Ontario houses more than 20 rides and attractions including bumper boats, a children's play area, pedal boats, Mega Maze, miniature golf, a motion simulator ride, Soak City Waterpark, and five Olympic-sized beach volleyball courts.

> **Ontario Place**
>
> **Hours:** May 18-June 7, Weekends only. June 8-Labour Day, 10 am-midnight. Attraction times vary. Cinesphere open year round.
>
> **Cost:** Play All Day passes range from $12 for kids to $25 for adults. Grounds admission is $10 but doesn't include rides, IMAX film, or access to the water park.
>
> **Directions:** On Lake Shore Blvd just west of Strachan. If you're on the Gardiner Expressway going east, exit at Spadina Avenue and drive west along Lake Shore Blvd. Turn left at Ontario Place Blvd. From the west, exit the Gardiner Expressway at Jameson Avenue and drive east along Lake Shore Blvd. to Ontario Place. Follow the signs for parking. You can also take the 511 Bathurst streetcar service from Bathurst Station or use the free shuttle bus from Union Station (runs 8:30 am to 8:30 pm in the summer season only).

Chapter Three

Ontario Place

Teens and child-free grown-ups head to Adventure Island, with its concert stages, bumper boats, canoe rentals, and attractions such as the Mars Simulator, the Mega Maze, and the Wilderness Adventure Ride.

Kids and families head eastwards to the award-winning Children's Village and Soak City, the water park. Under giant awnings, kids race up and down tunnels, through a maze of giant soft punching bags in the Foam Forest, and get buried in the Ball Crawl. Nearby is a new Festival Stage that features children's performers like television's Arthur, which is so popular it draws kids out of the water park. And as for rides, well, the little folk are spoiled these days. New rides have been added just for the tiny set, though with names like Cyclone and Free Fall, I wonder how tame they can really be? We still haven't had a chance to try them, though as far as Max is concerned, he'd just as soon spend the entire day on the track racing the Whiz Kids mini race cars.

The Play All Day passes are the way to go here, as they include admission to Splash City, all rides, entrance to the HMCS *Haida*, plus the Cinesphere's IMAX films as well.

HMCS Haida Naval Museum

Ontario Place
955 Lake Shore Boulevard West
Toronto, ON, M6K 3B9
(416) 314-9755
www3.sympatico.ca/hrc/haida

HMCS Haida

"Wow, cool!" is the reaction from most kids when they first spot the impressive HMCS *Haida*. It's been said that the Tribal class of destroyers were "magnificent in appearance, majestic in movement, and menacing in disposition". I'd have to agree. The *Haida* still looks as though she could sail silently into battle and win. In fact she looks like she wants to.

The Tribals had the most advanced naval architecture, marine propulsion systems, and weaponry of their time, and the *Haida* put it to good use, sinking 14 German ships and numerous U-boats. After helping to secure the Channel for the D-Day invasion, she went on to serve two tours in Korea, earning the title of the Fightingest Ship in the Royal Canadian Navy.

Toronto's Lakeshore and Islands

This is a great place for exploring and for pretending. Climbing up and down the staircases from deck to deck, your young sailors will feel like they're part of the 200-man crew. They can send Morse code messages from the Radio Room and use the voice pipes in the bridge to "talk" to the captain in his cabin. But it's wise to leave babies behind, as the terrain is definitely not stroller-friendly.

> **HMCS Haida Naval Museum**
>
> **Hours:** Open from Victoria Day until mid-September. Call for hours.
>
> **Cost:** General admission (ages 5-54), $3.95; Seniors, $2.95; Families, $9.95; free with an Ontario Place Play All Day pass.

Take a tour given by interpreters dressed in the jaunty uniform of a 1950s sailor. And make sure to get here by noon to hear the daily firing of the forward guns as a naval salute.

Canadian Automotive Collection and Motorsport Hall of Fame

Sports Hall of Fame
Exhibition Place
Lake Shore Blvd, between Strachen Ave and Dufferin St
Toronto, ON, M6K 3C3
(416) 597-2643
www.canadianautomotivecollection.ca

My son Max despaired when the Motorsport Hall of Fame disappeared from the corner of College and Bay Streets. We had promised him a visit for almost a year, but always seemed to pass it by on our way to Riverdale Farm. Then one day the sleek old racing cars were gone. We wondered if we'd ever get a chance to see them up close until we heard that it had a new home in the Sports Hall of Fame Building on the Exhibition grounds. This is a candy store for young boys who love the car racing circuit. You'll find Jacques Villeneuve Sr.'s 1983 Indy March car, a 1959 Porsche 356A once driven by Walt Mackay, and a 1984 KR 5 Frisbee driven by Villeneuve Sr. and Paul Tracy. It's a sizeable hall of fame with more than 90 inductees, and gleaming trophies catch the eye from a display case near the entrance, fuelling dreams of future glory in the minds of little boys.

> **Canadian Automotive Collection and Motorsport Hall of Fame**
>
> **Hours:** Mon-Sat, 10 am - 6 pm.
>
> **Cost:** Suggested fee of $2 per person, $5 per family.
>
> **Directions:** Take the Toronto-bound Queen Elizabeth Way or Lake Shore Boulevard and follow the signs to Exhibition Place

Chapter Three

Historic Fort York

100 Garrison Road
Toronto, ON, M5V 3K9
(416) 392-6907
www.city.toronto.on.ca/culture

Historic Fort York
Hours: Summer hours (mid-May to early Sept.): Daily 10 am - 5 pm. Rest of the year: Mon-Fri, 10 am - 4 pm and Sat-Sun, 10 am - 5 pm.
Cost: Adults, $5; Students (13-18), $3.25; Kids (6-12), $3.
Directions: Off Fleet Street, between Bathurst and Strachen Streets.

   Tucked away in a strip of forgotten wasteland beside the Gardiner Expressway, Fort York can be easily overlooked by visitors. Yet, as Canada's largest collection of original War of 1812 buildings and the site of Toronto's founding in 1793, it deserves more visibility. Fortunately, the site is slated for a major upgrade in the upcoming redevelopment of Toronto's waterfront.

   This small British fort surrounded by a dry moat is best known for the Battle of York in 1813, when soldiers awoke to find 14 American ships in the harbour. The battle raged for some six hours before the British commander ordered his men to blow up the Fort's magazine, along with the boat they were building for Sir Isaac Brock, a prominent British commander who would later die defending Niagara. Many American soldiers were killed in the ensuing blast and fire, while their compatriots took revenge on the citizens of York by looting and pillaging and setting fire to the Parliament buildings. Stung badly by this defeat, the British retaliated the next year by burning down the White House.

   You can take a guided tour of the Fort throughout the year, but if you're here for Canada Day (July 1) or in mid-July, take in Fort York's special events. Danielle Urquhart was our splendid guide on Canada Day, giving us a rousing rendition of the story of the battle, putting us squarely in the shoes of the British soldiers. Kids will enjoy the military reenactments complete with musket drills and much marching about. If you're lucky, shortbread cookies might be coming out of the historic oven when you arrive. They're very good about sharing them with 21st century visitors.

Soldier at Historic Fort York

Courtesy Ontario Tourism

Toronto's Lakeshore and Islands

City Centre Airport

60 Harbour Street
Toronto, ON, M5J 1B7
(416) 203-6942
www.torontoport.com/TCCA

> ### City Centre Airport
> **Hours:** Ferries run every 15 minutes from 6 am until about 11 pm, but the time to watch planes is weekdays during morning and afternoon rush hours.
>
> **Cost:** Ferry: Adults, $5; Kids, $2.

The Island Airport (as it's known to most Torontonians) is one of the busiest in the country, with a steady stream of small planes taking off and landing on the three runways. It's mostly small single engine planes and Dash-8 commuter planes flying to Montreal and Ottawa, but you can also see executives and sightseers hopping into helicopters, and seaplanes taking millionaires to cottage country and fishermen to lakes in northern Ontario. Grab lunch or a coffee at the Druxy's deli located upstairs in the terminal and drink in the atmosphere of this WWII-era building. The passenger and vehicle ferry, Maple City, makes the round trip across the 121 metre-wide (400 feet) Western Channel every 15 minutes during airport operating hours. It's the shortest ferry ride in the world, taking less than a minute to cross.

Toronto Music Garden

475 Queen's Quay West
Toronto, ON, M5V 3A6
(416) 973-3000
www.city.toronto.on.ca/parks/music_index

> ### Toronto Music Garden
> **Hours:** Never closes.
>
> **Cost:** Free.
>
> **Directions:** Between Spadina and Bathurst on Queen's Quay.

The Toronto Music Garden was the serendipitous result of a collaboration between renowned cellist Yo-Yo Ma and landscape designer Julie Moir Messervy, who used nature to interpret Johann Sebastian Bach's first Suite for Unaccompanied Cello. The project was so successful they decided to create a garden based on the suite, and approached the city of Boston to host the site. When that plan fell through, Toronto's mayor at the time, Barbara Hall, jumped at the opportunity and gave the project a prime piece of Toronto's waterfront.

This garden is a riot of color, texture, and motion throughout the four seasons, thanks to the ingenious use of rocks, plant materials, and man-made sculptural elements. Kids have endless fun racing up and down the grassy steps of the amphitheatre, playing hide and seek among the bushes, or giving impromptu performances in the pavilion. You can rent an audio tour of the garden, narrated by Mr. Ma, explaining all the nuances of the garden and how they reflect the six distinct movements in the First Suite.

In summer, volunteers give 45-minute garden tours on Wednesdays at 11 am and 6 pm. Self-guided audio tours are also available 10 am - 8 pm daily. Go to the Marina Quay office just south of the park to rent one for $5. Concerts are given in the pavilion on Thursday nights at 7 pm and Sunday afternoons at 3 pm. Check the schedule on the website to find out who's playing. Seating is limited so get there early or bring a folding chair.

Chapter Three

Harbourfront Antique Market

390 Queens Quay West
Toronto, ON, M5V 3A6
(416) 260-2626 or (888) 263-6533
www.hfam.com

Harbourfront Antique Market
Hours: Tues-Sun, 10 am - 6 pm.
Cost: Free.
Directions: One block south of the Skydome on Queen's Quay.

If you're ever down at the lakeshore, waiting for rain to let up or for a concert at the Music Garden to begin, this is the place to kill time. Kids will adore exploring some of the exhibitors' booths here, with old toy cars, comic books and more to tempt them. It might be too frustrating to bring toddlers, with all the breakables in this place, unless you find them a toy and take them upstairs to Sophie's Café. We found a box of old matchbox cars and trucks for a buck each, which made Max happy and allowed us to enjoy a coffee upstairs.

Our favourite booth is Yank Azman's, who has long supplied props to Toronto movie sets, and to "men and fearless women since 1969." In fact his shop looks like an enormous Ralph Lauren ad with its leather luggage, vintage sports equipment, and elaborate trophies. Teens who are otherwise thrown by the antiques might enjoy celebrity spotting; Hollywood A-list types like Jane Fonda, Meg Ryan, Catherine Deneuve, James Woods, and Matt Dillon have all shopped here.

Harbourfront Centre

235 Queen's Quay West
Toronto, ON, M5J 2G8
(416) 973-3000
www.harbourfront.on.ca

Harbourfront Centre
Hours: York Quay opens at 8 am and shuts as late as 1 am in the summer.
Cost: Many activities and performances are free, but some festivals have ticketed events as well.
Directions: From Lake Shore Boulevard, all downtown exits access Queens Quay West and Harbourfront Centre.

If I had to say where Toronto's heart lies, I'd pick Harbourfront, no question. It may not be the geographic heart of town, but it's certainly the spiritual heart, where Toronto's many nationalities gather to celebrate their national days and other special occasions with festive music, dance, theatre, and lots of great traditional food.

Summertime brings a whole roster of themed weekends under the banner Rhythms of the World. Recent years have included the Ritmo y Color (Latin music) festival, Ashkenaz: a Festival of Yiddish Culture, the JVC Jazz festival, a blues festival, and many other intriguing events and mini-festivals. Alongside all that entertainment is an International Marketplace where a constantly changing selection of vendors provides an endless variety of treasures from around the world. And the best part is that virtually all of it is free.

In the fall, Harbourfront hosts the world-renowned Author's Festival, when literary giants gather to give readings, take part in panels, and have the rare pleasure of mingling with other writers. In May, the renowned Milk International Children's festival takes over

Toronto's Lakeshore and Islands

the centre, and in summer a roster of day camps keeps more than a thousand kids busy all day. Winter brings a series of Cushion Concerts for kids, and the pond turns into a wonderful harbourside skating rink.

Visual art also thrives at the York Quay Gallery, where the emphasis is on drama. Kids adore watching the glassblowers work miracles with the molten material and peruse the displays full of their work with interest trying to guess whose work is whose.

We tend to come here spontaneously, and always have a terrific time. On a recent Sunday afternoon we caught an awesome pop band from Senegal. Another time we listened to a star from the Canadian Opera Company belt out arias over the bright blue waterfront. Other days we've arrived in the middle of a food festival. Sometimes I wonder what we'd be doing on weekends without Harbourfront.

The Power Plant

231 Queens Quay W. (at York St.)
Toronto, ON, M5J 2G8
(416) 973-4949
www.thepowerplant.org

Before London had the Tate Modern, Toronto had the Power Plant, a contemporary art gallery where you'll see today's rising stars of the local and international art scenes.

You might see found art sculptures, multimedia installations, or giant canvases covering the pristine white walls of this renovated power plant, though whatever is being displayed has always seemed to intrigue our kids. Like the gallery, the art tends to be large-scale as well, so visitors can usually see everything in less than an hour. The best part for families is that kids under 12 are free, so the financial risks of turning your kids onto modern art are nil, and they might end up discovering that they like it. Tours happen every Saturday and Sunday at 2 and 4 pm, and also on Wednesday nights (when admission is free from 5 to 8 pm) at 6:30 pm.

The Power Plant

Hours: Tues-Sun, noon - 6 pm; Wed, noon - 8 pm; Holiday Mondays only, noon - 6 pm.

Cost: Adults, $4; Kids under 12, free; Wed, 5 - 8 pm: free.

Directions: Beside York Quay at Harbourfront.

Chapter Three

Queen's Quay Terminal

207 Queen's Quay West
Toronto, ON, M5J 1A7
(416) 203-0510
www.queens-quay-terminal.com

Queen's Quay Terminal is a handsome old waterfront warehouse that was renovated into a high-end mall and condominium complex back in the 1980s. Because it was originally built for the cold storage of fruits and vegetables, the walls were extremely thick – so thick that developers thought better of tearing it down and built condos on top of it instead. Today it's one of the most pleasant shopping malls in town and one of the last reminders of what Toronto's harbour was like at the beginning of the last century.

While we find the shopping a little pricey, it's fun to browse in all the one-of-a-kind boutiques. This is also where to come if you'd like a good meal; you can choose from about a dozen restaurants and cafes, some with dockside patios. These are easily the best seats in town on a sultry summer night, particularly when the tall ships are in town (see Places to Eat and Shop at the end of the chapter).

Toronto Harbour Tours

145 Queens Quay West
Toronto, ON, M5J 1B7
(416) 868-0400
www.torontotours.com

Toronto Harbour Tours

Hours: Tours leave every half hour in summer. Winter hours vary; call for times.

Cost: Adults, $23.75; Students (13+), $19.75; Children (2-12), $9.75.

Directions: Tickets can be bought right on Pier 6 at the foot of York St. next to the Second Cup café.

Next to the ferry, Toronto Harbour Tours is our favourite way to see the harbour. If you get a guide like Brendan, you'll get an insider's take on Toronto, past and present. We heard hilarious stories involving landmarks like the Skydome (i.e. the one about the honeymooners in the hotel room) and were entertained for the better part of an hour as we were spirited around the harbour and islands. I loved hearing about the three island yacht clubs and some of the boats' better names, like the neurologist and gynecologist who dubbed their sailboat 'Heads or Tails'.

Enjoy the best view of Toronto's skyline on this tour, and get insight into how the Islands developed into one of North America's most unique residential communities. We were surprised to find out that a freak storm 'created' the islands in 1858; prior to that they were connected to the mainland by a series of sandbars.

Take a tour early in the morning or just before sunset when the views are especially impressive. Be warned that it can get very breezy and cold out on the water, so check the weather before you go. Also know that there's not much room to roam on this boat (in fact it's a sit-down experience) so if your kids are restless and need to stretch their legs occasionally, I'd opt for the Mariposa harbour tour instead.

Toronto's Lakeshore and Islands

Mariposa Cruise Line

207 Queen's Quay West
Toronto, ON, M5J 1A7
(416) 203-0178 or 1-800-976-2442
www.mariposacruises.com

Mariposa Cruise Line

Hours: Mid-May to September, 11 am, 12:15 pm, 1:30 pm, 2:45 pm, 4 pm. Call for extended season hours.

Cost: Adults, $16; Students (12-17), $14.50; Kids (4-11), $11.

A harbour tour is even more fun when you do it on the *Oriole*, a replica of a Great Lakes steamship that operates as a tour boat each summer. We admired Toronto's scenic skyline from a distance, and watched the tourists snapping away while we took in the sights of the islands, the island airport, and the fabled Gibraltar Point Lighthouse. Though we've not done it ourselves, Mariposa offers a two-hour Sunday brunch cruise and a three-hour dinner cruise as well.

Toronto Islands Ferries

Foot of Bay St, at Queen's Quay
Toronto, ON
(416) 392-8193
www.city.toronto.on.ca/parks/to_islands/ferry.htm

Most Torontonians don't realize that the islands weren't always islands, but were once a series of sandbars linked to the mainland. In 1858, a fierce storm was responsible for creating the familiar chain of islands we

Courtesy Ontario Tourism

know today. Three ferries make the short journeys out to the islands nowadays, packed with families toting coolers and pushing bikes. Depending on where you want to go, you can take a ferry to Centre Island, Ward

Toronto Islands Ferries

Hours: Ward's Island ferry: Daily, 6:35 am - 11:45 pm; Centre Island ferry: Daily, 8 am - 11:45 pm; Hanlan's Point ferry: Weekdays, 9 am - 10:30 pm; Weekends, 8 am - 11:15 pm. It's always best to call as hours fluctuate throughout the year.

Cost: Adults, $5; Students (under 19), $3; Kids (under 14), $2; Kids under 2, free.

Directions: Main entrance to the ferry dock is at foot of Bay St on Queens Quay. Enter through a walkway between Harbour Castle Westin Hotel and Harbour Castle condominiums.

Island, or Hanlan's Point. But it really doesn't matter which you take, since all the islands are linked together by paths and bridges, and you can return on whichever ferry you like.

Chapter Three

The Toronto Islands Park

(416) 392-8193
www.city.toronto.on.ca/parks/to_islands/island_index

The Toronto Islands Park

Cost: Free.

Hours: Dawn to dusk.
See ferry schedule for
first and last sailings.

Directions: The Islands are across
the water from downtown
Toronto. The only way to get to
them is by water taxi or by ferry.

In less than 10 minutes, a ferry transports you to a chain of idyllic islands crisscrossed by bike paths and quiet waterways. What better place to spend a glorious summer day, watching a regatta, lying on a beach, trout fishing, or canoeing.

The three major islands – Centre Island, Ward Island and Hanlan's Point – each have their own unique atmosphere, drawing over one million people to their shores each year. Families come for the expansive parklands, the car-free bicycle paths, and the wonderful beaches and pool. You can bring bikes across on the ferry or rent them on Hanlan's Point or at the Lookout Pier on Centre Island. To better plan your day, make sure to pick up a map at the information booth upon arriving at the ferry dock. If you want to know beach conditions in advance, call the beach hotline at (416) 392-7161.

Centre Island

Centre Island is most popular with families, with its huge picnic areas, playground, cedar hedge maze, beach, and award-winning gardens. The big draw is Centreville – an amusement park for the 2 to 12 set – with 30 rides, a petting zoo featuring farm animals and pony rides, and picturesque "swan" boats circling a small lagoon.

Centreville Amusement Park

On Centre Island
(416) 203-0405
www.centreisland.ca

For years, Centreville has been my son's absolute favourite thing to do on a summer afternoon. For one thing, you have to take a ferry to get there (oh joy!). But the best thing about this family amusement park is that the rides are geared to little ones, starting with the first ride you see, the popular Bumblebee. Other favourites are the Fire Engine and the motorboats, but there are 30 in total to try. Older kids will enjoy the Log Flume ride, which seemed thrilling enough for the pre-teens we saw riding it.

Centreville Amusement Park

Toronto's Lakeshore and Islands

After a fun-filled hour or two on the ferris wheel, antique carousel, motorboats, pony ride, water slide, and miniature golf course, families can enjoy picnics and train rides, or stroll through the Far Enough Farm. The island's quiet beaches provide the perfect escape from the bustling city. There's no admission fee for Centreville, but all-day ride passes are available for the attractions. We usually buy a bunch of tickets, and end up wishing we had bought the passes, which are a bargain.

> **Centreville Amusement Park**
>
> **Hours:** May 18-Sept. 2 (Opening weekend May 4 & 5): Daily, 10:30 am - dusk. Open weekends only in May and September. Times subject to change without notice, weather permitting.
>
> **Cost:** Day passes: Individual pass, $22; Children under four feet tall, $15.50; Family Fun Ride Pass for four, $72.
>
> **Directions:** The only way to get to Centreville, on Centre Island, is by ferry. See Toronto Islands Ferries listing in this chapter or call (416) 392-8193 for departure times. The Toronto Ferry Docks are located at the foot of Bay Street and Queens Quay. Once on Centre Island, follow the signs to the left of the ferry terminal.

Hanlan's Point

Hanlan's Point is a quiet corner of the park, where the historic Gibraltar Point Lighthouse still keeps a watch – though not in the direction of its other main attraction, Toronto's only nude beach!

Interestingly, this serene spot was once a thriving summer resort, nicknamed the Coney Island of Canada, with hotels, a vaudeville theatre, dance halls, and an amusement park. One of the main attractions in those days was a horse that dove, headfirst, off a high pier into the lake. Another famous resident, Edward "Ned" Hanlan, put Toronto on the map by earning international recognition as a rower holding numerous world records. By the turn of the century, Hanlan's Point had grown to be a "summer suburb of the city." Even in winter, people came to fish, skate, and sail their iceboats here.

In 1897, a baseball and lacrosse stadium was built on the site of the present-day Island Airport. It was here that Babe Ruth hit his first major league home run! And it was during this time that numerous cottages began to appear, as city residents embraced the landscape and lifestyle of the Island. When the stadium was demolished to make way for the airport, the tattered amusement park and summer village had seen better days. Today, much of the area is a nature preserve, along with the popular beach, parts of which are family-friendly and clothing compulsory!

Ward's Island

Ward's Island, the easternmost, is where all the island residents live today, in about 100 small cottages surrounded by lovely, whimsical gardens. Come and stroll around their lovely streets, enjoy the best family beach on the islands, and imagine what it would be like to live here! There's also a great place to eat, the Rectory Café, (416) 203-2152, just a short walk from the Ward's Island ferry.

Chapter Three

Air Canada Centre

40 Bay Street
Toronto, ON, M5J 2X2
(416) 815-5982
www.theaircanadacentre.com

Air Canada Centre

Hours: May-Sept, tours leave hourly
10 am - 4 pm.

Cost: Adults, $12; Students, $10;
Children (12 & under), $8.

There's an old saying among Torontonians: We love the Leafs – and all the other teams, if they're winning. Nothing beats the loyalty Torontonians have for their blessed Maple Leafs, a team that hasn't won a Stanley Cup for over 30 years. But who cares about winning, when it's the Leafs, right? While Maple Leaf Gardens was the home of the Leafs forever and a day, today it's the sparkling Air

The Maple Leafs

Canada Centre that plays host to NHL hockey, the NBA's Toronto Raptors, as well as myriad entertainment spectacles throughout the year.

Coming here for a game is the best possible way to see it, but a one-hour behind-the-scenes tour exposes the inner workings of this state-of-the-art facility. Kids ooh and ahh as they drink in the luxe interior of an executive suite, walk the hallowed floor, and tour the team dressing rooms and Raptors practice facility. But the piece de resistance for hockey fans is the Esso Maple Leaf Memories & Dreams Room. A must-see for any Leafs fan, it's like a de facto hockey museum devoted to Our Team. The nostalgia here will strike a chord with any fan, young or old. Leaf legends are honoured, memorabilia is displayed, and a replica of a Leafs locker room – showing lockers from 1931 and from 1999 – is like an answering goal to the Montreal Canadiens locker room in the Hockey Hall of Fame, just up the street from here.

Call in advance, as events mean that tours are subject to cancellation or changes.

Toronto's Lakeshore and Islands

Toronto Maple Leafs

Air Canada Centre
40 Bay Street
Toronto, ON, M5J 2X2
(416) 870-8000 for advance tickets.
On game day tickets available at the
Air Canada Centre box office, in person only.
www.nhl.com/lineups/team/tickets/index.html

> **Toronto Maple Leafs**
>
> **Cost:** Ticket prices range from $24 to $390.
>
> **Hours:** Schedule varies, but game nights are generally Monday, Tuesdays and Saturdays.

It's not easy to get tickets to a Leafs game – unless you're willing to part with a few hundred dollars! But should you score tickets, you'll be treated to a piece of Canadian hockey lore. Torontonians (and people across Canada) love their Leafs – even though they haven't won the Stanley Cup since 1967. They forge on, with some impressive teams, but not enough to topple Detroit, New Jersey or any of the other teams they've lost to in the playoffs recently. On game days near the end of the season, you're apt to see Torontonians wearing the blue and white to work. We live in hope!

Toronto Raptors

Air Canada Centre
40 Bay Street
Toronto, ON, M5J 2X2
(416) 872-5000 for advance tickets. Tickets are also available one week ahead of games at the Air Canada Centre box office, in person only. Groups of 20 or more can purchase tickets through the team line, 416-366-DUNK (3865).
www.nba.com/raptors

Torontonians have taken to The Raptors in a big way since the team's first NBA season in 1995. The fledgling team sprang onto the basketball scene with a brand new player named Damon Stoudamire, who was the Raptor's top scorer that year and went on to become the league's Rookie of the Year. Every year they get better, and under coach Lenny Wilkens,

> **Toronto Raptors**
>
> **Cost:** Ticket prices range from $10.50 to $625.
>
> **Hours:** Schedule varies but game nights are generally Sundays, Wednesdays and Fridays.

they've seen their best seasons yet. Star forward Vince Carter, the Raptor's main man, posted a 24.7 points per game average in 2002 and heads up a team that had a strong start to the 2002-2003 season. You can't go wrong taking the gang to a Raptors game, and the team frequently has family ticket deals. Check the website for current offers.

Chapter Three

Redpath Sugar Museum

95 Queen's Quay West
Toronto, ON, M5E 1A3
(416) 366-3561
www.redpath.com

Redpath Sugar Museum

Hours: Weekdays:
10 am - 12 pm, 1 - 3:30 pm.

Cost: Free.

Directions: Walk east past the Westin Bayshore, and you will see it just beyond a large parking lot.

The last industrial site on Toronto's lakeshore is the Redpath Sugar Factory, allowed to continue operating because of its clean steam-driven technology. It's an easy 10-minute walk from Harbourfront or the Island Ferry dock and makes for an interesting (and free) hour. The museum's curator, Richard Feltoe, knows exactly what fascinates kids about sugar, so take him up on the offer of a tour.

He explains how sugar was once so expensive that only kings and queens and the very rich could afford it. "As an example," he says, "sugar was 100 dollars per kilo 500 years ago, 30 dollars 200 years ago, and how much today?" We can't guess, so he tells us: "Only about 90 cents!" My son quickly determines that we should be buying more candy, since sugar's so cheap. An interesting conclusion.

A couple of 19th century political cartoons stop us in our tracks. One links sugar to slavery (and urges a boycott) and another depicts the trade wars that broke out between sugar cane and sugar beet producers. Other neat artifacts are the metal cone-shaped molds that used to be the standard way that sugar was packed, shipped and sold.

Much of the museum traces Redpath family history, which could be dull except for a number of fascinating artifacts from the early days of the company. An old punch clock, vintage photos, and elaborate programs from company picnics (with a formal games schedule that included spoon and egg and fat man races) inspire lots of discussion. But the neatest thing on display is a love letter that was written three times over in three different directions – up, down and sideways, still surprisingly legible for all that ink. And though there's no candy on offer (Max was hoping…) there is a case of elaborately decorated cakes that display the artistry involved in sculpting and molding sugar. Our favourite is a guitar-shaped Beatles cake, with wonderfully rendered faces of the Fab Four.

Tommy Thompson Park

Lake Shore Boulevard at Leslie Street
Toronto, ON
(416) 661-6600
www.trca.on.ca/parks_and_attractions/places_to_visit/tommy_Thompson

Tommy Thompson Park is a long expanse of urban wilderness created from the dustbin of Toronto's history – quite literally. The Leslie Spit, as it's still widely known, is a man-made peninsula intended to serve as an outer harbour to accommodate expanded shipping. For years, trucks dumped construction waste and landfill here, beginning in the 1950s. In total, more than four million loads have been deposited here to form the park that attracts so much wildlife.

Toronto's Lakeshore and Islands

Named after former Metro Toronto Parks Commissioner Tommy Thompson, who was well known for his phrase "Please walk on the grass," the park is a prime piece of the Toronto waterfront park system, offering families great recreational opportunities. Most people cycle the Spit, though it's great for a leisurely stroll with impromptu bird watching. Should you tire mid-stroll, you can hop on the official shuttle van that takes visitors around the park free of charge in summer.

Tommy Thompson Park

Hours: April-Oct, Weekends and holidays: 9 am - 6 pm; Nov-March, 9 am - 4:30 pm. Closed Christmas, Boxing, and New Year's Days.

Cost: Free.

Directions: Travel east on Lake Shore Boulevard to Leslie Street, then south half a kilometre to the park entrance. Hop on free transportation anywhere along the trail from early May to October. The shuttle van runs between the main gate and the pedestrian bridge within the park.

Wetlands meadows and forests cover the park nowadays, and you can spot some of more than 290 bird species that have been observed on site. Many of them nest here, including the Ring-billed Gull, Herring Gull, Common Tern, Black-crowned Night-heron, and Double-crested Cormorant. During the summer, catch the innovative mobile nature display called the "Spit Cart." And check the information board at the park entrance for information on interpretive programs and nature talks being offered. In the fall, you can see Monach butterflies massing by the hundreds, in preparation for their long migration south as far as Mexico.

The Docks Drive-In

11 Polson Street
Toronto, ON, M5A 1A4
(416) 461-DOCK (3625)
www.thedocks.com/nav/drivein

Remember drive-ins? Those staples of our childhood, now confined to the outer reaches of suburbia (if you can find one at all). Now Torontonians can eyeball the world's largest drive-in movie theatre screen at The Docks, a lakeside pleasure

The Docks Drive-In

Hours: Tues & Fri-Sun, 9 pm.

Cost: Adults, $12 ($6 on Tuesdays); Kids under 12, free.

Directions: The drive-in is located on The Docks Driving Range at The Docks Entertainment Complex. Drive south on Cherry Street from Lake Shore Boulevard. After Knob Hill Farms, turn right into Polson Street and drive to the end.

palace for the 20-somethings. While we've avoided The Docks ever since we had kids, the lure of the giant screen was too much to resist. So we popped the kids into pajamas and drove down to the drive-in. They run a double bill of first run movies every night, plus triple bills on long weekends. Check the website or call to find out what's playing.

There's a snack bar called Spike's, and after the show, you can access the entire Docks facility – nightclubs, patio, pool tables, sand beach, rock-climbing wall, a ride called Screamin' Demon, and much more. Not for us with small kids, but a good deal for a family with older kids or teens wanting a night out. The outdoor patio also has an amazing view of the Toronto skyline – a super photo op at night.

Chapter Three

Places to Eat

Most of the better restaurants along the lakeshore are in Queen's Quay Terminal, listed below. If you're looking for a snack or fast food, there are always hot dog vendors around during the summer months, and Harbourfront often has ethnic food festivals that feature food stalls on their main lawn area. An especially good one, called the Hot and Spicy Food Festival is held in late August.

Il Fornello
Queen's Quay Terminal
(416) 861-1028

Does Il Fornello or Terroni's make the best pizza in Toronto? They're both best, depending on where you are at the time. If we're at Harbourfront and in the mood for a big meal, this is our first choice. Get a table out on the patio and watch the ever-changing parade of boats that dock right in front of the restaurant.

Spinnaker's
Queen's Quay Terminal
(416) 203-0559

Spinnaker's is next door to Il Fornello and serves great seafood along with a classic kids' menu (chicken fingers, fish and chips, grilled cheese, pink lemonade, etc.)

Tim Horton's
Queen's Quay Terminal
(416) 214-9474

A mainstay with Canadian families, Tim Horton's built its reputation as a donut shop, but has evolved into a full-service fast food restaurant. The menu is soup and sandwich fare that is fast and fresh. On a hot day, we can't resist the iced cappuccinos – half the price of Starbucks and every bit as good.

Queen's Quay Food Court
Queen's Quay Terminal, 2nd Floor

Sometimes a food court is the only way to go. The second floor of Queen's Quay has four choices: burgers, Chinese, Japanese, and a deli. Plus lots of elbowroom in a big open space where kids can run around or watch the boats coming and going.

Places to Shop

Queen's Quay Terminal is the only shopping centre down at the Lakeshore. That and the Harbourfront Antique Market are the main sources for interesting browsing and souvenir shopping. All the shops listed below are located at Queen's Quay.

PROUD Canadian Design
Queen's Quay Terminal
(416) 603-7413

PROUD features furniture, housewares, and small decorative accessories by Canadian designers from coast to coast. You'll find no funkier shop for artful souvenirs of Toronto.

Toy Terminal
Queen's Quay Terminal
(416) 203-3385

Great educational toys from Lamaze Infant Development to Smithsonian Institution Chemistry Sets. Something for every age and interest.

Dollina
Queen's Quay Terminal
(416) 203-0576

A pleasure palace for little girls and boys who love dolls and teddy bears.

Chapter Four

Toronto's Downtown

Toronto's best-known district is Bay Street, the financial heart of Canada set in the heart of Toronto's downtown. All five major national banks have towers in this area, the stand-outs being Mies van der Rohe's sleek black towers for the TD Bank, and the Royal Bank tower's gleaming gold facade, which employs 7,000 kilograms of real gold to get that glorious glimmer.

To the west lies trendy Queen Street West and the Entertainment District, made up of theatres along King and Peter Streets, nightclubs on Adelaide and Richmond Streets, the Skydome, and music venue Roy Thompson Hall. On the east side is Toronto's most historic district, the original City of York dating back to the 17th century. This is one of Toronto's best strolling neighbourhoods, where you can visit St. Lawrence Market, admire beautiful St. Lawrence Hall, pop into St. James Cathedral for an organ concert, and see numerous other evocative buildings along the way.

Downtown attractions are all within walking distance, or you can hop on the Double Decker Bus and see it from on high. To see Toronto's skyline properly, you have to get out on the water. Take the ferry over to the Islands (see page 52) or hop on one of the harbour tours. Another great vantage point, especially at sunset, is from a patio seat at The Docks, (see page 57) an entertainment complex in the Portlands.

Chapter Four

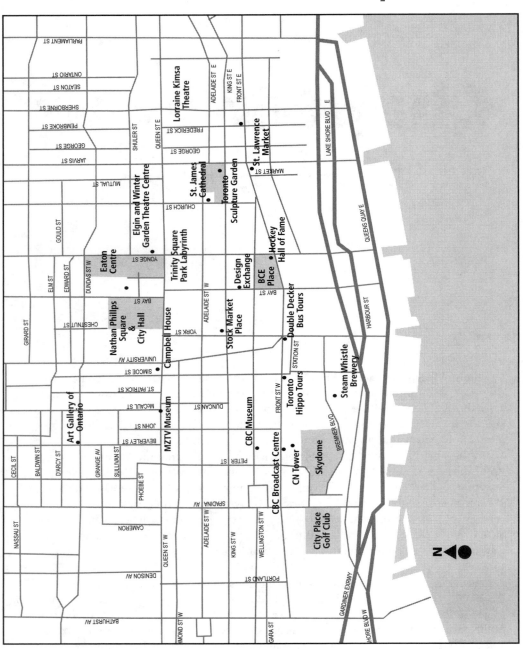

Toronto's Downtown
Things to Do
City Tours

Starting off with a city tour is always a good idea, but only you know the ability of your kids to sit still and listen to a tour guide for an hour or more. If my kids are any indication, most won't have the attention span required for the typical city tour. Fortunately, Toronto offers a few city tours that are stand-outs with kids: harbour tours (one of them on a schooner), an amphibious bus tour, and a double-decker bus tour. Any of these is a novelty for most kids and will engage them long enough for you to enjoy the tour as well!

Double Decker Bus Tours

123 Front Street West
Toronto, ON, M5J 2M2
(416) 594-3310

What kid wouldn't love to see the sights from atop the heights of a genuine double-decker bus? Indulge them with this well-narrated two-hour tour, or use the hop on/hop off service to explore Toronto on your own terms. The buses stop at more than 20 major destinations around town including Casa Loma, Harbourfront, and Chinatown, making this a great alternative to taxis or mass transit. Buses come every 35 minutes, and your ticket is good for a full 48 hours, allowing you to take all the time you need at every stop.

> **Double Decker Bus Tours**
>
> **Hours:** April-Dec, daily, 9 am - 4 pm.
>
> **Cost:** Adults, $31; Students, $28; Children (5-12), $16.
>
> **Directions:** Tours start in front of Nicholby's souvenir store at 123 Front Street West.

Toronto Hippo Tours

151 Front Street West
Toronto, ON, M5J 2N1
(416) 703-HIPO (4476); 1-877-635-5510
www.torontohippotours.com

This is a bus that is also a boat that will take you on a 90-minute tour of Toronto's major sights, including Front Street, up Yonge Street to Elm Street, then south on Bay up to University for a loop around Queen's Park and the University of Toronto, and then through the Fashion District to Ontario Place. That's where it heads down a ramp and into the lagoons around Ontario Place, Toronto's funky space age amusement park on the lake. It spends about 30 minutes plying around the park's pod-like structures and swinging by the impressive HMCS *Haida*, before rolling back onto shore and back to the starting point.

> **Toronto Hippo Tours**
>
> **Hours:** May-Nov, hourly, 11 am - 6 pm.
>
> **Cost:** Adults, $35; Students (13-17), $30; Children (3-12), $23; Family, $100 (two adults and two children).
>
> **Directions:** Board the bus at the corner of Simcoe Street and Front Street West.

Chapter Four

It's a funny-looking vehicle with hippos emblazoned on its sides and life preservers hanging off the back, so be prepared for lots of stares as you get wheeled and jetted around town. My only complaint is that the commentary wasn't nearly as good as some of the other tours we've taken.

Royal Ontario Museum (ROM) Walks

Tours take place all over the city. Check website or call for information
(416) 586-5513
www.rom.on.ca

> ### Royal Ontario Museum (ROM) Walks
> **Hours:** Wed, 6 pm and Sun, 2 pm.
> **Cost:** Most ROMWalks are free.
> **Directions:** Call for schedule and location.

ROM Walks take you through points of historical and cultural interest in Toronto, narrated by volunteers from the Royal Ontario Museum. These are always enlightening and fun for older kids – though it always helps to take treats and drinks along to keep them energized! There are 10 free walks that are offered up to four times each during the spring, summer, and fall. Just call the museum for the starting time and place and, upon arriving, look for the volunteer guide carrying a blue umbrella – rain or shine. Don't forget to pack your sneakers! Some of the more interesting titles include Sacred Stone and Steeples, Along the Front, and Cathedrals of Wealth and Commerce.

Discovery Walks

City Hall
100 Queen Street West
Toronto, ON, M5H 2N2
(416) 338-0338
www.city.toronto.on.ca/parks

Discovery Walks were created by the city's Parks and Recreation department to allow people to discover areas of Toronto through well-marked, self-guided pathways linking ravines, parks, gardens, beaches, and neighbourhoods. Each one has its own distinct flavour, some with public art and historic buildings along the way, others with natural features like ponds, marshes, and forests. They are all designed to take between two to four hours to walk at a reasonable pace, and have good surfaces for even the smallest walkers.

The guides can be found on the city's website (see above). They can be printed easily as PDF files (free PDF Reader available at www.adobe.com). Walks include: Downtown Toronto, Uptown Toronto, Eastern Beaches and Ravines, Humber River, Old Mill and Marshes, and Don Valley Hills and Dales.

Toronto's Downtown

Downtown West (West of Yonge)

CN Tower

301 Front Street West
Toronto, ON, M5V 2T6
(416) 868-6937
www.cntower.ca

Toronto's best-known landmark is the CN Tower – the world's tallest free-standing structure at 1,815 ft, 5 inches tall (553 metres) or about five and a half football fields stacked end to end. It's been a feature of the skyline since 1976.

People have tackled its heights (and made the Guinness World Book of Records) by pogo-sticking up the stairs – all 1967 of them – and tumbling down them (a movie stuntman did this on his day off). But the fastest and most scenic way up is by taking one of the six glass-fronted, high-speed elevators to the observation deck. Shooting up 20 feet per second, you reach the LookOut Level (at 346 metres/1,136 feet) in just under a minute's time – about the same rate of the ascent as an airplane.

Once you're up there, start by taking the stairs down to the Glass Floor, which was built to withstand the weight of 14 large hippos, so no worries! Myself, I can't go near it, let alone watch the antics of my husband and son, as they proceed to jump all over it. Take the famous glass floor photo, which involves lying on the floor, spreading your hair out, and pretending you're in free fall. You'll also find an excellent revolving restaurant called, fittingly, 360. Despite its reputation as a gourmet and wine-lover's mecca, it welcomes kids and is worth checking out for their outstanding kiddie cocktails and breathtaking view. It takes 72 minutes (and possibly three Shirley Temples) for a full rotation.

CN Tower

Hours: Open year round. Phone for seasonal hours. Closed Christmas Day.

Cost: Look out and glass floor: Adults, $15.99; Kids 4-12 $10.99; Under four, free. Additional $6.50 per person for the skypod; Simulators $7.50 each, but kids must be 42 inches tall to go in. Total tower experience is $29.99 per person. There are other variations on the pricing, call ahead.

Directions: Take the subway to Union Station and walk west on Front Street or take the Spadina streetcar to Front Street and walk two blocks east to reach the tower. When in doubt look up!

Now that you've gone this far, pay the extra four bucks and go up another 33 storeys to the Sky Pod, at 447 metres (1,465 ft). Equivalent to 142 storeys, Skypod is the world's highest observation gallery – next stop the International Space Station! Here you get a perfect unobstructed 120 kilometre (75 mile) view that is like nothing so much as the

Chapter Four

view from an airplane window. On a clear day you can see Rochester, NY, across the lake, the mist rising above Niagara Falls, and way out to the suburbs. But according to my son, the neatest thing is simply being above the clouds.

There's lots to do at the bottom of the tower, beyond shopping. The fifteen-minute film about the building of the Tower is called "To the Top" and may interest Bob the Builder fans who like nothing better than watching cranes in operation. But we find the simulators a lot more fun. These are state-of-the-art films that put you squarely in the pilot's seat, but kids have to be at least 42 inches tall to take part. "Wings" features the five most famous aircraft that advanced the science of flight. The other one is "Wildfire," which takes you along on the most dangerous peacetime air mission: fighting a wildfire! Hover over a mountain in the enormous Skycrane helicopter as you fill your tanks with water and then douse the flames below.

Tips: Go early on a clear day and take your camera (duh!). Leave strollers at the bottom. For less expensive dining than the luxurious 360, try Horizons café on the LookOut Level or the Marketplace Café on the ground floor, where you'll find reasonably priced, kid-friendly food.

Skydome

1 Blue Jays Way
Toronto, ON, M5V 1J3

Courtesy Ontario Tourism

The Skydome and CN Tower

> **Skydome**
>
> **Tours: (416) 341-2770;**
> **Box Office: (416) 341-1234**
>
> **Hours:** Tours are offered daily, but not on game days. Roof tours are irregular; call for more information.
>
> **Cost:** Skydome tours: Adults, $12.50; Youth (12-17), $8.50; Kids (5-11), $7. Roof tours, when available: $25 per person.

The Skydome evokes a mix of emotions for Torontonians, who either love it or hate it. It cost taxpayers about half of the total $500 million price tag (government and business interests pitched in the rest) but for that hefty amount, they did get the world's first stadium to have a fully retractable roof. Plus, according to *Toronto Life* magazine, they got "an architectural dialogue between ancient design concepts and computer-age technology, with its antecedents in Greek open-air theatres-in-the-round and in ovoid Roman auditoriums, the Colosseum being the most famous example." Now that's gotta be worth something!

Home to the Toronto Blue Jays of baseball's American league, Skydome seats about 37,000 (when the Jays are doing well), and considerably less when the team is in the doldrums. At full capacity, it can hold 60,000. It also hosts the Toronto Argonauts football team (part of the Canadian Football League), and numerous monster truck shows, circuses, and rock concerts throughout the year. Taking the Skydome tour is well worth it, whether your kids are sports fans or not. It's an awesome feeling to stand in the middle of the field, with the

Toronto's Downtown

roof open and the CN Tower looming right above you. If a roof tour is available, you'll experience the regular tour plus another half hour up on the network of catwalks, 36 storeys high above home plate. The tour starts in a museum-like area where all kinds of curious things (crockery, a cannon) that were unearthed during construction are displayed. Next you'll see a 13-minute film that recounts the building of the dome. Then the real fun begins as you begin a walking tour that might take you to the pressbox, a private Skybox, or a visit to a team dressing room (tour itineraries change depending on what's going on in the building that day).

Try to see a game here on a Saturday afternoon if you can, when kids are treated to all kinds of pre-game fun. If it's your birthday, Skydome will put your name up on the world's largest JumboTron scoreboard (about three storeys high). For another kind of thrill, get a table at the dome's Hard Rock Café with field-view seating, or really splurge and book a suite that faces the field in the Renaissance Skydome Hotel.

Toronto Blue Jays

1 Blue Jays Way
Toronto, ON, M5V 1J3
(416) 341-1234; 1-888-654-6529
www.bluejays.com

It seems like a long time since the Jays were contenders, even though it was only 10 years ago that they walked off with the World Series and repeated the very next year. In contrast, the last couple of years can be described as underwhelming, with the odd bright spot, here and there. Manager Carlos Tosca doesn't mince words in interviews when he explains that all he wants right now is to see what his guys can do and what positions they should be playing. "This is our mulligan year," he said during the summer of the 2002 season. In other words, they're rebuilding. Good news is that it's easy to get tickets for all the games, and the owners are offering all kinds of incentives to get you there. The very fact that they play in Skydome should make you want to go. If you do, pick a balmy summer afternoon when the roof is sure to be open, and you'll get an amazing view of the CN Tower, one you'll never forget.

> **Toronto Blue Jays**
>
> **Hours:** Gate 9 Box Office: Game days: Mon-Fri, 8 am - 1/2 hour after game; Sat-Sun, 9 am - 1/2 hour after game or 5 pm. Non-game days: Mon-Fri, 8 am - 8 pm, Sat-Sun, 10 am - 6 pm.
>
> **Cost:** Tickets from $7 to $39 for field level, bases.
>
> **Directions:** The Blue Jays play in the Skydome, right next to the CN Tower.

Chapter Four

Toronto Argonauts

1 Blue Jays Way
Toronto, ON, M5V 1J3
(416) 545-1777
www.argonauts.on.ca

In existence since 1873, this franchise was initially an amateur rugby team before they joined with three other teams in forming an organized football league known as the Canadian Football League (CFL). Today, the Argos are the team of the decade with three Grey Cup victories in the past ten years and 14 in total. With three downs instead of four and 12 players per side, the game is uniquely Canadian, but with the same entertainment value as its American counterpart. High profile alumni include Buffalo Bills QB Doug Flutie and ex-NFL great Joe Thiesman. They're coached by Mike "Pinball" Clemons, ex-Argo and all-time leader in all-purpose yards with 25,396.

After a game you might want to check out Soupy's, an eatery devoted to football, the Canadian kind, owned by a former Ottawa Roughriders player. (376 Dundas Street East; (416) 964-0584)

> **Toronto Argonauts**
>
> **Hours:** Off Season: Mon-Fri, 9 am - 5 pm; Season: Daily, 9 am - 6 pm; Game Night: 9 am - 9 pm.
>
> **Cost:** Tickets are available from the SkyDome Ticket Office or by telephone and range in price from $15 for end zone to $35 for sideline. There is also a club section available for $41 per seat.

Steam Whistle Brewery

255 Bremner Boulevard
Toronto, ON, M5V 3M9
(416) 362-2337
www.steamwhistle.ca

A few years ago a group of beer enthusiasts seized upon the long-neglected train roundhouse behind the Skydome and turned it into Toronto's most unique brewery. It makes exactly one kind of beer – a nice light pilsner great for summer sipping. While kids are not going to be joining in on the tastings, the whole family can enjoy a brewery tour. My son Max is a Thomas the Tank Engine buff, so it didn't take much convincing to interest him in a tour of a real roundhouse – complete with turntable still in front. Each tour ends with a chance to pull on the famous steam whistle.

These enterprising young businessmen also want to create a train museum here so there'll be that much more to see at the brewery. It makes for a nice detour when you're making your way between the Skydome and Harbourfront, and rumour has it they want to open an eatery as well.

> **Steam Whistle Brewery**
>
> **Hours:** 12 - 7 pm; Open later during music and art evenings.
>
> **Cost:** Tours cost $3, but include a tasting and a souvenir glass or a bottle opener. Tours begin daily at 1pm and run every hour.
>
> **Directions:** Look for the roundhouse behind Skydome.

Toronto's Downtown

City Place Golf Club

2 Spadina Ave
Toronto, ON, M5V 3P3
(416) 640-9888
www.tee-off.ca/courses/on701

Look just to the west of Skydome, and you'll see a sight to make a golfer's pulse quicken. The City Place Golf Club course is a little nine hole, par three course designed with the busy executive in mind. But don't let that stop you and the kids from having a whack. It's irresistibly located in the midst of many of Toronto's best attractions, and it's affordable too. Toronto execs come down here to play a quick nine holes on their lunch break, have lunch on the patio, and get back to the office in plenty of time. To top it off, the owners made sure the seasons would pose no problem for this state-of-the-art driving range: the 250-yard, two-tiered beauty is heated, which means fanatics can practice their swing all snowy winter long.

> **City Place Golf Club**
>
> **Hours:** 7 am - midnight.
>
> **Cost:** Mon-Fri, 9 holes, $22; 18 holes, $33; Weekends, 9holes, $20, 18, $30. Club rental, $5 and $7. Driving range, 40 cents per minute, about $12 per half hour; Unlimited balls, and two complimentary clubs provided. Before noon, green fees are half-price. No tee-off times; first come, first served. Call ahead to confirm there are no course closures for special events planned.
>
> **Directions:** Access is via Spadina Avenue, south of Front Street.

CBC Broadcast Centre Behind the Scenes Tour

250 Front Street West
Toronto, ON, M5V 3G5
(416) 205-8605
cbc.ca/aboutcbc/discover/tours

Growing up in the 60s and 70s, there was little other than CBC on television, but we didn't mind. Shows like Hockey Night in Canada, The Beachcombers, and Mr. Dress Up provided more than enough entertainment in those days. Today the venerable national broadcaster is still pumping out the programming, and the public (who own the network after all) are invited to see how it all gets done.

> **CBC Broadcast Centre Behind the Scenes Tour**
>
> **Hours:** Mon & Tues, 1 and 3 pm; Wed-Fri, 11 am and 3 pm; Sat, 12:30 and 2:30 pm.
>
> **Cost:** Adults, $7; Students and children, $5.
>
> **Directions:** In the Broadcast Centre at John and Wellington Streets.

Both national radio and TV networks are based here, so it's a real treat to visit Master Control and learn how the network distributes national and local programs across the country. Sit in Peter Mansbridge's seat and pretend to anchor the nightly news from the national news desk. You get a detailed explanation of all the production required to get a newscast on the air, and what can go wrong at the last minute. Then it's up to the 10th floor studios where favourites like "Royal Canadian Air Farce", "The Red Green Show", and other programs and movies are shot. Once we walked in on Danny DeVito directing a scene from *Death to Smoochie*, but had to leave once a production assistant noticed us. But not before hearing DeVito say the magic Hollywood words, "Quiet on the set." For the next month that's all Max would say, while doing a pretty good imitation of DeVito pacing the set.

Tours are an hour in length, but leave a few minutes before or after to visit the CBC Museum (see below).

Chapter Four

CBC Museum

250 Wellington Street
Toronto, ON, M5V 3P6
(416) 205-5574
www.cbc.ca/museum

CBC Museum
Cost: Free.
Hours: Mon-Fri, 9 am - 5 pm; Sat, 12 - 4 pm.
Directions: At John and Wellington Streets, inside the Broadcast Centre.

   The CBC museum has photos, archived footage, costumes and props from many of CBC's best-loved programs, plus a changing exhibit on some aspect of broadcasting in Canada. As this book went to print, a new exhibit called "Ballet from Stage to Screen" looked at the challenges of shooting ballet for television, and the adjacent Graham Spry theatre showed ballet productions filmed for television from 1954-86.

   Watch classic television moments on vintage TV sets, like Paul Henderson's winning goal in the Canada-U.S.S.R. series of 1972. Or listen to the radio clip of legendary hockey broadcaster Foster Hewitt shouting his famous phrase, "He shoots, he scores!" We also learned that in 50 years of broadcasting, Hewitt didn't miss a single game. And after exploring the CBC museum, we're sure they have every one of those games in the vaults somewhere.

Kidz Rave Party

To be determined; contact email below
Toronto, ON
(416) 593-5771
email: kidzrave@hotmail.com

Kidz Rave Party
Hours: Oct-April, Sat, noon - 3 pm.
Cost: $5.

   Here's a unique way to spend a weekend afternoon with the kids. Every Saturday, from Halloween to the end of April, pre-schoolers to pre-teens gather for their own knees-up. This interactive dance party has been going since 1996 under the direction of founder and chief ravemeister Lily Champniss. There's a kid's menu, a live DJ that plays current hits and old favourites, and entertainment (break dancers, magicians, or bands) between dance sets.

   But the chief activity for kids is getting down and shaking their tiny booties – along with their parents, who love the concept and the music, which ranges from Britney to the Beatles. All kids must be accompanied by adults, and there are crafts, prizes, and face painting every week, plus special parties celebrating every major holiday. This is a Barney-free idea whose time has come!

   Note: while the Kidz Rave was always held at a popular nightclub on Queen Street West called the Bamboo Club, as this book went to press the Bamboo announced plans to move to the Harbourfront area. So email or call Ms. Champniss to find out where the raves are being held, as it wasn't clear they were necessarily going to follow the Bamboo to their new location.

Toronto's Downtown

MZTV Museum

277 Queen Street West
Toronto, ON, M5V 1Z9
(416) 599-7339
www.mztv.com

MZTV Museum

Hours: Guided tours Mon-Fri, 12 pm, 2 pm, 4 pm.

Cost: Adults, $6; Students, $4, Families with ID, $18.

The name Moses Znaimer may not ring a bell with you, but Torontonians know him as the founder of City TV, a television station that revolutionized newsgathering and delivery, and influenced stations like Channel One in New York City and many others around the world. The MZTV was created as a showcase for Znaimer's huge collection of televisions, a passion that began with his first television – a Philco Predicta. As he began to search for rare and unusual televisions, he noticed that, "There are fewer pre-war televisions left in the world than Stradivarius violins." He felt an urgent need to collect what few did remain to catalogue the development of one of the 20th century's most important inventions. The museum is a fun look at something we all take for granted. And it's interesting to note that the trendy flat panel television of today had its precedent set way back in the 1950s.

Campbell House

160 Queen Street West
Toronto, ON, M5H 3H3
(416) 597-0227
www.advsoc.on.ca/campbell/GoCampbellHouse

Campbell House

Hours: M-F, 9:30 am - 4:30 pm; Weekends, Victoria Day-Thanksgiving, noon - 4:30 pm.

Cost: Adults, $4.50; Students, $3.50; Children, $2; Family $10 (two adults, two children).

Directions: At University and Queen St West, at Osgoode Station.

One of Toronto's oldest buildings, this Georgian house was built in 1822 in the heart of the old city of York. The home of William Campbell, sixth Chief Justice of Upper Canada, and his wife Hannah, it was moved to its present location in 1972, and restored with late 18th and early 19th century furniture and artifacts. Tours are given continuously by a costumed guide, though it's best to come for a special event. Kids will enjoy the Canada Day Celtic festival, Heritage Day in February, Law Day in April, and International Museum's Day in May. Other events have an admission fee and celebrate historical anniversaries and cultural traditions like Simcoe Day, Labour Day (a herbal event), and Halloween, which features Ghost Tours. During the Christmas season, kids can discover how houses that predate the Victorian period were decorated (i.e. don't look for a Christmas tree as that tradition hadn't taken root yet!).

Chapter Four

Art Gallery of Ontario

317 Dundas Street West
Toronto, ON, M5T 1G4
Family Fun hotline (416) 979-6615; (416) 979-6648
www.AGO.net

The collection of Henry Moore is renowned and kids love to explore the skylit room housing his large and lumpy sculptures. Other notable favourites are the second floor contemporary art galleries and special exhibits like the recently-mounted Yoko Ono and William Wegner retrospectives which have had great appeal for kids.

> **Art Gallery of Ontario**
>
> **Hours:** Tues, Thurs, Fri, 11 am - 6 pm; Wed, 11 am - 8:30 pm, Sat-Sun, 10 am - 5:30 pm. Closed Mondays.
>
> **Cost:** Suggested donation $6 per person. Super Sundays $25 per family. Special shows have separate admission.
>
> **Directions:** Corner of Dundas & McCaul Streets, three blocks west of St. Patrick Subway Station.

In fact, the AGO has been very successful at bringing families into the gallery largely due to their Family Sundays, which are regularly packed. Families are treated to special interactive activities and can spend time in Off The Wall!, the gallery's art-based play space. Kids learn the fundamentals of printmaking, drawing, painting, sculpting, and collage painlessly and get a chance to dress up as an old masterpiece. (Cameras compulsory!) Activities range from making interesting art sculptures in the studio to traveling into the past to learn about the historic house, The Grange, the AGO's first home.

The last time we were there, kids were asked to record a conversation between two paintings they saw. Another memorable afternoon was spent making music that we felt matched some of the abstract paintings in the collection. Each month the activities are linked to a different part of the collection or special exhibition, so visit often throughout the winter to see the range of what is offered. Since the AGO's collection ranges from 15th century European paintings to international contemporary works of art, kids are exposed to the full spectrum of Western art, as well as Inuit sculpture.

The AGO's Super Sundays take place the first Sunday of every month and include the same fun and entertainment as Family Sunday, but offer a little more, making it an extra special day for children. All the arts are combined into an extravaganza including the visual arts, drama, and music. In addition, there are always lectures, workshops, staff talks, live performances, and gallery tours, plus daily film and video screenings in Jackman Hall.

Cap off your visit with a bite at the casual Cultures Market. Or even better, head to Baldwin Street, just two blocks north, for a more substantial meal. You'll be able to choose from about a dozen great eateries on this charming little street (see Where to Eat listings).

Toronto's Downtown

The Textile Museum of Canada

55 Centre Avenue
Toronto, ON, M5G 2H5
(416) 599-5321
www.textilemuseum.ca

The Textile Museum of Canada

Cost: Adults $8, Students and children $6, Under 5's are free, Family (2 adults, 3 kids) $22. Pay what you can on Weds from 5 to 8 pm.

Hours: Tues, Thurs, Fri 11 am - 5 pm, Weds 11 am - 8 pm, Sat, Sun 12 - 5 pm. Closed Mondays.

Directions: One block east of University Ave., south of Dundas St.

If your kids are clothing horses, or have an interest in knitting, embroidery, fashion design or weaving, bring them to the Textile Museum for a fascinating look at the importance that cloth has had over the centuries. Exhibitions examine the cultural, religious, or political significance of textiles from its collection of over 10,000 ceremonial cloths, garments, carpets, quilts, and related artifacts from over 35 countries around the world. You might see rugs from Central Asia, 19th century batiks from Java, or lavish Tibetan silk robes. Or you might catch an exhibit of contemporary fibre and textile artists, who are making some of the most innovative and interesting art being created today.

And this is a museum that likes to have fun. If you have any goths in your family, they'd have enjoyed a recent exhibit called Moral Fibre, Dress Codes from Purity to Wickedness. Black PVC cat suits worn by members of the contemporary demi-monde hung next to Afghan modesty robes to illustrate how the clothes we wear speak volumes about our own attitudes toward society's implicit (and sometimes explicit) dress codes.

Textiles are meant to be touched as well as seen, and in a unique resource center called fibrespace, you are invited to do both. Creator Penny Bateman has tucked away treasures in drawers that you can open, and displayed industrial fabrics like fishnets and landscaping fabric to illustrate the multiple uses of textiles. Get hands-on experience at different techniques used in making textiles. Try hooking a rug, weave a few rows on a floor loom, or embroider a swatch of fabric to add to the Visitor's Patchwork. Learn how the plants and flowers in your own backyard can be used to dye fabric. And much, much more.

As Bateman says: "Textiles are worn, walked on, lived in and slept under... In fibrespace I want the visitor to become absorbed by the creativity inherent in producing any textile." Having seen kids completely immersed in fibrespace activities, I'd say she's more than succeeded.

Chapter Four

Stock Market Place

130 King Street West
Toronto, ON, M5X 1J2
(416) 947-4674; 1-800-729-5556
www.tse.com/visitor

Stock Market Place
Hours: M-F, 9 am - 5 pm.
Cost: Free.

My kids are blissfully unaware of the stock market – for now at least. But if you've got older kids who've come of age during the ups, downs, bubbles, and crashes of recent years, a visit to Stock Market Place is in order. This brand new interactive centre has games that will challenge your investment skills and teach you all about the games people play with their money. At least that's how I look at it! For instance, see if you can find the top five investments that made the most money on the TSE in the past 20 years. Learn how short-term investing works, or choose from 20 long-term investments to build a virtual portfolio and see how it fares. The Money Go Round explains how money moves in the economy, while Capital Moves lets you be CEO for a day, making decisions that real world CEOs face. Good fun, even for the investment challenged like me!

Design Exchange

234 Bay Street
Toronto, ON, M5K 1B2
(416) 363-6121
www.dx.org

Design Exchange
Hours: Tue-Fri, 10 am - 6 pm; Sat-Sun, noon - 5 pm.
Cost: Adults, $5; Students, $3.50.

If your kids are interested in why things are made the way they are, a quick stop in the Design Exchange might be a place to relax and recharge. This gallery exhibits the latest in fashion, graphic design, and ergonomics, and is located in an interesting building, the former Toronto Stock Exchange. Have a peek at the original trading floor with its historic murals still intact. International, national, and local designers are on display in the exhibition hall and, while there is an admission charge to view their creations, the Design Effectiveness Centre is free of charge.

City Hall/
Nathan Phillips Square

100 Queen Street (between Bay St and University Ave)
Toronto, ON, M5H 2N2
(416) 392-1111; (416) 338-0338
www.city.toronto.on.ca

City Hall/ Nathan Phillips Square
Hours: City Hall: M-F, 7:30 am - 10:30 pm; Sat-Sun, 8 am - 10:30 pm. Nathan Phillips Square never sleeps.
Cost: Free.

In 1957, Toronto held the largest architectural competition ever and invited 520 architects to submit their ideas for a new city hall. After a year of debate, Finnish architect Viljo Revell won the competition and gave Toronto one of the world's great buildings. Cultural critic Robert Fulford notes that Torontonians needed to make a psychological leap, and believes that Revell's avant-garde design seemed to single-handedly shake off the dowdy old image of Toronto held in the minds

Toronto's Downtown

of many of its citizens. The building gave the city the psychic lift it needed, bringing it into the modern world kicking and screaming. If only we had a few more of those rare moments of clarity! (And a few great buildings to go with them.)

Looking at City Hall, you may see it, as the author of a letter to the editor did, as two boomerangs over a half-grapefruit. The architect envisioned it as an "eye" with the two semi-circular buildings representing the upper and lower eyelids, and the council chambers in the center as the pupil. But an eye is not what most people saw. Perhaps it was the space age tenor of the times, but many saw UFOs and flying saucers. And it did once appear in a Star Trek episode.

Nathan Phillips Square is a gathering place where people feel right at home in the heart of the big city. Some of Toronto's best-loved events take place here, including the Outdoor Art Festival, Winterfest, the Christmas Market, and the annual Canada Day celebration. In winter, the reflecting pool turns into a giant skating rink, and summer brings a weekly farmer's market into downtown. In July and August, Kids' Tuesdays draw families to free performances by well-known kids entertainers, plus crafts and activities, while Wednesdays feature live performances by some of Toronto's most popular acts. And should you be there on a day when nothing is happening, kids can take advantage of a playground for preschoolers, or you can have a bite in the café in City Hall.

Courtesy Ontario Tourism

City Hall!

Chapter Four

Toronto Eaton Centre

220 Yonge Street
Toronto, ON, M5B 2H1
(416) 598-8700

When it was built in 1979, the Eaton Centre was an anomaly in Canada: a downtown mall that improved upon the suburban model. You can see the antecedents – the natural light, the trees and fountains – which we now take for granted. Today it might seem old hat, but the Eaton Centre still boasts the highest sales per square foot of retail space (at $746) in North America. And it remains the number one tourist attraction in Toronto with one million

Courtesy Ontario Tourism

Eaton Centre

visitors a week. In fact, long before Sunday shopping was allowed, Eaton Centre was permitted to open, because of a bylaw classifying it as a tourist attraction.

There are more than 285 shops, restaurants, and services to wind your way through, not to mention a movie theatre, a ticket kiosk for same-day, discount theatre tickets, and a police station. The Yes Toronto! shop features clothes and tchotchkes perfect for last-minute souvenir purchases.

Two notable features are Michael Snow's sculpture of Canada geese called Flight Stop and the Centre Court's famous fountain. Outside, at the Yonge and Dundas corner, street vendors sell their wares while buskers perform for passersby, lunch crowds, and throngs of teens. There's a peaceful side to the west, on the City Hall side, where you'll find Trinity Square. It's a nice place for a rest, or to walk the labyrinth (see below).

Trinity Square Park Labyrinth

10 Trinity Square
Toronto, ON, M5G 1B1
(416) 534-4053
www.city.toronto.on.ca/parks/labyrinth

A group of citizens called the Toronto Labyrinth Community Network wanted to create a labyrinth as a millennium project, and with the blessing of city council and Trinity went about creating this peaceful spot as a gift to harried downtown workers. It is the exact copy of the 13th century stone labyrinth at Chartres Cathedral in France. The idea is that people should have a place they can go to release stress and recharge. Unlike a maze, a labyrinth has a single path and is intended for meditation and reflection. Walking it is indeed a very relaxing thing to do, and can take up to 30 minutes to follow and complete depending on your pace. Kids tend to move through it more quickly, needless to say!

Toronto's Downtown

Elgin and Winter Garden Theatre Centre

189 Yonge Street
Toronto, ON, M5B 1M4
(416) 314-2874; Ticket Info: (416) 872-5555
www.heritagefdn.on.ca/Heritage/housecall-cent

This is the world's only surviving example of a double-decker vaudeville theatre, built in 1914. While your kids may not even know the meaning of vaudeville, the gilded romance of these theatres should bring the period to life for them as soon as they step into the ornate lobby.

As our guide told it, when they opened the creaky doors of this magnificent structure back in 1981, historians were delighted to find much of it intact. Over 110 pieces of vaudeville scenery originally used in the Elgin and Winter Garden Theatres are still here, including palaces, rustic cottages, woods, and four house interiors.

Kids will enjoy experiencing the very distinct atmospheres of the two theatres. The Elgin is all gold leaf and rich fabrics, with ornate boxes like an opera house, and plaster cherubs. The Winter Garden is a fantastical trip through a magical garden, its walls covered in murals to resemble a garden, its ceiling hung with branches taken from real beech trees that twinkle with fairy lights. The theatres played host to such greats as George Burns and Gracie Allen, Sophie Tucker, Edgar Bergen and Charlie McCarthy, and Milton Berle.

In 1928, vaudeville was in decline, and the Winter Garden closed for over 50 years, becoming a time capsule of sorts. The grand old Elgin continued on as a movie house, gradually falling into disrepair with the passing of each decade. Now renovated by the Ontario Heritage Foundation, it hosts theatre productions, special screenings, stand-up comedians, and special events all year long. Many years ago I saw *Cats* here, as well as Australia's fabulous *STOMP!*, The Who's *Tommy*, and *Joseph and the Amazing Technicolor Dreamcoat*.

> **Elgin and Winter Garden**
> **Theatre Centre**
>
> **Cost:** Adults, $7; Students, $6.
>
> **Hours:** Year round guided tours: Thurs, 5 pm; Sat, 11 am.
>
> **Directions:** Across Yonge Street from the Eaton Centre.

If you can see a live performance here in either of the theatres, by all means do. Catch the annual Christmas pantomime if possible. If there's nothing on, then take the tour given by some of the terrific volunteer guides, who will tell you about the ghosts and unusual people who have connections with the theatres. Ask about the unusual way they restored the beautiful hand-painted murals and tree branches. If only these walls could talk!

Chapter Four

Hockey Hall of Fame

BCE Place
30 Yonge Street
Toronto, ON, M5E 1X8
(416) 360-7735
www.hhof.com

Hockey Hall of Fame
Hours: M-F, 10 am - 5 pm; Sat, 9:30 am - 6 pm, Sun, 10:30 am - 5 pm.
Cost: Adults, $12; Kids 4-18, $7; Families, $32.

As exciting and loud as the game it celebrates, the Hockey Hall of Fame gets a visit from us whenever visitors come to town. We can't get enough of its great mix of hockey artifacts and memorabilia with state of the art exhibitry and interactive technology. It's an ideal venue for an intergenerational visit: while Grandpa checks out a recreation of the Montreal Canadiens dressing room or listens to legendary broadcaster Foster Hewitt call a game, the grandkids can try to stop slap shots from the likes of Wayne Gretzky or Mark Messier. Upstairs in the ornate original bank building a more respectful calm predominates as visitors file by the many trophies, awards, and portraits of Hall of Famers. A highlight is the original Stanley Cup on display in the bank vault. You can have your photo taken with it, or make like a pro hockey player and give it a big kiss!

Courtesy Ontario Tourism

The Stanley Cup

Downtown East (East of Yonge Street)

St. Lawrence Market

91-95 Front Street East
Toronto, ON, M5E 1C2
(416) 392-7219
www.stlawrencemarket.com

If you want to partake in a shopping ritual that's about 200 years old, come to St. Lawrence Market on a Saturday morning. Since 1803, when the land north of Front Street, west of Jarvis, south of King, and east of Church was designated as Market Block, merchants have sold their wares here.

St. Lawrence Market
Hours: Tues-Thurs, 8 am - 6 pm; Fri, 8 am - 7 pm; Sat, 5 am - 5 pm. Closed Sun-Mon.
Cost: Free to browse.
Directions: On Front Street West at Jarvis.

Beginning at 5 am, you'll see the sights of the city's rich diversity, the sounds of brisk trade, the smells of a gourmet paradise of foods. Everybody has their favourites, including most of Toronto's finest chefs who can be found here browsing.

Toronto's Downtown

Today the south building's 70-odd stores are chockablock with fresh and bulk foods, from organic sprouts to caviar. The fish is famous, as are the bagels at St. Urbain's. Go downstairs to find all the spice and bulk foods, plus most of the eateries. Fresh bread and sweets are worth sampling at Future Bakery, as are the astounding small-batch cheeses you can find at Alex's Farms and Olympic Food & Cheese. Right in the center, there's a kitchen store where I always manage to find rare items I can't get elsewhere – like a grapefruit knife that I had looked for for years.

Eating here is a snap: pick up fresh bread, cheese, and fruit for an afternoon picnic, or sample some of the market's dozen or more restaurants and food stands. Everybody has their St. Lawrence Market favourites: a steaming bowl of soup at Neil's Soup Kettle, Carousel Bakery's famous peameal bacon sandwiches, or mouth-watering chicken sandwiches from the famous Churrasco St. Lawrence.

The North Market, across Front Street, was demolished in the 60s and replaced by a rather ordinary building that is redeemed only by the merchants who crowd there on the weekends. The Saturday Farmer's Market is held here, and on Sundays, the same space is filled with over 80 antique dealers that spill into the surrounding plaza, displaying their wares from dawn to 5 pm. Admission is free.

Courtesy Ontario Tourism

The St. Lawrence Market

Chapter Four

St. James Cathedral

65 Church Street
Toronto, ON, M5C 2E9
(416) 364-7865
www.stjamescathedral.on.ca

St. James Cathedral is one of several magnificent churches in Toronto, along with St. Michael's Roman Catholic Cathedral and Metropolitan United Church, both located a short distance north of St. James. The Gothic Revival Anglican cathedral has its origins in the 1790s when the government set aside the land on which it sits for the Church of England. Today's cathedral, which opened in 1853, boasts Canada's tallest steeple, beautiful stained glass windows created in Toronto, New York, Britain, and Germany, a glorious organ, and various memorials to Toronto's old Anglican elite.

On summer Sundays at 4 pm, you can hear the sound of 5,000 pipes ring out during the pre-evensong organ recital here. From September to June, you can catch the Tuesday one-hour recitals beginning at 1 pm.

Toronto Sculpture Garden

115 King Street East at Jarvis
Toronto, ON, M5C 1G8
(416) 515-9658
www.city.toronto.on.ca/parks/parks_gardens/sculpturegdns

Toronto Sculpture Garden
Hours: Dawn to dusk throughout the year.
Cost: Free.

If you're ready for something a little different in the way of art, this sculpture garden, across from St. James Cathedral, features bi-annual exhibits created by various Canadian sculptors in a fresh outdoor setting. If you're looking for a bite just then, La Marquette restaurant has a lovely terrace overlooking the garden where you can sit and take in the atmosphere as sensual floral fragrances waft past.

Toronto's Downtown

Lorraine Kimsa Theatre for Young People

165 Front Street East
Toronto, ON, M5A 3Z4
(416) 862-2222
www.lktyp.ca

For generations, Toronto kids have been entertained by the award-winning Lorraine Kimsa Young People's Theatre, where many of Canada's finest actors and directors got their start. Launched in 1966, in 1977 it moved into what was originally a stable for about 500 horses that pulled Toronto Street Railway Company's streetcars. The building's Victorian industrial past can sometimes provide an interesting background for plays, as with a recent production of Oliver Twist. Today the theatre is surrounded by the St. Lawrence district, noted for its first-rate urban design and one of Toronto's most distinctive family neighbourhoods.

Families can usually count on shows suitable for kids aged three and up, as well as teens, in addition to their core audience of six to 12 year-olds.

> ### Lorraine Kimsa Theatre for Young People
>
> **Hours:** Several matinees on weekends and holidays. Some productions have an evening show at 7 pm. The theatre is dark in the summer. Call ahead for show times.
>
> **Cost:** Ticket prices vary from $16 to $28 per show; packages of seven plays are $110, four plays $66, and three plays $58. Discounts available for previews and pay-what-you-can performances. Special prices also for balcony and mezzanine seating. Call for more information.

Places to Eat

Downtown West (West of Yonge)

Terroni's

720 Queen Street West
Toronto, ON, M6J 1E8
(416) 504-0320

106 Victoria Street
Toronto, ON, M5C 2B4
(416) 955-0258

Toronto has great pizza, but this is standout, in two equally funky, casual settings. The Victoria location is around the corner from Eaton Centre, Hockey Hall of Fame, and City Hall. Fantastic sandwiches, pizzas, and pastas starting at about $5.

Le Select Bistro

328 Queen Street West
Toronto, ON, M5C 2A2
(416) 596-6405

The owners are French and the food's fantastic. Classic bistro menu, with a great kid's menu as well, bien sur!

Rivoli Café

334 Queen Street West
Toronto, ON, M5V 2A2
(416) 596-1908

The Rivoli's menu is a hodge-podge but well-executed and able to please every palate. It's also a very funky hip place to be seen, which teens might appreciate.

79

Chapter Four

Queen Mother Café

208 Queen Street West
Toronto, ON, M5V 1Z2
(416) 598-4719

There's a bit of everything here, from Thai and Laotian to standard diner fare and brunch specials. Busy at lunch with the working crowd, but very kid-friendly at other times. Nice desserts too.

Tiger Lily's

257 Queen Street West
Toronto, ON, M5V 1Z4
(416) 977-5499

A funky décor here as well as an awesome menu, for anyone who loves noodles done every which way. Try the chicken potstickers for something hardy, or the mix and match soup bowls done as you like it!

Shopsy's TV City Deli

284 King Street West
Toronto, ON, M5V 1J2
(416) 599-5464

A classic deli serving the stacked high-cholesterol sandwiches you know and I love, plus Toronto favourites named after some of the city's best-loved personalities. Try the Dan Aykroyd, the Shania Twain, or the Jim Carrey, or just stick to the pastrami. Kind of a sports bar too, with tellies everywhere.

Downtown East (East of Yonge)

Siegfried's Dining Room

300 Adelaide East
Toronto, ON, M5A 1N1
(416) 415-2260

Come here before or after a play at the Young People's Theatre, just around the corner. Home to Toronto's most exclusive chef's training school, you can eat fabulously here for a fraction of what it would cost to eat at Scaramouche or North 44. Not quite student's prices, but very high concept, artful food at café prices. Serves lunch and dinner Tuesdays to Fridays.

Old Spaghetti Factory

54 The Esplanade
Toronto, ON, M5E 1A6
(416) 864-9761

You know the drill: pick your pasta, pick your sauce, a full meal deal. Kids love it and it's consistently good. Gotta love that sourdough too!

Toronto's Downtown

Places to Shop

West of Yonge
(West of Yonge)

F/X

515 Queen Street West
Toronto, ON, M5V 2B4
(416) 504-0888

Come to F/X for a real Queen Street shopping experience. Not only can you find excellent glad rags, but shoes and accessories to go with them, make-up, candy, ice cream, and lots more. One-stop shopping for the gals in your entourage!

Misdemeanours

322-1/2 Queen Street West
Toronto, ON, M5V 2A2
(416) 351-8758

The romantic, theatrical clothes created by Toronto designer Pam Chorley for her Fashion Crimes boutique are also available in tiny sizes at her Misdemeanours shop across the street. If you want your kids to look as hep as you do, come here.

Silver Snail Comic Shop

367 Queen Street West
Toronto, ON, M5V 2A4
(416) 593-0889

Toronto's oldest comic shop, they carry mainstream and alternative books, as well as trading cards, figurines, role playing games, and other assorted paraphernalia. A friend of ours still regrets selling his comic book collection to the Snail – way back in the early 80s.

Modrobes

239 Queen Street West
Toronto, ON, M5V 1Z4
(416) 595-9555

Sometimes I wonder what Max will be wearing when he's 16 while I'm browsing the rack at Modrobes. Maybe vintage stuff from here, I think, talking myself into buying something to be recycled at a later date. This is the spot for urban street wear in Toronto right now, with two locations – here and on Yonge Street as well. If you've got teens or pre-teens itching to buy, this is the spot to buy instant street cred.

ROOTS

356 Queen Street West
Toronto, ON, M5V 2A2
(416) 977-0409

Truly a retailing phenomenon, ROOTS has become Canada's most outwardly patriotic store, celebrating the outdoorsy Canadian lifestyle with aplomb and great clothes and gaining fame worldwide as the outfitters for the Canadian Olympic team (and now the American and British teams as well). A great stop for a souvenir, the clothes are comfy and well-made – in Canada!

Legends of the Game

322 King Street West
Toronto, ON, M5V 1J2
(416) 971-8848

Sports fans will want to stop in at Legends of the Game. Doors with baseball bat shaped handles open onto an emporium that features the Wall of Fame and every conceivable sports collectible.

Chapter Four

Sugar Shack Candy and Fun House

322 King Street West
Toronto, ON, M5V 1J2
(416) 348-9202

Right under Legends of the Game, this has retro-candy (pop rocks, gold nuggets, pixie sticks) as well as your kid's favourites. Stock up on pre-theatre treats before Lion King, just up the block.

Mountain Equipment Co-op

400 King Street West
Toronto, ON, M5V 1K2
(416) 340-2667

This is the place to buy sporting equipment – great kid's outdoor gear you can hand down from kid to kid endlessly. It's a co-op too, so prices are great and the small membership fee of five dollars is minimal compared to the high quality and selection that MEC provides. Once you've returned home you can continue to order from MEC's great online store (www.mec.ca).

Downtown East (East of Yonge Street)

Ontario Specialty Co.

133 Church Street
Toronto, ON, M5B 1Y4
(416) 366-9327

Directly across from St. James Cathedral (see page 78), this is a must-see for any nostalgia buffs. Come see a magical little shop devoted to tin toys, vintage sunglasses, and all manner of neat collectibles. Run for decades by the Geller family, Ontario Specialty Co. is like an attic where boxes of brand new items that have sat for decades untouched are opened up and sold. The likes of Beck and U2 have shopped for their sunglasses here, but for me the big draw is all the spring-loaded toys from all over the world.

Frida Craft Stores

39 Front Street East
Toronto, ON, M5E 1B3
(416) 366-3169

This reminds me of shopping in the Fleetwood Mac era. Piled high in this shop's two floors of imported goods from Asia and South America, you'll find clothing, glassware, incense, jewelry, linens, and all kinds of small toys and decorative items perfect for kid's rooms.

Flatiron's Toronto

51 Front Street East
Toronto, ON, M5E 1B3
(416) 365-1506

This unique gift shop is worth browsing for its tremendous inventory of fun tchotchkes – from martini glasses to piggy banks. I dare you to try to resist its charms. This shop also stocks gorgeous Christmas ornaments year-round, including delicate hand-painted baubles from Europe and Mexico.

Chapter Five

Toronto's Midtown

Midtown Toronto is a wide swath of land extending north from Chinatown up all the way past Queen's Park and the university to St. Clair Avenue. Bloor Street is the heart of Midtown, with the Bloor east-west subway line running underneath it.

Attractions in Midtown run the gamut from Riverdale Farm in leafy Cabbagetown to the medieval-style castle called Casa Loma perched on a hill just south of St. Clair. But Midtown may be best known for its dining and shopping, with Bloor Street a veritable feast of high-end boutiques and glamorous designer shops. Between Avenue Road and Yonge Street, Prada, Tiffany, and Chanel share the sidewalk with Canadian brands like ROOTS and luxury department store Holt Renfrew. For kids there ain't much, so I'd advise walking one block north to Yorkville.

This tony shopping district, with galleries, restaurants, and shops to fulfill every imaginable wish is where Toronto ladies go to lunch and shop, shop, shop. Hard to imagine then, that Yorkville was the centre of Toronto's hippie culture in the 1960s. Flower children from across North America flocked to the area to hang in the many coffee houses, and watch-up-and coming folksingers like Neil Young and Joni Mitchell begin their careers. The vestiges of that past are still present today in the narrow streets and Victorian houses that were retained and updated, lending it a village-like air that makes it one of the more pleasant places to stroll in Toronto. Make sure to walk through Old York Lane, one of Toronto's quaintest passageways. And have a look at the old firehouse and library – both still in use.

Chapter Five

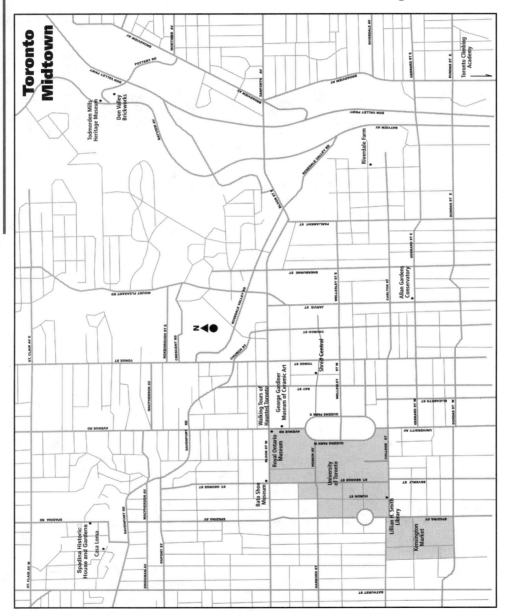

Toronto's Midtown

Today Yorkville's streets are among the city's liveliest, filled with some of the most avid shoppers and most interesting niche shops in Toronto. And it's not devoid of fun, with some great novelty shops and jeans boutiques that should appeal to teens.

For a break from all the commerce, grab a snack at one of the nearby cafes and enjoy the wonderful Village of Yorkville Park. The result of a global design competition, this creative space does a great job of rendering the varying topography found in Southern Ontario. The avant-garde garden features a birch grove, a curtain of water that recalls the gentle fall of rain, and, just for kids and mountain goats, a massive granite outcropping.

Things to Do

A Taste of the World

(416) 923-6813
www.torontowalksbikes.com

A great way to see Toronto is on foot, and if you're going to take a walking tour, let it be one of these. For 10 years, foodie and fan of the offbeat, Shirley Lum, has been giving tours of Toronto's nooks and crannies that are sadly skipped by most guides. A recently added tour – Haunted Kensington, Chinatown and Grange Walk – has proven very popular as has More Than An Island Bike Tour: Summer & Fall Colours. There's a bikes and bakeries walk, a culinary tour of the St. Lawrence Market, and a Charles Dickens walk that harkens back to his visit to Toronto, captured in his book, *American Notes*. They're all served up with Lum's renowned sense of humour and great knowledge of her subject.

Her original Chinatown walk elicits a great response from kids, especially from boys. "I take them to a Chinese herbalist and show them a whole row of glass cases with trays of dried scorpions, octopuses, sea horses and lizards, which are completely flattened. The boys love that. Anything that's gross they love." The highlight of the tour is a leisurely dim sum lunch at one of Chinatown's best spots. Check out the timetable on her website to find a tour, but give yourself lots of time as they sell out quickly in the summer.

A Taste of the World

Hours: Mon-Sat, 11 am - midnight; Sun, 11 am - 10 pm.

Cost: Walking tours, $15 to $35; bike tours start at $45.

Directions: Where you'll meet your guide depends on which tour you take. Call to book a tour and find out where you'll be meeting up.

Chapter Five

Walking Tours of Haunted Toronto

100 Queen's Park
Toronto, ON, M5S 2C6
(416) 487-9017
www.ontarioghosts.org/walkingtours

Walking Tours of Haunted Toronto

Hours: Haunted Streets of Downtown Toronto: Mon & Wed, 7 pm; Ghosts of the University of Toronto: Mon & Wed, 10 pm.

Cost: Adults, $7; Students, $5; Kids under 8, free. Call ahead and let them know you're coming.

Directions: Tours depart from the front of the ROM (Royal Ontario Museum), 100 Queen's Park, southwest corner of Bloor Street West and Avenue Road.

All cities worth visiting have their share of mysteries, urban legends, and ghost stories, and that's certainly true of Toronto. Take either of these two walking tours and you'll get insights into (and sightings of?) the ghosts from Toronto's past that still haunt the present.

Start off at the Royal Ontario Museum, where, as tour guide Richard Fiennes-Clinton informs you, a long-deceased curator still stalks the halls clad only in a nightshirt. Fiennes-Clinton cuts a dramatic figure himself, resplendent in a top hat and cape, and carrying a lantern. He clearly relishing re-telling all the chilling tales, and gives participants a thorough grounding in all things spectral in Toronto's downtown.

The University of Toronto tour is especially popular since its gothic architecture inspires a mood of foreboding even before the tour begins. Young children may not fare too well on these tours, although a wee one in a backpack dozed off while her parents listened in rapt attention to the ghost stories. I especially loved hearing the story about a famous author (I won't tell you who – go on the tour) who vowed to return from the grave to haunt Massey College.

Is it Toronto the Good or Toronto the Ghoulish? You decide!

Royal Ontario Museum

100 Queen's Park
Toronto, ON, M5S 2C6
(416) 586-5549 or (416) 586-8000
www.rom.on.ca

Royal Ontario Museum

Hours: Mon-Sat, 10 am - 6 pm;
Fri, 10 am - 9:30 pm;
Sun, 11 am - 6 pm.

Cost: Adults, $15; Students with ID, $10; Children, $8; Under four, free On ROM Friday Nights after 4:30 pm, and one hour before closing every day, admission is free (except during feature exhibitions when admission is offered at a reduced rate).

Directions: The ROM is centrally located in midtown Toronto at the corner of Bloor Street West and Avenue Road, at the Museum subway station.

With exhibits ranging from suits of armour to Victorian lamps, from mighty carved crest poles to massive dinosaurs, Toronto's venerable Royal Ontario Museum – known locally as the ROM – is a crowd-pleaser, with something for everyone from the smallest to the biggest kid. The largest museum of human civilization and

Toronto's Midtown

natural history in Canada, and the fifth largest museum in North America, the ROM's 45 galleries have brought it international recognition, as has its slate of ongoing research projects around the world.

Long-time family favourites include the Dinosaur Gallery, with its 13 dinosaur skeletons displayed in realistic environments. If you dare (this can scare little ones a bit), venture into the dark, winding Bat Cave which has 3,000 life-like bats roosting and flying through the air as well as other cave-dwelling insects and rodents.

On a cold winter day, you'll find us at the ROM where we became members after making three visits here just in the month of February alone. After saying hello to the giant bronze Buddha in the atrium (a family tradition), it's off to the Discovery Gallery, a place of hands-on activities and real artifacts. Here you can dig for dinosaur bones, walk through a crystal cave, dress-up in traditional costumes or armour, and play in an enchanting forest. A perfect introduction to the ROM's diverse galleries and subject areas, the Discovery Gallery is staffed with facilitators who aid in ongoing adventures for family members of every age.

If your kids are into volcanoes, rocks, and minerals don't miss the spectacular, award-winning Dynamic Earth: Inco Limited Gallery of Earth Sciences. Combining dramatic lighting, sound, and visual effects to envelop the visitor in the magnificent wonders of the planet, the gallery provides a better understanding of the forces that continue to shape it. Visitors can step inside the Volcano Theatre to view a film projected onto the floor, experience the evolutionary stages of the Earth in six experiential rooms, view a rainbow of magnificent mineral specimens in the Hall of Treasures, and marvel at the beauty of the S. R. Perren Gem and Gold Room.

Finally there's Hands-on Biodiversity where environmental exhibits explore the amazing natural interdependence of plants and animals (including humans) in Ontario and the rest of the world. There are hundreds of authentic specimens to examine up-close, and even a living stream and a buzzing beehive that Max always gravitates to first! We see how long it takes him to find the elusive queen bee. (Hint: she's the one with the blue spot marked on her back for easier identification.) Visitors can also learn practical nature conservation tips, such as instruction on planting wildflower gardens and building bird boxes.

The ROM has two very different dining options: the more kid-friendly of the two is Druxy's Famous Deli Sandwiches; but if your kids are sophisticated enough, you can try Jamie Kennedy at the Museum (known as JK ROM), an elegant dining lounge on the 4th floor, featuring a great view of midtown Toronto. Don't miss the shopping – the kid's shop is downstairs and full of great games, souvenirs, and toys inspired by the ROM's collections.

Chapter Five

George Gardiner Museum of Ceramic Art

111 Queen's Park
Toronto, ON, M5S 2C6
(416) 586-8080
www.gardinermuseum.on.ca

George Gardiner Museum of Ceramic Art
Hours: Mon, Wed, Fri, 10 am - 6 pm; Tues, Thurs, 10 am - 8 pm; Sat-Sun, 10 am - 5 pm. Closed November 20, Christmas Day, and New Year's Day.
Cost: Adults, $10; Students and children 5-12, $6; Under 5, free; Families, $24. Free on the first Tuesday of every month.
Directions: Across from the Royal Ontario Museum, at the Museum subway station.

While the gorgeous Meissen coffee sets and Renaissance maiolica pieces do nothing for a preschooler, the funny animal shapes and hilarious expressions to be found on some of the pre-Columbian work can pique a kid's imagination. Come on a Sunday afternoon and let them loose in the Clay Pit, a hands-on workshop where kids can sculpt anything they want from clay. The fee is nominal ($5 for kids, $8 for adults), professional potters are on hand to help, and you can pay extra to have your piece glazed and fired. The only catch is you'll have to return to collect it, but why not turn an occasional visit into a new hobby, as many visitors have done?

Concerts and family activities are also offered here from time to time, usually in conjunction with the opening of a new exhibit. Check local listings or give the museum a dingle. In the past, we've enjoyed many great films and talks, a special Mexican Day of the Dead celebration, and an annual fundraising treat called The Twelve Trees of Christmas. The latter features some of Canada's best interior designers who decorate trees that are auctioned off to raise money for the museum, then donated to local hospitals and charities. One year the theme was Art through the Ages, and designers created trees honouring Joan Miro, art deco and 'Tree-historic' art, which didn't need much decorating at all!

Bata Shoe Museum

327 Bloor Street West
Toronto, ON, M5S 1W7
(416) 979-7799
www.batashoemuseum.ca

Bata Shoe Museum
Hours: Tues, Wed, Fri, and Sat, 10 am - 5 pm; Thurs, 10 am - 8 pm; Sun, 12 - 5 pm. Closed Mondays.
Cost: Adults, $6; Students (15 and older), $4; Kids (5-14), $2.

Definitely one of Toronto's quirkier spots, this museum has amassed over 10,000 pairs of footwear and related artifacts from 2500 BC to the present day. Since founder Sonja Bata (of the global shoe manufacturing Bata family) began collecting shoes in the 1940s, pop stars, politicians, and everyday folk have all entrusted their shoes to her. When she decided to open a museum, Toronto architect Ray Moriyama designed a cunning shoebox-like structure whose "lid" seems to be lifting off. Those with an eye for detail might notice that the building's signage incorporates leather, that staple of the cobbler's trade.

There are neat surprises everywhere here, like chestnut crushing shoes from France

Toronto's Midtown

and platform running shoes worn by Ginger Spice. Exhibits change regularly, but starting at the lower level, you'll find a neat overview of the history of shoes and a sampling of extraordinary shoes that reveal the breadth of the collection.

Hands-On Wednesdays are a good day for families to come, when you can get close to artifacts from the collection and find out more from the people who know. Spring Break week is very popular with families, when special workshops and events are held every day.

Lillian H. Smith Library

Osborne and Merrill Collections
239 College Street
Toronto, ON, M5V 1R5
(416) 393-7753

Lillian H. Smith Library

Hours: M-F, 10 am - 6 pm; Sat, 9 am - 5 pm.

Cost: Free.

Directions: On College Street at Huron, one block east of Spadina. About four blocks north of the Art Gallery of Ontario

I'll admit I'm partial to this branch of the Toronto public library system: it's our local branch where we've spent many rainy afternoons and where my daughter took her first tentative steps. But it's also one of the most interesting buildings in town, with architecture that's as appealing to kids as it is to adults. Two enormous bronze griffins stand guard outside this playful castle-like building, with a grand circular staircase leading upstairs and down. In the moody, dungeon-like basement where films and puppet shows are often presented, try an experiment. Stand in the middle of the circular lobby and whisper something. Some rare feat of physics amplifies and throws your voice – great fun if you can get the kids to keep the volume down!

People do come for the books, however, and two special collections draw people from around the world. The Osborne Collection of Early Children's Books traces the development of children's literature, starting with a fourteenth century manuscript of *Aesop's Fables*. The collection originated with a visit to Toronto in 1934 by English librarian Edgar Osborne. Osborne was so impressed with Toronto's Boys and Girls House (the first children's library in the Commonwealth) and the work of its librarian and custodian, Lillian H. Smith, that in 1949 he signed over his 2,000-volume collection to the library.

Come up to the fourth floor and see temporary exhibits and rare items. Kids love the pop-up books that are occasionally displayed, some of them so elaborate it's a miracle they survived someone's childhood! Gems you might see are early original illustrated letters written by Beatrix Potter, or one of the books belonging to Florence Nightingale's childhood library.

If your kids are sci-fi buffs, stop off at the library's other notable collection – the Merrill Collection of Science Fiction, Speculation and Fantasy Literature. The Merrill is one of the top five collections of its kind in the world with over 55,000 items. The last exhibit I saw there was called "They're Green: Creatures from the Pulps," which featured all the magazines in the collection with slimey green monsters and little green men on their covers. A sci-fi feast for the eyes!

Chapter Five

Shred Central

19 St. Nicholas Street
Toronto, ON, M4Y 1W5
(416) 923-9842
www.shredcentral.com

Shred Central is Toronto's only indoor skatepark where your skater dude or dudette can practice their nollies, ollies, caveman crooks, and noseblunts in relative safety. The park includes a bowl, quarterpipe, half-pipe, flatbank, and more. There's a skate shop onsite, and best of all, girls skate for free! Note: Kids under 18 must bring a waiver signed by their parents to get in. You can download a waiver from the website.

> **Shred Central**
>
> **Hours:** Tues-Fri, 3 - 9 pm; Sat, 12 - 9 pm; Sun, 12 - 8 pm. Closed Mondays.
>
> **Cost:** Daypass $10. Kids under 18 must bring a waiver signed by their parents. Waiver can be downloaded from the website.
>
> **Directions:** Just north of Wellesley subway station, off Yonge St.

Casa Loma

1 Austin Terrace
Toronto, ON, M5R 1X8
(416) 923-1171
www.casaloma.org

One of Toronto's notable oddities is Casa Loma, the medieval castle built between 1911 and 1914 by Toronto financier Sir Henry Pellat. There it sits on the top of a hill overlooking midtown Toronto, inspiring local poet Dennis Lee to write this little poem in his famous book *Alligator Pie*:

> *Wiggle to the laundromat,*
> *Waggle to the sea;*
> *Skip to Casa Loma*
> *And you can't catch me!*

By 1911, Pellat had made a huge fortune on land speculation and other industries and had the hard cash to build his dream home. He hired society architect E.J. Lennox to design it and to manage the 300 craftsmen required to build it. Construction began in 1911, lasted three years, and cost $3.5 million. Then Pellat spent another $1.5 million on furnishings.

This was a castle with as many modern conveniences as rooms. Fittingly, the man who held the monopoly on electricity for Toronto street lights at the time had the castle completely wired. Fifty-nine telephones were installed as well, all wired into a central phone exchange. (In fact it's been said that more calls were made at Casa Loma in one day than in the entire city of Toronto.) In keeping with the overblown size of the castle, the ovens in the kitchen were large enough that an entire ox could be cooked in them. Not only that, but when Sir Henry and Mary moved in, the home had three bowling alleys, 30 bathrooms, an elevator, a shooting gallery, a wine cellar, a pipe organ, and one of the first built-in vacuum systems in the world.

Toronto's Midtown

Pellat's dream lasted only a few years, when a series of unsound investments evaporated his wealth and the City of Toronto hit him with a huge property tax bill. After occupying the castle for only nine years, Sir Henry signed it over to the city. Suddenly Toronto city council had a castle, but didn't know what to do with it. It sat neglected for over a decade until 1937 when the Kiwanis Club struck a deal to manage it. Casa Loma has remained open for tours ever since.

Today Casa Loma is a grand place for kids to explore, with its overwhelming Great Hall rising to a dizzying 60 feet. The library is another favourite, with shelves that can hold 10,000 books and a herringbone oak floor of myriad tiny pieces that took many months to assemble. A magnificent stained glass dome covers the Conservatory, with its walls and floors of Italian and local marble. Outdoors, Pellat had steam pipes installed under the flowerbeds to ensure a beautiful garden would thrive even in the depths of a harsh Ontario winter.

And what castle worth its salt doesn't have some secret passageways? Casa Loma doesn't disappoint, with several threaded throughout. A case in point is Sir Henry's study, which has two doorways hidden on each side of the fireplace. Visitors can take the passage to the left of the fireplace to reach the second floor, or they can take the easy way up and use the staircase in the Great Hall.

Be sure to walk the 240m (800 ft) underground tunnel leading to the stables, where Pellat housed his beloved horses in grand style. While you're there, do walk the magnificent grounds where kids can search for the secret garden. You can take snacks out of the castle café to enjoy there, and during holidays when the castle is decorated for the season, live pantomimes and Santa Claus visits make a visit to the castle extra special. After seeing Santa Claus at the castle one year, my son Max still believes he lives at Casa Loma, for at least part of the year!

Casa Loma

Hours: Daily, 9:30 am - 5 pm. Christmas show runs from mid-Nov - early Jan.

Cost: Adults, $10; Youth 14-17, $6.50; Children 4 -13, $4.50; Under 3, free.

Directions: You can approach it from the north or south on Spadina Road.

Casa Loma

Chapter Five

Spadina Historic House and Gardens

285 Spadina Road
Toronto, ON, M5R 2V5
(416) 392-6910
www.city.toronto.on.ca/culture/spadina

Spadina Historic House and Gardens
Hours: Tues-Sun, 12 - 5 pm.
Cost: Adults, $5; Youth, $3.25; Children, $3.
Directions: Take the 127 bus north from Spadina station to Davenport Road.

Spadina House would be even more impressive, if it weren't overshadowed by Toronto's resident castle, Casa Loma, right next door. But do include it in a visit: it's a grand old house with original furnishings and fine art dating back to 1866, on six acres of extensive Edwardian and Victorian gardens. Built by banker James Austin in 1866, the last member of the family lived here until 1982, when the house was entrusted to the city cultural department. The best rooms by our reckoning are the billiards room and the solarium, which have excellent views onto the surrounding forest the natives called Espanidong, which was anglicized into Spadina (pronounced Spa-deena).

Small musical ensembles perform in the gardens every Sunday afternoon in spring. In June, people flock to its annual Strawberry Fair, which features luscious berry desserts, Edwardian children's games on the lawns, and music throughout the day. Another great time to tour the house is at Christmas when the house is festooned with authentic period decorations.

Allan Gardens Conservatory

19 Horticultural Avenue, at Jarvis & Gerrard Streets
Toronto, ON
(416) 392-1111
www.city.toronto.on.ca/parks/parks_gardens/allangdns

Allan Gardens Conservatory
Hours: M-F, 9 am - 4 pm; Sat-Sun, 10 am - 5 pm.
Cost: Free.
Directions: South of College, between Jarvis and Sherbourne Streets.

On a winter's day there's nothing quite as nice as inhaling the heady fragrance of tropical blossoms. This stately Victorian conservatory is in what was once one of Toronto's grandest neighbourhoods. Of botanical importance since 1858, the conservatory boasts a "Palm House" (1909) modeled after similar structures in the United States and England. Today its environs are a bit down at heel, but the six greenhouses are meticulously kept, each displaying different plant collections in 16,000 square feet of space.

Seasonal flower shows like the Victorian Christmas Show, the Spring Display, and the Fall Flower show draw people from all over Toronto. At any time of the year, children love watching the water wheel turn and the goldfish milling about in the pond. In fact, it was hard to get my son to budge until I told him we might see Wile E. Coyote among the cactus in the Desert and Succulent Garden. After experiencing an entire year of changing displays, kids are also able to guess what flowers might be on display. Christmas means it's time for... poinsettias! Easter brings... lilies! Have a look on your way to Riverdale Farm (see below), or after a heavy snowfall for a real midwinter lift.

Toronto's Midtown

Riverdale Farm

201 Winchester Street, in Cabbagetown
Toronto, ON, M4X 1B8
(416) 392-6794
www.city.toronto.on.ca/parks/riverdalefarm

Riverdale Farm

Hours: Daily, 9 am - 5 pm.

Cost: Free.

Directions: At Sumach Street between Carlton and Winchester Streets.

My family has literally grown up at this amazing place, where baby animals arrive each spring, chicks are hatched regularly, and events make weekends here extra special. A day at the farm in the middle of a big bustling city – that's what visitors to Toronto's Riverdale Farm get to experience. Nestled in a picturesque Victorian neighbourhood called Cabbagetown, this working farm boasts rare breeds of pigs, poultry, sheep, cows, and draft horses. My kids have spent hours – in both winter and summer – watching farm staff milk the cows and goats and helping them gather eggs in the poultry barn. Plus there are regular demonstrations of butter churning, spinning wool, and ice-cream making during many of the seasonal events held here. Drop by the Meeting House where free craft-making and other activities are offered throughout the year.

The adjacent park is perfect for picnics, with a wading pool in summer. Every October, the Great Pumpkin Festival brings hundreds of families to the park where food stalls and a mini-midway are set up, and merchants sell crafts of all kinds.

In the summer, drinks and snacks are sold in the farmhouse, but our favourite treat is to stroll Cabbagetown's leafy lanes over to Parliament Street where a number of eateries offer kid-friendly fare, or at the very least, ice cream.

Kids and a kid at Riverdale Farm

Courtesy Ontario Tourism

Chapter Five

Todmorden Mills Heritage Museum

67 Pottery Road
Toronto, ON
(416) 396-2819
www.city.toronto.on.ca/todmorden

Todmorden Mills Heritage Museum

Hours: Summer: May-Sept:
Tues-Fri, 11 am - 4:30 pm;
Sat-Sun, noon - 5pm.
Fall: M-F, 10 am - 4 pm.
Dec until Christmas:
Sun, noon - 4 pm.

Cost: Adults, $3; Students and seniors,
$2.25; Children 6-12, $1.50.

Directions: Pottery Road is easily
accessed from either Broadview
or Bayview.

One of the nicest historic homes in Toronto isn't Casa Loma or Gibson House, it's the Terry House at Todmorden Mills, a village in the Don Valley built by English settlers. In the 1830s, the Terry family built a Regency-style cottage that stays cool in the summer, and throws brilliant light into every room. Long before feng shui came along, this house seems to have known the secret, giving off a wonderful feeling of well-being. Take a peek into the cupboards in the parlour, and you'll find a Noah's Ark – the only toy that children were allowed to play with on Sundays back then. The other house on the site is the Helliwell's, a family that brewed beer and distilled whiskey for early Torontonians. Their house is bigger, and more modern, with an upstairs full of beds for some of their 17 children! As I write, the Mill (dating from the 1790s) was being renovated to accommodate large groups and an art gallery.

The site offers wonderful March Break and summer programming for kids. Recent summer courses included an outdoor art program for seven to 11 year-olds, a one-day watercolour class, and Crafty Millers, which introduces five and six year-olds to life in the 1830s. At Christmas, kids are invited to print their own greeting cards using woodblocks.

A nature trail winds through the trees to a wildflower preserve and pond that hops in summer with toads, ducks, and frolicking dragonflies. The entire loop takes about ten minutes and is stroller-friendly (with just a short set of steps to negotiate). It starts at the bridge and finishes in the parking lot.

Toronto's Midtown

Don Valley Brickworks

Bayview Extension, south of Pottery Road
Toronto, ON
(416) 392-8186
www.city.toronto.on.ca/culture/the_donvalley

> **Don Valley Brickworks**
>
> **Hours:** Parklands always open.
>
> **Cost:** Free.
>
> **Directions:** Take the 8 Broadview bus from Broadview station to Pottery Rd or access it from Bayview Avenue.

When a farmer named William Taylor realized his land was nothing but clay, he decided to turn a curse of Nature into a profitable industry. He founded the Don Valley Pressed Brick Company with his brothers in 1889, which operated as one of Toronto's most successful industries for one hundred years. You can still read the word "Valley" set into the russet bricks of the last remaining smokestack (of four).

Bricks from the Don Valley works literally built the city. The enormous crater the factory left behind is studied by geologists for the one million year span of history it reveals. In recent years, the Weston Quarry Garden has been established within the mammoth excavation, in an attempt to re-naturalize the valley. Many of the old brick-works buildings are structurally unsound, though a long-term plan to restore them is underway. Interpretive panels will have to do in the meantime. It's a great example of Victorian industrial architecture and a perfect place to set off on a walk or a bicycle ride through the valley.

Toronto Climbing Academy

100A Broadview Avenue
Toronto, ON, M4M 3H3
(416) 406-5900
www.climbingacadeny.com

> **Toronto Climbing Academy**
>
> **Hours:** M-F, noon - 11 pm; Sat-Sun, 10 am - 10 pm.
>
> **Cost:** Sat morning kids climbing clinic, $20. Advance sign-up required.
>
> **Directions:** At Queen and Broadview.

Sasha Akalski is a rock climber with impeccable credentials, having coached Bulgarian and Canadian champions. He's set up Toronto's best climbing facility with state-of-the-art World Cup walls designed by Solid Rock and the French company Pyramide.

The best part is that kids six years-old and up can learn, and on Saturdays a clinic called Kids Love to Climb costs just $20 for a two-hour introductory lesson. For more experienced climbers, the centre's 13,000 square feet of multi-dimensional climbs features overhangs, caves, and bouldering spread out in 10 different climbing areas. There's a full range of classes for every level, and you can work your way up to belaying – or leading other climbers – which is vital if you're going to take the sport up for real. And why not? The Niagara Escarpment, with its giant rock face, is only 40 minutes away.

Chapter Five

Kensington Market

www.kensingtonmarket.org

Kensington Market
Directions: Just west of Chinatown, between College and Dundas, and Spadina and August Streets.

If you visit just one neighbourhood in Toronto, make it Kensington Market. I'm partial to its lively, if tattered, streets, full of interesting shops, galleries, and cafes. To me, it's the most typically Toronto neighbourhood in the city, a microcosm of the larger multicultural mix of folks who make their home here.

Today it's a vibrant area lined with shops selling fresh produce, cheese, meat, fish, and a range of other products, but it wasn't meant to be this way. When John Graves Simcoe, Lieutenant Governor of Upper Canada, parceled out 100-acre lots to his deputies in the mid-1800s, he envisioned grand country homes on huge estates. But many of the recipients sold their land, subdividing it into tiny plots. Instead of grand estates, Kensington became a closely-knit grid of streets lined with modest houses, perfect for the first major wave of immigrants to Toronto. The first settlers were mostly labourers and tradesmen from the British Isles, reflected in the market's street names, Oxford, Kensington, Baldwin, and Wales. After a generation or so, they moved up to more affluent districts, and a new wave of immigrants moved in. Soon the neighbourhood was filled with Europeans, mainly Italians and Jews. By the 1920s, 80 per cent of the city's Jewish population lived in and around Kensington, worshipping at over 30 local synagogues. You can still see two of them on the edges of the market: the Anshei Minsk on St. Andrew's and the Kiever on Bellevue Square.

It was during this period that the market came into being, in a process of evolution that began with merchants selling goods from hand-pushed carts. When merchants parked their carts on the front lawns of their homes, the area became known as the Jewish Market. By 1930, the parlours of their homes had become store fronts, attracting other merchants and shops to the area, and soon Kosher meat processing plants and chicken slaughterhouses emerged.

After the Second World War, immigrants from war-torn Europe – mainly Ukrainians, Hungarians, Italians, and Portuguese – moved into the neighbourhood. By the 1960s, the Portuguese community was dominant, and today they still are, joined by the Chinese from nearby Chinatown.

During the 60s, urban renewal was the clarion call from City Hall. But residents resisted the pressure to demolish the old houses and lobbied hard to maintain the historical storefronts and character of the market. The residents and government worked together to make some necessary changes. The residents won some battles (the umbrellas and canopies over the sidewalks stayed), but lost others (the live chickens went).

Kensington Market

Courtesy Ontario Tourism

Toronto's Midtown

A Brief Walking Tour

I can still recall my first visit to Kensington in 1985, when live chickens were still being sold and slaughtered in the market. Today you won't find any live animals, but a plethora of green grocers, meat and fish shops, cheese and spice shops. Just walk into the market and start exploring. Make a stop at **Casa Acoreana - Nuts Make The World Go Around**, on the corner of Baldwin and Augusta Streets. You'll find every spice known to man, bulk food, nuts and coffee, plus all kinds of specialty candies and baking ingredients. Buy the kids a candy whistle here, and indulge in some grown-up treats too – you may find long-lost favourites among all of those jars!

Another 'sweet stop' is **The Chocolate Addict** (185 Baldwin Street), a relative newcomer to the market scene. Their high quality chocolate truffles, lollies, and chocolate-dipped rice crispie squares are all scrumptious and not expensive. We are addicted to their chocolate sauce, which we use on ice cream and for strawberry dipping, available in dark, milk, and champagne chocolate flavours. A great find.

Come on a Saturday morning to soak up the atmosphere when the market is in full throttle. **European Meats** (174 Baldwin Street) a carnivore's paradise with 20 or more staff running circles around each other trying to fulfill shoppers' orders, is a mob scene after 10 am. Ditto the cheese shops on Kensington, which have doled out dozens of generous samples to our hungry kids over the years. Explore some of the market's restaurants, like the eatery that specializes in both Thai and Hungarian food. Or for upscale fare, you can venture north on Augusta to **La Palette** (256 Augusta Street) for perfectly authentic French bistro fare.

Where else but Kensington would you find an egg shop, which sells nothing but eggs – of every possible variety. Where else could you witness the shameless flirting that goes on between certain West Indian ladies and their Portuguese fishmongers – a little taste of what Saturday night in Toronto is all about. But I digress. While the prices are a fraction of those in a grocery store, don't think this is a down-market market. You can find quality here too. In fact Toronto's finest chefs and foodies come here on regular pilgrimages for exquisite wild mushrooms, exotic fruits and vegetables, delectable homemade Middle Eastern spreads, and the best empanadas north of Santiago. Come to Kensington, meet real people and taste their real food in this gloriously disheveled corner of the city.

One last plug: if you have fashion-conscious kids, they'll adore the market's second-hand clothing boutiques amassed along Kensington Street. Don't miss **Courage My Love** (14 Kensington Avenue), famed for its amazing imported finds and superb vintage clothes and jewelry. You could spend a whole afternoon going through all their drawers, bins, and racks, but make sure to save time for some of the other schmata shops, like **Dancin' Days** (17 Kensington Avenue), **Asylum** (42 Kensington Avenue), and **Exile** (20 Kensington Avenue).

Chapter Five

Places to Eat

Yorkville

Toby's Goodeats

725 Yonge Street
Toronto, ON, M4Y 2B5
(416) 925-9908

Just south of the Mink Mile on Bloor Street West, you can savour milkshakes, floats, and burgers in a funky, 1950s-style joint that kids adore.

Green Mango

730 Yonge Street (near Bloor)
Toronto, ON, M4Y 2B5
(416) 928-0021

The Green Mango always has a line-up at lunch, but it's a great spot for quick pick-ups of pad thai, lemon coconut soup, and green curries. Just a block south of pricey Yorkville.

Movenpick

133 Yorkville Avenue
Toronto, ON, M5R 1C4
(416) 926-9545

Excellent value, famous coffee and gigantic desserts make this an appealing spot, justly famous for its Sunday brunch. It has a special kids' menu, colored pencils and drawing paper too. We find ourselves here quite often, usually when we have something to celebrate. Right in the heart of Yorkville.

Greg's Ice Cream

200 Bloor Street West
Toronto, ON, M5S 1T8
(416) 961-4734

Try Greg's famous roasted marshmallow flavor, and you'll be experiencing the same flavor that countless Hollywood stars adore. Come here for an icy treat after a day at the ROM or the Gardiner, and experience the all-too-rare taste of all-natural ice cream. Available by the cone or in litre containers.

Cake Master

128-1/2 Cumberland Street
Toronto, ON, M5R 1A6
(416) 925-2879

Do not be deterred by the dull exterior – the fluffy poppyseed buns here are ethereal. Get a coffee from one of the cafes and soak up the atmosphere of the award-winning Village of Yorkville Park, across the street.

Toronto's Midtown

Little Italy (College St. west of Bathurst)

Cafe Diplomatico
594 College Street
Toronto, ON, M5G 1B3
(416) 534-4637

Last time we were here, we saw Mike Myers and his bro having lunch. Nothing-special Italian fare, but the patio is the definitive Little Italy place to be seen, and kids are very welcome. Actually refreshing in contrast to the typical louche, leather-jacketed types usually seen here.

Tavola Calda
671 College Street
Toronto, ON, M6G 1B9
(416) 536-8328

A no frills café serving old-school Italian home-style favourites like spaghetti and meatballs at bargain prices. They do a marvelous eggplant parmigiana and a bread pudding to die for. Much better than the Dip, and just down the street. Closed Mondays.

Mars Diner
432 College Street
Toronto, ON, M5T 1T3
(416) 921-6332

This is an old neighbourhood hang-out that serves breakfast all day with a smile. It's got a pretty classic diner menu, so kids can get a grilled cheese, a burger, and an old-fashioned milkshake. The colossal muffins are justly famous, too.

Bloor St/ University of Toronto

Kensington Kitchen
124 Harbord Street
Toronto, ON, M5S 1G8
(416) 961-3404

The owner's collection of old toy airplanes delights kids. Great Middle Eastern fare with lots of choices for kids, like pita pizzas and pastas. For grown-ups, I recommend the couscous, limburgers, and spicy Moroccan merguez sausages.

Nataraj
394 Bloor Street West
Toronto, ON, M5S 1X4
(416) 928-2925

Our neighbourhood Indian – good food, nice atmosphere, pleasant service, tolerant of kids. What more can you ask for? Try the decadent kebab lebabdar for a kid-friendly (but rich) entree.

Baldwin St. (near the Art Gallery of Ontario)

Yung Sing Pastry
22 Baldwin Street
Toronto, ON, M5T 1L2
(416) 979-2832

This family-run operation is packed with customers on a Saturday morning and at lunch hour during the week. They make all kinds of Chinese savouries: steam buns, deep-fried shrimp wontons, taro root buns, and great dim sum dumplings. Closed Wednesdays.

Chapter Five

Café le Gaffe

24 Baldwin Street
Toronto, ON, M5T 1L2
(416) 596-2397

A popular student haunt, but make no mistake, this is a very talented kitchen. Nice patio out front and back and very happy to serve kids to boot.

Margarita's Fiesta

14 Baldwin Street
Toronto, ON, M5T 1L2
(416) 977-5525

Traditional fare, with enormo Margaritas. Two front patios, one on top of the other, make this an obvious choice on a hot summer afternoon. The food's great, if not remarkable.

John's Italian Café

27 Baldwin Street
Toronto, ON, M5T 1L1
(416) 598-8848

More than a few films have used John's as a location, its front window still adorned with Hebrew letters from its previous life as a kosher food shop. John's does marvelous gnocchi, pizza, and bruschetta, with a relaxing vibe that has people lingering (for hours) over a meal. Afternoons are quiet, so we often head here for a light snack, early dinner, or a coffee and dessert after a visit to the Art Gallery.

Chinatown

King's Noodle

296 Spadina Avenue
Toronto, ON, M5T 2E7
(416) 598-1817

If you want Chinese food fast, come to King's. Their steamed-up window brims with the usual carnivorous savories: barbecued duck, roast pork, sweet sausages, etc. But have a bowl of soup to start. There's always a pot boiling away in the open kitchen, and it's why we head here as soon as the days start to cool down in September.

Lee Garden

331 Spadina Avenue
Toronto, ON, M5T 2E9
(416) 593-9524

My husband's family practically grew up in Lee Garden, coming here for Sunday night dinner for years. This is the best meal in Chinatown, hands down. Ask Bill to recommend some dishes, and you'll be in heaven.

Pho Hung

350 Spadina Avenue
Toronto, ON, M5T 2G4
(416) 593-4274

An old stand-by for Vietnamese victuals – great pho, but everything we've had here has been A1. Service is quicksilver fast, so you can order spring rolls for cranky kids and be all sorted out in five minutes.

Toronto's Midtown

Greektown/Danforth

The Friendly Greek

551 Danforth Avenue
Toronto, ON, M4K 1P7
(416) 469-8422

Large-scale murals that set the scene, a bustling kitchen, and souvlaki that rocks. Serves late at night.

Astoria

292 Danforth Avenue
Toronto, ON, M4K 1N6
(416) 466-5273

Astoria has a wonderful patio in summer. Very reliable Greek fare catering to families.

Magic Oven

788 Broadview Avenue
Toronto, ON, M4K 2P7
(416) 466-0111

Excellent pizza, pasta, and sandwiches, including tons of vegetarian options. Neat pizza toppings for eclectic tastes.

Places to Shop

Yorkville

Ice

163 Cumberland Street
Toronto, ON, M5R 1A2
(416) 964-6751

Great shop for purses, jewelry, body lotions and soaps, magnets, home furnishings, Paul Frank stuff, and all the next-biggest-things. This is where all the movie stars come during the Film Festival (it's handily located a stone's throw from the Four Seasons Hotel). In fact, Ice has opened up a second shop in Hollywood just to cater to their celebrity fans.

Over the Rainbow

101 Yorkville
Toronto, ON, M5R 1C1
(416) 967-7448

Jeans, jeans, and more jeans by Teenflo, Dex, Inwear, and all the brands your teens adore.

Kidding Awound

91 Cumberland Street
Toronto, ON, M5R 3N7
(416) 926-8996

Wind-up toys, music boxes, and vintage collectibles. This is where Candice Bergen found a rare ventriloquist puppet of her father, and where Hollywood types up for a shoot or the film festival can be found perusing the glass cases.

Chapter Five

The Toy Shop
62 Cumberland Street
Toronto, ON, M4W 1J5
(416) 961-4870

A great two-storey toy shop with all the usual suspects, (Brio, Playmobil, Lego) plus charming European toys and well-chosen educational toys, too.

Bloor/Bathurst

The Beguiling
601 Markham Street
Toronto, ON, M6G 2L7
(416) 533-9168

One of the best comic book shops in North America. They've also got a great selection of underground literature, magazines, and Japanese anime that'll knock the obi socks off fans.

Yesterday's Heroes
742 Bathurst Street
Toronto, ON, M5S 2R6
(416) 533-9800

Max always wants to stop in here mainly because of its amazing Spiderman sign out front. Truth be told, it's more of a grown-up and teen shop with comics, sci-fi collectibles, including *Star Wars* stuff, model kits, action figures, and trading cards.

Honest Ed's
Corner of Bathurst Street and Bloor Street West
Toronto, ON, M6K 1G3
(416) 537-1574

Owner and theatre impresario Ed Mirvish invites you to "come in and get lost" at Honest Ed's, his labyrinthine bargain palace. Toronto's most famous department store boasts cheap prices on just about everything including porcelain Elvis busts. It's also lit up at night like Times Square, with over 10,000 lightbulbs pulsing away. A Toronto legend and a must-see if you're in the area.

Little Italy

Red Pegasus
628 College Street
Toronto, ON, M6G 1B4
(416) 536-3872

This shop suits the hip feeling of Little Italy with its whimsical house-wares, jewelry, and accessories. You'll have trouble telling the kids' stuff from the grown-ups'. Plus stuff for your funky pet, too.

Animal Kingdom
593 College Street
Toronto, ON, M6G 1B2
(416) 531-6067

A kid's clothing store that caters to the neighbourhood, with licensed products you won't find many other places, i.e. Thomas the Tank Engine t-shirts. A nice selection of books, sequin-covered party shoes for girls, and other handmade items set this shop apart.

Chapter Six

North York, Etobicoke, and Richmond Hill

North York encompasses an enormous swath of land north of Toronto, where post-war babies were reared in neat brick houses. Its chief claim to fame is probably the long reign of Mayor Mel Lastman, who courted big business very successfully and convinced many companies to base their head offices there. For his efforts, North York has grown into Toronto's northern business hub, with high-rises spread out along Yonge Street and around Mel Lastman Square, forming a downtown of shops, restaurants, and entertainment venues. Attractions run the gamut from a pioneer village to the world–famous Ontario Science Centre. But get used to driving up here: nothing is close in Lastman–land.

Just west of Toronto is Etobicoke, once its own municipality, now part of Greater Toronto. A mix of luxury neighborhoods like The Kingsway, and working class areas like Rexdale, Etobicoke grew up as a more industrialized sister city to Toronto. Less business, more manufacturing. But it has some of the more interesting venues, like Woodbine Race Track and Ontario's largest indoor amusement park.

As you continue north along Yonge Street, you arrive at the pleasant town of Richmond Hill. One of the fastest-growing municipalities in Canada, its early develop-ment was closely linked with the passage of farmers and goods along Yonge Street down to Toronto. While it continues to expand into the countryside, the old village core and early hamlets have retained their visual identity, and preserve Richmond Hill's unique character.

Chapter Six

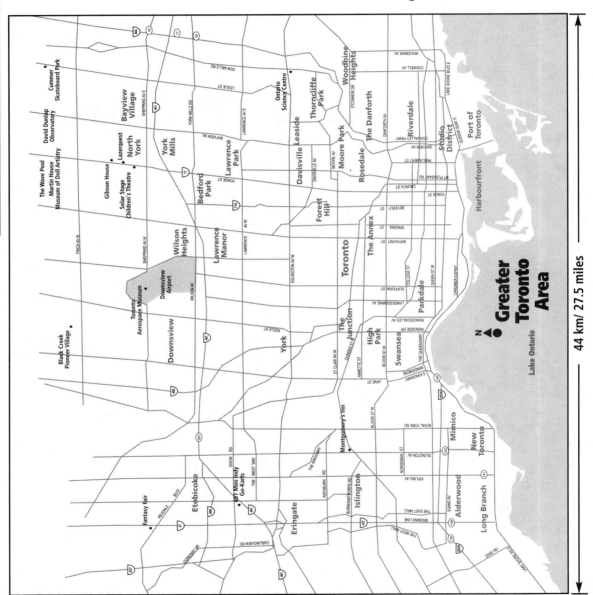

North York, Etobicoke, and Richmond Hill

Things to Do

Black Creek Pioneer Village

**1000 Murray Ross Parkway
North York, ON, M3J 2P3
(416) 736-1733; 1-888-872-2344
www.trca.on.ca/bcpv**

Black Creek Pioneer Village
Hours: May 1- Dec 31: M-F, 10 am - 5 pm; Sat-Sun, 9:30 am - 4 pm.
Cost: Adults, $10; Kids 5-14, $6; 4 and under, free.
Directions: From Finch subway station take Steeles bus 60 West B, D, or E. From Jane subway station take, Jane bus #35.

Roaming around Black Creek Pioneer Village is a real "step back in time" to 19th-century Canada. Unlike the costumed interpreters I've seen in some historical parks, I found the denizens of this village quite eager to share their stories. So, soon after arriving, we found ourselves hearing the tale of a U.S. Civil War widow. (Surprising perhaps, but a lot of Canadian men enlisted). The poor woman had just gotten word of her husband's death and had been hanging black veils over all her mirrors when we arrived. My son Max was soon wrapped up in her life story, the spell only broken by the sounds of a cannon being wheeled up the street. The battle was beginning. Up and down Queen Street the soldiers

Soldiers lining up at the Black Creek Pioneer Village

fought, advancing, filling their muskets, and then marching five abreast into battle once again. By the time it was over, my eardrums ached and smoke was everywhere, forcing us to take refuge in a nearby dry goods shop. Though it was not a normal day at Black Creek (the Civil War reenactment is an annual treat held in mid-July), it is typical of the very good programming they do all through the year.

There are special events all year round, but Christmas is an especially wonderful time with Victorian celebrations. If you work up an appetite roaming the streets, try the Half Way House Restaurant (11 am - 4 pm) for good old country fare. And finding a souvenir is easy at the Laskay Emporium or Visitor Centre Gift Shop, both of which are well-stocked with historical toys and country wares.

Chapter Six

Gibson House

5172 Yonge Street
North York, ON M2N 5P6
(416) 395-7432
www.city.toronto.on.ca/culture/gibson_house

Gibson House
Hours: Jan-Aug, Oct, & Nov 1-12: Tues-Fri, 9:30 am - 4:30 pm; Sat-Sun/holidays: noon - 5 pm. Sept: Tues-Fri, 9:30 am - 4:30 pm; closed Sat-Sun. Mid-Nov -Dec 31: M-F, 9:30 am - 4:30 pm; Sat-Sun/holidays, noon - 5 pm.
Cost: Adults, $2.75; Youth 13-18, $2.25; Children 2-12, $1.75.
Directions: Between Finch and Sheppard on Yonge Street.

When kids walk into this farmhouse, circa 1851, they can't believe it was once surrounded by some of the best farmland and most contented cows in Canada. Today it's very much a city house, hemmed in by new condo towers and the hum of traffic on Yonge Street.

The museum is housed in the restored 1851 home of David and Elizabeth Gibson and their seven children. David Gibson was a land surveyor, local politician, and farmer. First elected in 1834, Gibson became disillusioned with the government's refusal to change, which led to his involvement in the ill-fated Rebellion of 1837. After their home was set on fire and they were exiled to the United States for 10 years, the family returned to Toronto and built a new house, which is today's Gibson House Museum. If your kids are interested in history, this family's dramatic tale of community and prosperity risked for principle is a really inspiring one.

Costumed interpreters set the scene most days. But the best part about Gibson House is its interactive Discovery Room where kids can open up activity boxes designed to get them thinking about what it would've been like to live here long ago. Puzzles, games, crafts to make and take, make this historic house the most fun to visit in Toronto. The summer and March Break camps here are wildly popular too, probably because kids associate Gibson House with having a good time.

Cummer Skateboard Park

6000 Leslie Street
North York, ON M2H 1J9

Cummer Skateboard Park
Hours: Daylight hours only.
Cost: Free.
Directions: North of Finch Avenue East and south of Steeles Avenue East, at Cummer Avenue. Adjacent to Cummer Community Centre.

The site of 100 gnarly skateboarders flying off dozens of man-made surfaces at every imaginable angle is what you'll find on an average weekend day at Toronto's first skatepark. Designed to replicate urban streets with stairs, railings, benches, and curbs, Cummer Skateboard Park offers an alternative to skateboarding in traffic. The park is next to a multi-purpose facility that includes a fitness centre, indoor pool, and an arena, so a family can make a day of it, each to his own. An adjacent park has playing fields for baseball and soccer, and tennis courts.

North York, Etobicoke, and Richmond Hill

David Dunlap Observatory

123 Hillsview Drive
Richmond Hill, ON L4C 1T3
(905) 884-2112
http://ddo.astro.utoronto.ca

The David Dunlap Observatory is a moody, atmospheric place that is all the more mysterious at night, when tours are offered. This is home to Canada's largest telescope, a 23-tonne Cassegrain brought over from England in 1933 and assembled in the white domed observatory where it's rested ever since.

Our evening of wonder starts with a half-hour introductory talk in the lecture room in the main building. We learn about the telescope, how it works, and what we'll (hopefully) be seeing. We leave the building and walk over to the dome, under a bright starry sky. The first glimpse of the telescope is so impressive, it seems a bit unreal, or out of a sci-fi movie at least. In the main room, the monster telescope points up out of a window into the night sky, not making a sound. One by one we all get up on the ladder and take turns peering way, way out into space.

Weather conditions can make it impossible to use the telescope about half of the time, so count your lucky stars if you're able to use it the night you're there. We had a clear night, but it wasn't easy to identify what I was seeing. It's a good thing that you can find amateur astronomers from the Royal Astronomical Society outside on the lawn. They often set up telescopes here on weekend evenings and are happy to let visitors have a look at what they've found.

> **David Dunlap Observatory**
>
> **Hours:** Tours: May-Sept, Fri-Sat nights, call for exact times. Friday tours are "family nights" and parents with children over 7 are encouraged to attend these tours. Tours are not scheduled on holiday weekends.
>
> **Cost:** Adults, $6; Children, $4. Tickets sold same-day, first-come first-served basis.
>
> **Note:** no children under 7 allowed.
>
> **Directions:** Hillsview Drive runs west off Bayview Avenue about 3 km north of Highway 7 and 1 km south of Major MacKenzie Drive. The DDO is the only property on the south side of Hillsview.

Chapter Six

Ontario Science Centre

770 Don Mills Road
North York, ON, M3C 1T3
(416) 696-3127
www.ontariosciencecentre.ca

Long before interactive displays became a mainstay of the museum world, the Ontario Science Centre had a thorough grasp of the concept. This world-renowned centre has been fascinating Toronto kids (and grown-ups) since 1969, and has hosted 30 million visitors since then. If you ask anyone who's visited the centre, they'll rave over the hair-raising electrical balls, lasers that burn through wood like butter, and flowers that shatter into icy shards.

With more than 800 exhibits and 13 exhibition halls, one visit is never enough. Plan to spend the day here, leaving some time at the end for some outdoor activity. I wouldn't recommend taking kids under 6 though, since finding exhibits they'll understand amid the hundreds of interactive modules is a challenge. And if they're like my son Max, whose first visit

Ontario Science Centre

Hours: Daily, 10 am - 5 pm; July-Aug, 10 am - 6 pm; closed Christmas Day.

Cost: Adult, $13; Youth (13-17), $9; Children (5 to 12), $7. The IMAX films have separate admission prices, but your best bet if you want to both visit the science center and see a movie is to get the combination admission ticket.

Directions: From downtown by car: take the Don Valley Parkway north to Don Mills Rd N and follow signs to Science Centre. From the North: Exit Hwy 401 E or W to Don Valley Parkway South. Exit Wynford Dr and watch for the signs.

Ontario Science Centre

was a disaster (he was three at the time), they won't want to return for quite some time! That said, we've been back and absolutely love this place for its sheer size, and kid-friendly interactivity (the hallmark of this place).

I'd recommend Space, Sport, the Human Body, and the Information Highway as a few of the in-depth exhibits worth exploring. Don't miss the Omnimax theatre presentations – whatever is showing is sure to be memorable. Shucks, even the introduction explaining all of the theatre's features is entertaining and suspenseful.

Be sure to find out the special events and demonstrations that are held throughout the year. The last time we visited, a man was casting a brass watchcase in the foundry in front of an audience of rapt 12-year-olds. In the middle of his spiel, he even tossed a barb at the Science Centre's downtown rival when he said, "If you can't guess what I'm going to do next, you'll have to spend all day tomorrow at the ROM." Cruel dude!

North York, Etobicoke, and Richmond Hill

Toronto Aerospace Museum

65 Carl Hall Road
Toronto, ON, M3K 2B6
(416) 638-6078
www.torontoaerospacemuseum.com

Toronto Aerospace Museum
Hours: Thurs-Sat, 10 am - 4 pm.
Cost: Adults, $5; Youth 13-18, $3, Children 6-13, $2; Under 6, free.
Directions: In Downsview Park between Allen Expressway and Keele, Sheppard exit.

Like many four-year old boys, my son dreams of flying an airplane some day, so a visit to Toronto's Aerospace Museum (TAM) was a stroke of genius one blustery spring afternoon. It's Toronto's newest museum, but one of their current projects should put them on the map. Volunteers are busy building a full-scale model of an Avro Arrow – the infamous fighter jet that was mysteriously destroyed under the orders of the Canadian government in 1959. The Arrow has been much celebrated for its ground-breaking technology, which many say would have made Canada a world leader in airplane design and manufacture. But all we have are memories, alas – and soon a model we can marvel at.

Like the Arrow, everything has a story here, so take advantage of the volunteer guides. For instance, we learned that an odd looking contraption is actually an early flight simulator called a Link. The Link was invented just in time for the Depression, when almost nobody was flying! So the inventor sold them to midways where people "flew" them for a penny. His luck changed with WWII, when virtually every airfield in North America needed a couple of Links for pilot training. An interesting feature of the Link is its use of bellows to simulate flight. Why bellows? Because the inventor's father was an organ maker.

The museum is housed in an old DeHavilland hangar, where the Canadian aerospace company built British-designed Tiger Moths out of cloth and wood, beginning in 1929. But the company wanted to design its own planes and started with the Chipmunk in 1946, which was sold to more than 60 countries. Buoyed by the Chipmunk's success, the company built subsequent planes and one, the Beaver, was recently named one of the top 10 engineering feats of the 20th century by the International Engineering Association.

Look for the enormous old Lancaster bomber, a CF-5 Freedom Fighter, and the tailfin from a British Nimrod submarine hunter which crashed at a Toronto air show a few years back. And soon the museum will have an exhibit explaining the design stages of an aircraft – from its start on paper, to the wooden mock-up stage, to its final Iron Bird stage, where a working cockpit helps designers to refine it before sending it out for testing.

Before you leave, ask to see the Institute for Aerospace's Project Ornithopter, which was still awaiting its first test flight when we saw it. Scheduled to take off sometime in 2002, it's a plane that will fly like a bird – by flapping its wings.

Chapter Six

Solar Stage Children's Theatre

4950 Yonge Street
North York, ON, M2N 6K1
(416) 368-8031
www.solarstage.on.ca

Solar Stage has been producing children's plays in North York for many years, with great success. Whether they're producing Hans Christian Andersen classics, or a brand new play based on Robert Munsch's books, you can be sure of a great afternoon out. In 2002, they added a concert series for the first time, which features first-rate Toronto-area performers.

Solar Stage Children's Theatre
Hours: Plays: Sat-Sun, 11 am and 2 pm. Concerts: Fri, 7 pm; Sat, 11 am. Concerts: Fri, 7 pm; Sat, 11 am.
Cost: $10 per show, or packages of up to 13 plays available at a savings. Concert series single tickets $12; full series of 6 concerts, $60.

Montgomery's Inn

4709 Dundas Street West
Etobicoke, ON, M9A 1A8
(416) 394-8113
www.montgomerysinn.com

Montgomery's Inn is like a film set of an old tavern, circa 1830. All the period furnishings are here in the original inn building that Thomas and Margaret Montgomery built and ran for 25 years. Kids enjoy the enormous fireplaces they can walk right into, the ample kitchen, which is often used for historical cooking demonstrations, and a tavern with a wooden bar hung with old ale mugs. The Montgomery's own rooms contain the telltale signs of family life – toys, needlework, and clothes – scattered throughout.

Montgomery's Inn
Hours: Tues-Fri, 9 am - 4:30 pm; Sat-Sun, 1 to 5 pm.
Cost: Adults, $3; Child, $2; Family, $8.
Directions: Corner of Islington and Dundas West in Etobicoke.

There were rooms to let at the inn, of course, but they were pretty spartan. Rooms under the rafters contained straw mattress beds, several to a room, with few windows. If you had a little more coin, you could get a private room with two beds and a fireplace – but you had to share it with strangers most nights. Outdoors, the inn has a kitchen garden with all the usual foods of the day, like gooseberries, rhubarb, turnips, beets, potatoes, tomatoes, and a wide assortment of herbs like parsley, sage, marjoram, dill, lavender, and lemon balm.

Throughout the summer, tea is served in the tearoom every afternoon from 2 to 4:30 pm. And old-fashioned toys like cast iron banks and Jacob's ladders are on sale in the gift shop. Special events include Scottish country dancing, a Canada Day strawberry tea, and a popular corn roast that brings out the whole community, held in September each year.

North York, Etobicoke, and Richmond Hill

Fantasy Fair

Woodbine Centre
500 Rexdale Boulevard, at Hwy 27
Etobicoke, ON, M9W 6K5
(416) 674-5437 ext 317
www.fantasyfair.ca

Fantasy Fair
Hours: M-F, 10 am – 8 pm; Sat-Sun, 10 am – 7 pm; Holidays, noon - 6 pm.
Cost: Day Passes: Adults, $10.95; Under 54", $12.95; Under 36", $9.95; Family, $41.95; Individual tickets $0.95.
Directions: Take Highway 427 North to Rexdale Blvd and Derry Road. Turn right on Rexdale Blvd. Woodbine Centre is just two stops lights away, at the intersection of Rexdale Blvd and Queens Plate Drive.

What to do in midwinter when Centreville and Ontario Place are but sweet memories of a summer long gone? Pack up the kids and head to Fantasy Fair where the weather's perfect all year round.

All the things that make a three year-old's heart go pitter patter are here at Ontario's largest indoor amusement park: bumper boats, a vintage train, a beautiful antique carousel, and a ferris wheel for a bird's-eye-view of the goings-on. In fact, the entire place looks like the set of *Chitty-Chitty Bang-Bang* with its turn-of-the-century storefronts, ice cream parlour, and old-fashioned midway.

The best tip I can give you is to go on a weekday, when it can be so quiet that kids can be ride-hogs and no one minds at all. "Let it snow, let it snow, let it snow," I sang to myself, as Max galloped his giant rabbit around the carousel for a third time. Then it was time to pilot an airplane high above the crowds. Next up was a trip around the world – Phileas Fogg-style – in a hot-air balloon. With my co-pilot tucked safely beside me, we soared up 32 feet and pretended we were Babar and Celeste, starting off on a new adventure.

Holidays are crowded, but that's when special events like face-painting and puppet shows are laid on. If you're taking older kids with you, the new Spinners ride, the bumper cars, and the computer games in Fantasy Station Arcade should keep them occupied. If that's still not doing it for them, they can catch a flick next door at the mall's Cineplex.

401 Mini Indy Go-Karts

37 Stoffel Road
Etobicoke, ON, M9W 6A8
(416) 614-6789

If your kids are 10- to 15-years-old and crazy about car racing, this just might be their favourite place in the world. They can zoom around on the 401 Mini-Indy's super wide, one and a quarter mile track in custom-designed go-karts. There are double go-karts for 5- to 9-year-olds, but they must be driven by an adult. I had a blast zipping over the banked turns and around the clover leaf over the highway, just like driving the 401, but without the insane traffic. If anyone bores of driving, there are batting cages, bumper cars, and a wacky golf course to try.

401 Mini Indy Go-Karts

Hours: Mid-June - Labour Day: Daily, 11 am - 10pm.

Cost: 10 laps, $8; 20 laps, $15; 30 laps, $20; GST extra. There is an additional two-year, $5 club-membership fee, but it will be waived with a minimum 10-lap purchase.

Directions: Hwy 401 to Dixon Rd West; Dixon Rd West to Kelfield Rd; left on Kelfield Rd to Stoffel Dr.

The Wave Pool

5 Hopkins Road
Richmond Hill, ON, L4C 0C1
(905) 508-WAVE (9283)
www.toronto.com/E/V/TORON/0002/41/19

Who needs a package holiday when you can swim in four foot waves, body surf, or just go with the flow on a giant water mat? The surf's always up at The Wave Pool.

Try riding the 160-foot twisting water slide, splash around in the shallow area, or warm up in the sauna. Little ones enjoy playing on the 'beach,' with its gently sloping entry into the water, while moms and dads can bask in the large 35C whirlpool or sit in the sauna. Flotation mats, beach balls, and life jackets are available too. Since this is Toronto's only indoor wave pool, the crowds can get big. To avoid being on a waiting list, try to avoid Spring Break or go early in the day.

The Wave Pool

Hours: Summer, M-F, 1:30 - 4:30 pm and Fri 5 - 8 pm; Sat-Sun, 1 - 4 pm and 4:30 - 7:30 pm. Winter: Fri, 2 - 4 pm and 5 - 8 pm; Sat-Sun, 1 - 4 pm and 4:30 - 7:30 pm.

Cost: Adults, $5.50; Children (3-15), $3; Under 3, free; Family, $12.75.

Directions: Drive straight up Yonge Street, turn west on Major Mackenzie Drive.

It's fun to make believe you're on holiday with the kids. Pack a special picnic filled with tropical treats, and enjoy your day at the beach with no worries about nasty under-tows, no sand in your bathing suit, and no sunburn!

North York, Etobicoke, and Richmond Hill

Laser Quest

9625 Yonge Street
Richmond Hill, ON, L4C 5T2
(905) 883-6000
www.laserquest.com

Laser Quest

Cost: $7.50 per person.
Groups of 10 are $6.50
per person.

Hours: Mon-Thurs 5-9 pm;
Fri, 4 to midnight; Sat, 12
pm-12 am; Sun 12-8 pm.
Extended summer hours;
call for more information.

Imagine a game of high-tech cops and robbers played in a giant maze and you're getting the flavour of Laser Quest. Up to 32 kids play at one time, each of them with a laser pack strapped on their back. Questors, as they're called, try to score as many points as possible by zapping the flashing targets on other people's packs without getting tagged themselves. The maze features ramps, catwalks, swirling fog, thumping music and sound effects. Kids as young as 7 have been known to jump right into the action, while older kids have been known to hang back – it all depends on the child. But you can usually just show up and join in the next game. Games begin every 20 minutes and last that long. Before entering the maze, Questors choose a codename and enter the Briefing room to take the Players Code of Conduct. They're taken through the Airlock, where they get their laser pack, and then they're off.

After finishing, Questors get a computer print-out detailing who they hit, how many times and what their ranking was. If your kids love the adrenalin pumping exhilaration of stalking and tagging opponents, then Laser Quest could become a regular haunt. Birthday parties are big as are corporate team-building sessions. There are several locations in the GTA; check the website.

Martin House Museum of Doll Artistry

46 Centre Street
Thornhill, ON, L4J 1E9
(905) 881-0426

**Martin House Museum
of Doll Artistry**

Hours: Mon-Sat,
10 am - 5:30 pm.

Cost: Prices range from a
few dollars for a bear to
thousands for collector's
bears and dolls.

Directions: Centre Street is
just off Yonge Street, a few
blocks north of John
Street in Thornhill.

Is this a shop or a museum? I challenge anyone to step inside Martin House and not be charmed by its extraordinary collection of dolls, dollhouses, and miniatures. Dolls and teddies are everywhere, many of them so lifelike you half expect them to start talking to you. See Corolle dolls from France, dolls by Madame Alexander, Lee Middleton, Aston-Drake, Annette Himstedt, and dozens of artist dolls and limited editions. And for teddy bear aficionados, there are Steiffs, Gunds, and one-of-a-kinds, plus classic characters like Curious George and Babar dolls that grab little boys as much as the dolls thrill their sisters.

Chapter Six

But above all, this is the source for dollhouse enthusiasts who will not compromise in their quest for authenticity and period detail. Kits and full-assembled houses are available plus all the furniture you'd need for your medieval castle, Victorian mansion, or 50s ranch style. Dollhouse do-it-yourselfers can buy everything from tiny shingles and wallpaper to marble tiling and hardwood flooring for their down-sized domiciles.

We saw miniature bathtubs, bottles of wine, chandeliers that are wired for electricity, a man's wallet with credit cards sticking out, and a vanity set fit for a lady's dressing table. My daughter squealed with delight as she spotted object after object that caught her fancy. Meanwhile, I was calculating how much a fully equipped house would cost, and it is staggering! Start with a fully-assembled dollhouse at $1200 and then count on spending an average of ten bucks for every item in it. But looking is free!

Places to Eat

Cuisine of India

5222 Yonge Street
North York, ON, M2N 5P6
(416) 229-0377

This Indian place is family friendly, in fact it teems with kids on weekends. They're good about letting them watch the chef making roti and naan bread in the tandoori oven, which can kill some time before dinner arrives. Try the fish curries and anything from the tandoori oven.

Centre Street Deli

1136 Centre Street
Thornhill, ON, L4J 3M8
(905) 731–8037

Centre Street Deli is said to be the best deli in all of Toronto – because the smoked meat comes from Montreal! If you're up this way, Centre Street is a good bet, with lots of things for the kids to nosh on. It's open seven days a week from 7 am to 8 pm.

Dante's

267 Bay Thorn Drive
Thornhill, ON, L3T 3V8
(905) 881-1070

A bustling place popular for take-outs, Dante's is notorious for its huge servings of wonderful Italian food. Go easy when ordering and share main courses. It's best to ask the servers how much to order.

Chapter Seven

Daytrips from Toronto

While I'm a city gal who used to cherish her lazy weekend routines, having a family changed all that in an instant. Now we're up at the crack of dawn, packed and in the car by nine o'clock, ready for a full day's adventure. So it's a relief to know that we'll probably run out of kids before we run out of day-tripping ideas, since Torontonians have an endless supply of terrific spots less than an hour's drive away.

To the west, it's the rocky outcropping of the Niagara Escarpment, where we can visit a re-created Iroquois longhouse. If we decide to go north, we may be headed to Kortright Centre for a nature walk. If we head east, we might catch a ride on a vintage train – the best way to see Ontario's stunning fall colors. And because Southern Ontario has the best farmland in the country, any direction you care to take will lead you to farms, many of which are pick-your-own operations. If you enjoy berry-picking as much as my family does, check out Harvest Ontario's website, www.harvestontario.com, so you can combine a day in the country with a harvest of your own.

We've discovered a lot of new places on these weekend jaunts, and most of them are listed in this chapter. So whether you want to go snow-tubing, try laserquesting, or want to make a festive journey to a Christmas tree farm, we've got the goods right here.

Chapter Seven

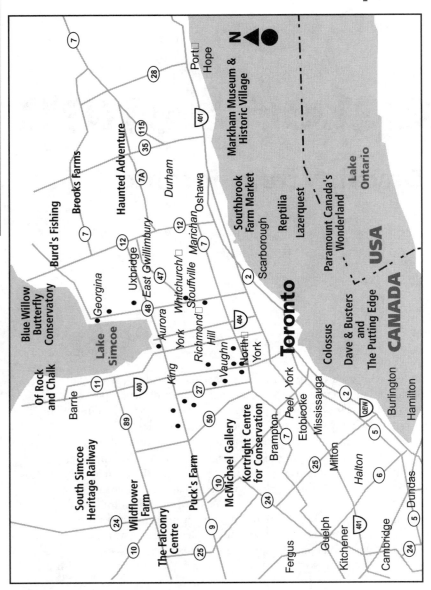

Daytrips from Toronto

North of Toronto: York Region

The York Region encompasses a huge area north of Toronto, with towns like Newmarket and Stouffville expanding rapidly to accommodate Torontonians fleeing the city for greener pastures. Among rolling farmlands and new subdivisions lie fun farms, zoos, historic towns, and dozens of other attractions. Because it's grown so rapidly in recent years, developments began to threaten the major natural feature of the region, the Oak Ridges Moraine. The Oak Ridges Moraine is a ridge of land up to 300 metres (900 feet) high that runs parallel and about 60 km (35 miles) north of Lake Ontario. Formed by glacial action during the last Ice Age, the Moraine forms the headwaters to more than 30 rivers, and is the major source of ground water for the region. The Moraine's varied geology has also spawned a great diversity of rare plants, including a few endangered species. It's hard to overstate how important a feature it is. So it was a great victory for local residents and environmentalists when the provincial government moved to protect it a few years back.

In the coming years, expect many more recreational opportunities to appear along this rich band of protected parkland. In the meantime, with established institutions like the Kortright Centre and the McMichael Gallery and newer attractions like The Putting Edge and Colossus, you'll see why it's worth getting to know York Region a lot better.

Things to Do

McMichael Collection of Canadian Art
10365 Islington Avenue
Kleinburg, ON, L0J 1C0
(905) 893-1121 or 1-888-213-1121
www.mcmichael.com

Tell your kids they're going to a cabin in the woods full of art and they probably won't believe you. But the McMichael Gallery is just that, and a whole lot more. The gallery started out as a lovely fieldstone and timber retreat for art lovers Robert and Signe McMichael, who were busy amassing one of the country's finest collections of Canadian art. When the collection outgrew their home, they felt it was time to share it with others. In 1965, they donated 184 paintings, their country home, and the rolling hill country that surrounds it to the province of Ontario. Soon their passion for the rugged Canadian landscapes of the Group of Seven painters

Courtesy Ontario Tourism

Chapter Seven

became a national one, and the gallery grew from a few thousand square feet to more than 80,000. Today the most popular of these paintings are national icons, celebrated on stamps, posters, books, and on walls all over the country.

A visit to the McMichael Gallery in Kleinberg is an all-day affair for my family, since we can't imagine coming here without doing one of the short hikes around the gallery. After seeing the magenta leaves of a Tom Thomson canvas, or the stark blue-white icebergs in a Lawren Harris, we simultaneously develop a sort of craving for the outdoors. And nature is all around you as you move through the gallery, with enormous picture windows framing superb vistas, glorious in every season.

We try to come on the second Sunday of each month, when the McMichael's huge atrium doubles as a performance space and art studio for hands-on activities. From 11 am to 4 pm, you might find artifact touch tables, storytelling, and music performances. Guided tours, available every Sunday, also depart from here.

Recently we came to see an exhibit of folk art by noted Nova Scotian artist Joe Norris. His work was especially popular with our kids, as they could easily relate to the everyday things and themes that inspired Norris. Kids made their own piece of genuine folk art afterward, and went home empowered by the thought that they too can be artists with a capital A.

Many people come to the McMichael specifically to see the work of the Group of Seven. The family-oriented Discovery Space deconstructs and explores these famous images in a playful way, and helps us to understand the imagery and symbols present in its superb collection of First Nations and Inuit art. Once we used felt pieces to shape an eagle symbol that was carved on a Tlingit blanket box. Another time we admired a group of artists' notions of what home means to them and were encouraged to leave our own versions on paper. Whether you think you're artistic or not, the McMichael will always let you have a go.

McMichael Gallery

Hours: Nov 1- April 30, 10 am - 4 pm; May 1- October 31, 10 am - 5 pm. Closed December 25.

Cost: Adults, $12; Students, $9; Family (1 or 2 adults & 3 children under 18), $25.

Directions: Take Hwy 400 north to Major Mackenzie Drive. Turn left (west) on Major Mackenzie Drive to Islington Avenue. Turn right (north) on Islington Avenue to the village of Kleinburg.

Daytrips from Toronto

Kortright Centre for Conservation

9550 Pine Valley Drive
Woodbridge, ON, L4L 1A6
(905) 832-2289

> **Kortright Centre for Conservation**
>
> **Hours:** Daily, 10 am - 4 pm.
>
> **Cost:** Adults, $5 ; Children, $3.
> Under five free. Parking is $2.
>
> **Directions:** 2 km west of Hwy 400,
> south of Major Mackenzie Dr.

When winter begins to drag on a bit, and museums and indoor playgrounds begin to lose their appeal, we head to the Kortright Centre for high quality edutainment. A regular program of nature-themed guided hikes begins in spring and lasts through the summer months, or you can walk some of their 800 acres of green space yourselves with the aid of a trail map available on site or from their website. On smoggy days, city folk look longingly at the centre's demonstrations of renewable energy technology, wishing the future would arrive a little sooner to help clear the skies.

Special events, workshops, and specially themed evenings are a few of the offerings, but the best thing to do is check the website for upcoming events. Our favourites include May's Warbler Week Birding Hikes, the Four Winds Kite Festival, the Spring Maple Syrup Festival in February, the Owl Prowl, or the Real Raptors (see Calendar of Events).

In summer, visit the Bee Space weekends from 1 to 3 pm, talk to the Bee Keeper, see the bees at work, and taste some Kortright Honey.

Join a Kortright naturalist to hike the trails looking for spring flowers, migrating birds, and other signs of spring. Check out Peeper Pond for a glimpse into the fascinating lives and behaviour of the small animal life which abounds in a spring pond.

Kortright offers over 10 km of hiking trails for you to enjoy throughout the year. You can explore forests and meadows, follow the boardwalk through the marsh, or take in the scenery from a lookout. Download a copy of the trail map to help guide you along your way.

Puck's Farm

16540 11th Concession
King Township,
RR3 Schomberg, ON L0G 1T0
(905) 939-7036; 1-800-621-9177
www.pucksfarm.com

> **Puck's Farm**
>
> **Hours:** M-F, 10 am - 2 pm; Sat-Sun, 10 am - 5 pm.
>
> **Cost:** $8 per person, includes most farm activities.
>
> **Directions:** 2-1/2 km (1-1/2 miles) south of Hwy 9, on the
> 11th Concession of King Township, near Schomberg.

Puck's is legendary among Toronto families, as one of the region's first fun farms. Music abounds (the owner is a longtime music industry member), and the farm actually has a recording studio onsite in one of the old barns. But unless your family's last name is Hanson or Moffat, you're probably looking for the farm. Admission includes unlimited hayrides and pony rides, cow milking demos, baby animals to meet and greet, and musical concerts performed by troubadours. Like other fun farms, Puck's has an annual sweet corn festival in August, a Harvest Festival in September, and a Pumpkin Festival in October. There are burgers and hotdogs on the grill, but picnics are welcome too.

If your kids enjoy picking flowers, the Wildflower Farm is just ten minutes away from Puck's.

Chapter Seven

Wildflower Farm

15485 10th Concession, RR 3
Schomberg, ON, L0G 1T0
(905) 859-0286; 1-866-GRO-WILD (476-9453)
www.wildflowerfarm.com

Wildflower Farm
Hours: May - mid-October: Daily, 10 am - 5 pm.
Cost: Free.
Directions: North on Hwy 27 to King Sideroad No 17; head west to first concession (No 10), north to first farm on the right; look for signs on Hwy 400 and Hwy 27.

Marian Goldberger is well-known for her wild-flower advocacy, peaceful farm, and fascinating nursery. You won't see most of the plants she cultivates in city nurseries, so prepare to be tempted. Opened in 1988, the garden has continued to expand. Visitors can start cutting their own perennial and annual flowers in the spring, can learn about Eco-Lawn (a low-maintenance turf grass developed on-site), pop into growing houses, catch a demonstration, and wander through a sunflower maze.

Perched on one of the highest points of the Oak Ridges Moraine, the 100-acre farm has glorious views over undulating countryside in every direction. Families can barbecue in a fieldstone pit while the kids swing and climb on the rustic playground, chase frogs in the miniature pond, or play in the old-fashioned sandbox.

For Max, the real draw is the tree house. We usually come with a picnic (or at least a snack) that we can all share high up in the branches, where clover-scented breezes waft over us and the sound of crickets is all that can be heard. It's a delightful, sensuous way to spend an afternoon in the country.

Southbrook Farm Market

1061 Major Mackenzie Drive West
Maple, ON, L6A 3P2
(905) 832-2548
www.southbrook.com

Southbrook Farm Market
Hours: Daily, 9 am - 6 pm.
Cost: Free.
Directions: On Major MacKenzie, a half mile east of Bathurst Street between Richmond Hill and Maple.

A visit to Southbrook Farm is a pleasant way to end a day of sightseeing around the North York region, after the McMichael Gallery or a ride on the South Simcoe steam train. The farm has some of the best fruit and vegetables in the province and is similarly famous for its winery's award-winning cabernets and framboise. Throughout the summer and early fall, the U-pick operation features dew-fresh strawberries, raspberries and pumpkins at the height of ripeness. If the thought of picking is exhausting, you can buy freshly-harvested fruits and vegetables in the market store, as well as pies, cookies, herbs, honeys, and all manner of condiments and sauces.

Daytrips from Toronto

South Simcoe Heritage Railway

South Simcoe Railway Station
Tottenham, ON
(905) 936-5815
www.steamtrain.com

Max's eyes grew as big as dinner plates as he watched the magnificent steam engine pull into Tottenham station. This is the genuine article – a 1883 steam train that hisses and chugs its way down the track just like the trains in *Thomas the Tank Engine*. And even the smallest Thomas fan will enjoy riding the South Simcoe, as the entire trip – from Tottenham to Beeton – lasts an ideal 45 minutes. Along the way a uniformed conductor provides interesting commentary about the area's history, and tells the story of a ghost train that disappeared one night long ago. He plays it up really well, blowing the train whistle three times in the hopes that the ghost train might answer back.

Santa trains and October fall colour trains are very popular, so come early for tickets if you want to stand a chance of getting on. But if you happen to miss getting tickets for the train, don't despair. Buy tickets for the next one (they leave every 90 minutes) and discover the many ways to spend that time – browsing the shops in town or having a picnic and swim at the conservation area across the road.

> **South Simcoe Heritage Railway**
>
> **Hours:** May-June, Sun only; July-Aug, Sun-Tues; Sept, Sun only; Oct, Sat-Mon. Generally 10 am - 3 or 4 pm. Check the website or call ahead for departure times.
>
> **Cost:** Adults, $10; Children (15 and under), $6.50; Children under 2, free. Tickets are first come, first served, so be there at least 30 minutes before departure.
>
> **Directions:** From Highway 400, take highway 9 west 20 km to the traffic lights at Tottenham Road. In Tottenham, turn left onto Mill Street at the first set of traffic lights and follow signs to free parking in the lot on Industrial Road.

The Falconry Centre

Line 2
Tottenham, ON, L0G 1W0
(905) 936-1033; 1-888-7-TALONS
www.falconrycentre.com

Walking over the drawbridge into this walled and turreted medieval compound is a treat in itself, but nothing beats seeing the art of falconry demonstrated in front of your eyes by master falconer Wilfred Emonts. His alter ego, King Wilfred, takes you on a fascinating educational journey into the world of falconry during the daily Raptors in Flight show. But first, grab a headset and tour this intriguing modern facility where over 200 birds of prey are housed and over a hundred young birds are bred each year. Along the way you might see Romeo and Juliet, secretive Northern Goshawks, rarely seen by people. In the nursery, you might see newborns, but go early in the season (mid-

> **The Falconry Centre**
>
> **Hours:** Mid-May - Oct, 10 am - 5 pm. Shows: July-Aug, 12, 2 and 4 pm; May-June and Sept-Oct, 2pm.
>
> **Cost:** Adults, $9; Children (3-12), $6; Family (two adults, two children), $26.
>
> **Directions:** On 2nd line near Tottenham. Take Hwy 400 northbound, then take Hwy 9 westbound. Turn north on Tottenham Road and take the first road westbound.

Chapter Seven

May) to see the down-covered babies peeking out of their nests. Birds grow incredibly fast, so make sure to go in May or June to see the downy babies. A baby Bald Eagle is about the size of a chicken egg when it hatches. Twelve weeks later this eagle is full-size with an eight-foot wing span. My favourite area is the Falcon Chambers where you can see breeding pairs behind a one-way mirror, which allows you to see behaviours like feeding, endangered species such as the Peregrine Falcon, Gyrfalcon, and Lugger Falcon brooding their eggs or feeding their young, totally oblivious to your presence.

All of the species bred here are either currently endangered or threatened, and many birds were acquired after being injured or spending many years in zoos. Some of them, like the goshawks, are extremely difficult to breed in captivity, but already the Falconry Centre has a reputation for making it happen. They have a strong conservation mission, and are dedicated to teaching others how to breed and train the birds. People come from all over the world to learn at the School of Falconry, and a quick glance at all the messages on the website shows the art is widely practiced not only in Canada, Europe, and the Middle East, but as far away as the Phillipines.

Note: There's an indoor café, a refreshment stand with hotdogs and drinks, and a covered playground for kids in case of rain.

Of Rock and Chalk

482 Ontario Street
Newmarket, ON, L37 2K7
1-888-248-7625
www.rockandchalk.com

Bruce Wilkinson's indoor rock climbing gym is a beehive of activity when I visit in mid-summer. Dozens of kids are attempting to climb the walls of the four main areas, one of which is seriously steep with the tiniest grips I've ever seen – definitely for those who want to get 'vertically challenged.' Wilkinson is constantly adding new environments and challenges to his facility. Kids as young as four can be taught the fundamentals of rock climbing, though Bruce says they don't go much higher than 7 or 8 feet up. He recommends birthday parties for kids 12 and up since any younger and they may not want to take full advantage of the experience, and the cost may seem exorbitant.

Of Rock and Chalk

Hours: M-F, 2 - 10 pm; Sat, 10 am - 7 pm; Sun, 12 - 6 pm.

Cost: Beginner's courses (12 and up), $35; Family day pass, including shoes and harnesses, $55; Kids Climb Time (for tots four and up), $15 per hour.

Directions: In downtown Newmarket, five minutes from Hwy 404.

Daytrips from Toronto

Burd's Fishing

13077 Highway 48
Stouffville, ON, L4A 7X8
(905) 640-2928

The boys at Burd's will do everything for you but catch the fish – that's still up to you. But they'll help you along the way by putting the worm on your hook, taking the fish off your line, and then cleaning it and packing it in ice for you to take home. And your kids are almost guaranteed to catch a live one, as the two ponds are stocked with more than 10,000 trout! The larger pond is stocked with bigger salmon trout, and is more accessible with a paved path around it. The smaller pond flashes with smaller rainbow trout.

This delightful spot (with churning water wheels) is ideal for introducing kids to fishing, but if that's not enough action for them, they can retire to the playground and let mom and dad catch a big one.

There are washrooms and a shelter in case of rain (all the better as fish will be biting!), plus a snack bar for peckish fishermen and women. Best of all, you don't need a fishing license to catch it and take it home with you.

Burd's Fishing

Hours: Call ahead for times.

Cost: $3 per person. Children under 7 fish for free. $3 for rod rental (bait included), plus 38 cents per ounce for the fish. Fish cost between $3-4 on average. Cleaning and packing in ice is free.

Directions: Take Hwy 404 north, turn right at exit 37 to Stouffville Road. Turn north on Hwy 48 and watch for the farm on your right.

Brooks Farms

122 Ashworth Road
Mount Albert, ON, L0G 1M0
(905) 473-3920
www.brooksfarms.com

Paul Brooks has had a ball transforming his family's 'back 40' into an entertainment venue that's getting attention across the country, thanks to a profile on national television. Beyond the standard petting zoo, visitors to the farm can snow tube in the winter, take a train tour around the farm, and pick berries all summer long. But the main attraction is their Fall Fun Fair weekends, held in October. Kids love the corn maze and the wagon rides out to the pumpkin patch where they can pick their own pumpkins. But lately it's been the pumpkin cannon and pig races that have got people talking. The

Brooks Farms

Hours: Oct Fall Fun Festival: Fri, dusk - 10 pm; Sat, 10 am - 10 pm; Sun, 10 am - 5 pm. Snow tubing: Christmastime-spring thaw. Pick your own strawberries and raspberries: late June-Aug, 8 am - 8 pm. Asparagus picking: April; Call ahead for availability.

Cost: Various costs depending on activity. Daytime fun, $3.75 per person; Nighttime haunted hayride and barn (not recommended for kids under 8), $8 per person;. Snow tubing, $9 for two hours; Children 2 and under, free, though pony rides and face painting are extra.

Directions: Travel north on Hwy 404 to Vivian/Mulock exit at Newmarket. Turn right on Vivian Road. Travel east to Hwy 48. Turn left on Hwy 48, right at Mount Albert Road (at the lights). Drive 2 km east to Durham 30 and Ashworth Road. Farm is straight ahead and to your left. Watch for our clear blue signs along the way.

piglets race around a track, sometimes getting sidetracked by clover or an interesting smell. The first year they held the races one fellow attached an engagement ring to one of the piglet's necks and proposed to his girlfriend who was teary-eyed by the end of it.

Then there's the pumpkin cannon, which jettisons pumpkins about 500 feet across a nearby field. The sound is impressive as the orange sphere makes its long arc across the autumn sky. But there's more coming down the pipe. Brooks' latest invention is the pumpkin gattling gun – which he says "should be able to launch 6 pumpkins in 10 seconds." My family will be there to find out if it can.

During the day, wagon rides take visitors out to the pumpkin patch so they can pick their own pumpkins for Halloween. They also grow squash, gourds, and "ghost" pumpkins, all for sale. For fall decorating, you can take some decorative corn, corn stalks, straw bales, and mini-bales back to the city to wow the neighbours.

During October weekends, the Haunted Hayride, a 25-minute tour into the surrounding countryside and cornfields, will raise a few goosebumps. Scenes animated by costumed actors and sound effects scare the pants off grown-ups and older kids. The bravest might carry on with a visit through the Haunted Barn's two levels, and its famous "Black Hole." Scary!!

Blue Willow Butterfly Conservatory

23834 Highway 48
Baldwin, ON, L0E 1A0
(905) 722-5849; 1-800-598-0041
www.bluewillowgarden.com

Blue Willow Butterfly Conservatory
Hours: Mon-Sat, 9 am - 6 pm; Sun, 10 am - 5 pm.
Cost: Adults, $4; Kids, $2.
Directions: 20 minutes north of Davis Drive on Hwy 48.

For a learning experience as beautiful as it is enlightening, nothing beats this bright new butterfly conservatory in Baldwin. Built by Roy Gucciardi as part of his family's successful nursery and landscaping business, the aim is to educate Canadians about all our native species and how we can attract them to our own gardens. The first stage of the project features strictly native species that can be found in Ontario gardens. Butterfly species include the giant swallow tail, mourning cloak, tiger swallow tail, and the familiar monarch.

Before you enter this unique habitat, which includes more than 30 species of native butterflies and moths fluttering among trees, shrubs, herbs, vines, flowers and grasses, take time to explore the excellent displays. Here the gorgeous electric blue wings of the morpho join lesser known exotics as well as native moths and butterflies and a few nightmarish creatures such as a tarantula and a gnarly goliath beetle. The 45-minute tour will tell you more about the life cycle, anatomy, and importance of butterflies to our environment than you'll find anywhere else. For instance, the black and amber viceroy butterfly manages to look enough like a noxious monarch to fool predators.

Daytrips from Toronto

If you're lucky, you'll see butterflies and moths emerging from their chrysalids and cocoons, to bask in the sun and warm their wings until they're ready to take flight. The big surprise for me were the moths, such as the enormous cecropia and the stunning jade-coloured luna, that buries itself under leaves in the fall and emerges with the fine weather in spring. "A lot of these moths, people will never have seen because they only fly at night," Mr. Gucciardi explained. A shame, because they are as intricately marked and coloured as the more-celebrated butterflies.

In addition to the conservatory, there is a children's playground, and display gardens featuring butterfly-attracting plants and drought tolerant plantings.

Colossus

3555 Highway 7 West
Woodbridge, ON, L4L 6B1
(905) 851-6400; (905) 851-1001
www.famousplayers.com

Colossus

Hours: Opens one hour before first movie screening.

Cost: Regular movie admission prices apply.

Directions: You cannot miss this giant spaceship if you are driving along Highway 400 north of Steeles and south of Major MacKenzie Road.

Ever since it "landed" in 1999, my son Max has wondered what the spaceship was doing on the side of Highway 400. One night when we saw its pulsating light show, with its laser-like searchlight beaming up into outer space, we knew we had to investigate. Entering the silver sphere we found a games zone packed with teens killing time before heading in for a movie on one of its 19 screens. Upstairs in a suspended cocktail lounge above the din, dating couples sat chatting. And families like ourselves were lined up at the usual fast food booths, or checking out the displays. Costumes, space ships, and other paraphernalia from recent space movies decorate the lobby along with real-life memorabilia from NASA and MIR. An IMAX theatre shows the latest 3D and large format films available, although the manager told us he tries to keep any space-themed films playing for as long as he can. The IMAX projection booth is visible from behind a transparent glass wall so you can see the world's most powerful projection system at work – amazing in itself.

Chapter Seven

Dave & Busters

120 Interchange Way
Vaughn, ON, L4K 5C3
(905) 760-7600
www.daveandbusters.on.ca

Dave & Busters

Hours: Sun-Wed, 11 am - 12 pm; Thurs, 11 am - 1 am; Fri-Sat, 11 am - 2 pm. After 9 pm, guests must be 19 years or older.

Cost: No entrance fees. Cards can be loaded with as little as $10.

Directions: Located at the intersection of Highways 400 and 7.

What happens when two entrepreneurs – one a restaurant owner the other an arcade owner – notice their customers going back and forth between their establishments? If they're savvy enough, they get together to create a single entity (a high-tech midway married with a bar and restaurant), and call it Dave and Busters, after who else but themselves. That's what happened almost 20 years ago down in Arkansas, and now the concept has arrived in Toronto. For families, it works splendidly, since kids can race around the Million Dollar Midway, playing games, winning points, and collecting prizes, while Mom and Dad relax at the bar, play virtual golf on a state-of-the-art simulator, or don virtual reality helmets and play a video game from the inside out. Rechargeable power cards allow you to play on any of the games. Whenever you win, you get a bunch of tickets which you collect until you have enough to claim a prize. It can be agonizing to watch a four-year-old spend 10 long minutes trying to decide between a hot wheels car and a baseball card. If you want to save up and come back to rack up more points, you can do that too. Bigger prizes include DVDs, cellphones, and other high-tech gadgetry. Just remember to have the kids out of the restaurant by 9 pm, when customers have to be the age of majority (19-years-old in Ontario).

The Putting Edge

60 Interchange Way
Vaughn, ON, L4K 5C3
(905) 761-3343
www.puttingedge.com

The Putting Edge

Hours: Winter, 9 am - 1 am; Summer, call for hours.

Cost: General (12 and over), $8.50; Youth (7-12), $7.50; Children (3-6), $5.00. Matinees: M-F before 6 pm, $6.50.

Directions: At the intersection of Hwy 400 and Hwy 7.

Has anyone invented a better family game than mini-golf? It appeals to every age group, and allows the tiniest to take part and even win. We tend to do these courses whenever we see them – whether we're on holiday or not. But our addiction has grown with the latest trend in mini-golf – glow-in-the-dark mini-golf. None of the courses we'd been on was as fun or as challenging as the dazzling, eye-popping colours of this course. Prepare to be amazed as you navigate through this trippy course toward the 18th hole, shaped like a tornado. If you get a hole-in-one, it'll flash like a lightning storm and should get you a round of applause.

The course takes about 45 minutes to an hour to complete. Colossus (see page 125) and Dave and Busters (see above) are close by in case you want to make a full day or night of it.

Daytrips from Toronto

Paramount Canada's Wonderland

9580 Jane Street
Vaughn, ON, L6A 1S6
(905) 832-7000
www.canadas-wonderland.com

Torontonians head to Canada's Wonderland for the ultimate amusement park experience with rides to suit every age group. Giant in size with more than 200 attractions, 65 rides, a 20-acre water park, and numerous live performances, one visit really isn't enough to see or do even half of it. A good strategy is to spend a few minutes looking over the map upon entering and deciding which areas interest your gang the most. Or, before arriving, check the website and click on the Visit Planner. There you can choose your children's age groups and get a list of suitable sights, shows, and rides. Then you can plan your route – though prepare to be diverted by all the action along the way.

Paramount Canada's Wonderland

Hours: Summer, 10 am - 10 pm; Call for other times.

Cost: Adults (7 to 59 yrs), $46.99; Children (3 to 6 yrs), $23.49; Grounds admission, $24.99; Deluxe 12-coupon book, $26.99; Guest with disabilities, $28.99; Family of four season pass, $327.63; Individual season pass, $99.92.

Directions: As this book went to press, rumours were flying that Wonderland might be moving to Niagara Falls and merging with Marineland. In the meantime, you can still find it just minutes north of Toronto off Highway 400, just 10 minutes north of Highway 401. Exit Rutherford Rd if heading north or south on Highway 400. By public transit the Wonderland Express "GO" Buses run regularly from Yorkdale and York Mills subway stations. Schedule operates throughout the day and evening through closing.

Max and I head toward Hanna-Barbara Land, as much a trip back to my own childhood as it is a preschooler heaven for three- and four-year-olds. KidZville right next door is for slightly more daring tikes, with attractions like Taxi Jam, a novice roller coaster parents and kids can ride together, and Chopper Chase, a monorail ride that offers a bird's-eye view of the park. Little boys fond of all things supercharged can catch planes, trains, and rocket ships in Zoom Zone. For older kids with the addicted-to-thrills gene, Silver Streak is the ultimate, Canada's first junior inverted coaster with a helix that puts young thrill seekers through dives, twists, and swoops along its suspended, zigzagged track.

Kids of all ages enjoy Wonder Mountain – a volcano that erupts with a fiery display of lifelike lava, smoke, and fire. Then take your water babies to Splash Works where they can cool off while trying its 11 new slides including Barracuda Blaster and Riptide Racer.

If you've got teenagers, they won't know which way to turn. Every corner has a roller coaster, and dedicated fans make the pilgrimage here to sample over 12 of them (the most of any park in North America), and always try The Mighty Canadian Minebuster, the largest and longest wooden coaster in Canada. But beyond nostalgia, there are plenty of cutting-edge roller coaster thrills: Vortex, Canada's first suspended roller coaster; the intense corkscrew design of The Bat; Skyrider's shark curves and side-winding helix (standing up, of course); Dragon Fire's two 360-degree loops, and the trek through Wonder Mountain (the symbol of the park) aboard Thunder Run. Every year the amuse-

Chapter Seven

ment park adds a ride or two, and 2002 was no exception with the launch of Psyclone, "the most powerful pendulum on the planet," that takes thrill seekers 120 ft into the air, while spinning on a giant disc.

There are different themes for almost every day in the summer, so consult the website to see if any are particularly popular with your gang. Stage shows based on popular television shows (we once saw a show based on Caillou here) and days devoted to celebrating a particular ethnic community are programmed throughout the summer.

After two visits, my family has only just scratched the surface of this park. No doubt one could grow up with Wonderland, much like annual trips to The Ex. A brief list of other attractions includes: the White Water Canyon Area, Paramount Action FX Theatre, Medieval Faire, and International Festival.

Tips: Best days to visit are during the week and the month of June to avoid crowds and line-ups. If you want to picnic, you'll have to exit the grounds and spread your picnic in the park just outside the gates. You can get a stamp to re-enter afterwards.

Reptilia

91 Fernstaff Court
Vaughn, ON, L4K 3L9
(905) 761-6223; 1-888-REPTILIA
www.reptilia.org

We finally get to see what we came for – Reggie, a giant reticulated python is eating a couple of rabbits for dinner – his first meal in a week or so. After watching the snake slowly coil around his prey (previously frozen and then microwaved to the right temperature) and constrict, I've had enough. I go back to the nursery where I much prefer watching baby pythons hatching out of their shells in the incubator.

Reptilia

Hours: Mon-Fri, 10am - 8pm; Sat-Sun, 10am - 5pm.

Cost: Free to browse during normal shop hours; Occasional presentations $5 per person, pre-registration required; Sat, 1 pm, see Lou the alligator being fed.

Directions: From the 401, take the Allen Expressway north past the 407 and Hwy 7 to Langstaff Road. Turn left onto the first street north of Langstaff.

We're in Reptilia, an education centre, retail shop, and breeding facility-cum-zoo, where fans of all things reptilian can come just to look or find a new pet. For years, Reptilia has been educating scout and brownie packs, school groups, and the general public on the biology and behaviour of reptiles. They're not as keen to encourage people to take them on as pets. In fact, they've had to rescue many reptiles (many obtained illegally) that have outgrown their owner's ability to keep them. For instance, we see an enormous and rather unattractive iguana lounging in a case, and Rodolfo, a staff member who's showing us around explains: "Green iguanas are really cute when they're small, but they lose their colour and get really big really fast. And then the owners don't want them anymore. That's why we've got him, and why we refuse to sell them." So a big part of their mission is to help hobbyists make responsible, ethical selections when buying reptiles and to try to ensure that people buying reptiles are up to the task of caring for them.

Daytrips from Toronto

Before the visit is over, we've met Lou, Reptilia's 6.5 foot American alligator, and spotted a couple of tiny tree frogs, not much bigger than your thumbnail. There are beautiful poison dart frogs, popular fire-bellied toads, geckos, skinks, frilled lizards, and colourful basilisks. Staff will generally take you around and answer your questions if they have time. Otherwise you're free to wander among the turtles, lizards, snakes, and toads – a little boy's paradise!

Reptilia offers fun and interactive presentations about reptiles on a regular basis for a small fee. If you're able to attend, look up and you'll see a veiled chameleon that lives in the classroom on a long bank of artificial vines. You can also check out the website to find out which public events they'll be at next. Coming soon to a neighbourhood near you!

Markham Museum & Historic Village

9350 Highway 48
Markham, ON, L3P 3J3
(905) 294-4576
www.markham.on.ca

> **Markham Museum & Historic Village**
>
> **Hours:** Mon-Sat, 10 am - 5 pm; Sun & Holidays, 1 pm - 5 pm. Closed weekends Sept-May, Christmas, New Year's, Good Friday, and Canada Day.
>
> **Cost:** Adults, $5; Students, $4; Children, $3; Family, $14. In winter, Adults, $3.50; Students, $2.50; Children, $2; Family, $10.
>
> **Directions:** Located on Markham Road at 16th Avenue, north-west corner.

Historical villages are rather like forts; unless they have something unique about them, they can all seem the same, and that sameness can be a bit bland. Fortunately, Markham Historic Village does a fine job of capitalizing on its strengths. Home to one of Ontario's finest collections of horse-drawn vehicles, the museum has taken some of the stand-outs and assembled them in a replica of the former Markham Carriage Works. The only downside for Max was the no-climbing rule, but compensation came in a cord that he could pull to ring some sleighbells. Locally-built wagons, an elaborate horse-drawn hearse that kids are very intrigued by, and a beautiful wooden sleigh are just a few of the old beauties on display here.

There are 17 heritage buildings on 25 acres, and nine of them are open to visitors. Two sites being developed currently are a Firehouse and an Implement House. The latter will display some of the best examples of tools, large and small, common to early settlers in these parts. When we last visited, staff were just finishing cataloguing some of the museum's 30,000-piece collection, and readying the Implement exhibit for visitors.

Self-guided exploration sheets outline a scavenger hunt for kids, from Tuesday through Friday during the summer, costumed staff demonstrate life in the village, cooking in a bake oven or making candles in a rustic Mennonite home from the 1820s. You can stroll through the apple orchard or shop in the 1875 dry-goods store. Make sure to see the restored railway station and the opulent Acadia, a railway car once used by Princess Margaret and other dignitaries.

One of the most popular annual events is the October Applefest, when the old cidermill gets going, churning out hundreds of gallons of apple cider. Other opportune times to visit are at Halloween, and during the holidays when Santa hosts a breakfast in the decorated village.

Chapter Seven

Haunted Adventure

Magic Hill Farm
13953 Ninth Line
Stouffville, ON, L4A 8A3
(905) 640-2347
www.magichill.com

Haunted Adventure

Hours: Oct: Fri-Sat and last two Sun, dusk - midnight.

Cost: Adults (12 and over), $16 for two attractions, $21 for three, and $26 for all four attractions; Kids (8 to 12), $11, $14, and $17.

Directions: Take Hwy 404 to Bloomington Sideroad, turn right on 9th line and look for signs.

There's a Jekyll and Hyde quality to Magic Hill Farm, just a half hour's drive up the Don Valley Parkway from Toronto. In October, it becomes the scariest place in the province, while in December, it's a bucolic Christmas tree farm, offering up hot chocolate, sleigh rides, and a magic show.

First the scary bit: the line-ups here are legendary on October weekends, when thrillseekers come from all over Ontario (and as far away as Buffalo) to experience the farm's Haunted Adventure. 'Grandpa,' the man responsible for the spectacle, employs about 120 actors who don ghoulish disguises and take their places in frighteningly realistic sets created by professional set designers, special effects masters, and make-up artists. In fact, they won't admit kids under the age of eight, nor do they want pregnant women to attend the spectacle. Haunted Adventure has a big reputation among haunted house aficionados for being really and truly frightening. This is really a show for the pre-teen and teen crowd who enjoy having the pants scared off them. Many first-timers go AWOL within minutes of the start. There are four attractions, starting with the Howling Hayride, followed by the Haunted Barn, Terror Trail Trek, and Black Cavern. The hayride takes you through farmers fields full of scary scenes and unexpected surprises. Next, walk through the hallways of the 150-year-old Haunted Barn getting the daylights scared out of you by actors, more ghoulish scenes, etc. The Black Cavern is another spooky walk through narrower and even darker hallways. Finally the Terror Trail Trek is like the *Blair Witch Project.* You make your way through a mine shaft, a Haunted Miner's cabin, through a forest, ending up in a maze. Drinks, snacks of all kinds, and pizza are available in the Munch House.

In December, the mood is entirely different as families follow a long tradition of driving into the country to choose their Christmas tree. The kid's play areas are open, hayrides are running, and Santa Claus and the elves are busy making toys. The Munch House hosts a magic show and serves up hot chocolate, soup, hot dogs, and cookies.

Daytrips from Toronto

Places to Eat

Main Street Grill

66 Main Street
Markham, ON
(905) 471-4227

A great family restaurant, for breakfast, lunch, or dinner. Specializing in burgers, halibut, and chips.

The Old Curiosity Tea Shop

91 Main Street North
Markham, ON
(905) 472-9927

A delightful Victorian-style tea shop where you can have high tea served by wait staff in period costume.

Places to Shop

Pacific Mall

4300 Steeles Avenue East (at Kennedy Rd.)
Markham, ON, L3R 9V4
(905) 947-9560

Pacific Mall
Hours: Mon-Thurs, 11 am - 8 pm; Fri-Sun, 11 am - 9 pm.

Ever since a coworker came to the office in an Astroturf mini skirt, I had to see this place. It's an Asian mall, full of shops catering to the Asian population with the latest in Japanimation.

This airplane hangar-sized installation at Kennedy and Steeles houses about 500 shops on two floors, laid out in a grid of avenues and pathways. The narrow, glass-fronted stores hawk the latest in Japanimation, clothing, fun and funky jewelry, and assorted decorative accessories for the home. Then there's the entertainment: behind a long, wavy façade of brushed aluminum on the second floor is MHQ Karaoke Box, a lounge with 20 sound-proof rooms, each containing low tables, biomorphic couches, and state-of-the-art technical equipment. Heritage Town, an additional section of diminutive shops on the second floor, has been decorated to reflect Asian visual arts and architecture. Storefronts sit on the opposite side of a pond with waterfalls splashing over stones imported from China. A footbridge spans the gap, allowing access to the beautiful structures with green-glazed terra cotta roofs, hand-carved wooden detailing, and individually painted lanterns hanging on their exteriors. A gold-encrusted stage – with carved red rosewood furniture, a superb sound system, and backstage dressing rooms – has been located near the food court and is intended for seasonal festivities and use by community groups, school choirs, and artists. Plans for an Italian month and a Greek food festival are in the works.

Chapter Seven

East of Toronto:
Scarborough and Durham County

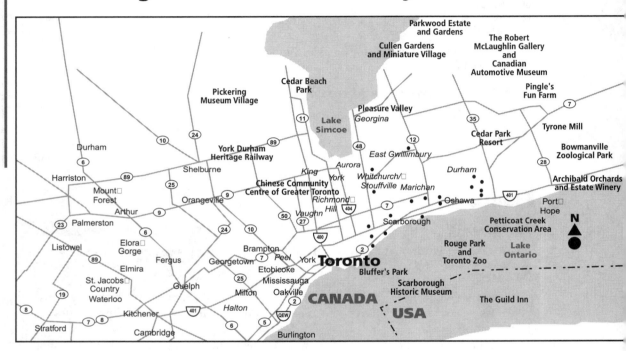

Scarborough

Scarborough has a reputation for being a bit bleak, earning it the nickname Scarberia. But the hometown of comedian Mike Myers has a wealth of natural areas and parkland within minutes of the town centre, which makes Scarborough a terrific destination for daytrips as well as a wonderful place to grow up.

For starters, Scarborough has the Bluffs, one of the most dramatic and under-celebrated natural features of the Toronto lakeshore. The Toronto Zoo is here, as well as Rouge Park, the largest urban park in North America. In fact, the two are across the street from each other and can be combined in a nifty weekend of urban camping and wildlife viewing.

Daytrips from Toronto

Toronto Zoo

361A Old Finch Avenue
Scarborough, ON, M1B 5K7
(416) 392-5900
www.torontozoo.com

Toronto Zoo

Hours: March-Victoria Day, and Labour Day-Thanksgiving, 9 am - 6 pm; Summer, 9 am - 7:30 pm; Winter, 9:30 am - 4:30 pm.

Cost: Adults, $13; Kids 4-14, $8; Parking $6.

Directions: From downtown take the Don Valley Parkway to Highway 401, go east until exit 389 at Meadowvale Road and drive one mile north to the zoo. By TTC, take the Bloor subway east to Kennedy station and transfer to bus #86A which stops right in front of the zoo entrance.

The Toronto Zoo was established in 1974 and instantly became a leader among the then-unenlightened world of North American zoo parks. The enclosures were huge compared to the small cages most zoos used, plus its sheer size (over 700 acres) and dedication to research and the breeding of rare and endangered species placed it at the forefront of progressive, positive zoos.

Today the zoo continues to maintain its reputation for excellent research and breeding programs, and houses more than 5,000 animals representing 459 wildlife species. It can be a daunting task just trying to decide where to begin. But I'd recommend starting with a look at the Daily Events board at the admission gates. There's often a Meet the Keeper event, special feedings, or newborn animals to visit, which can make a zoo visit extra special.

The zoo is sensibly arranged according to geographical zones. So, if your kids adore African wildlife you can skip other parts and head right there. Ditto for the Australasia, Eurasia, Canadian Domain, Indomalaya, or Americas areas. There are outdoor exhibits and indoor pavilions, so no matter what the weather,

Big Kitty relaxing at the zoo

you can see loads of fascinating creatures. If your kids aren't big on walking, for $3 per person, you can take the open-air Zoomobile to the far end of the zoo and walk back towards the entrance (our usual strategy). You can also rent strollers and wagons, though they aren't allowed on the Zoomobile.

The best-known exhibit has to be the Gorilla Rainforest, which just got a brand new pavilion making it the largest in North America. Celebrity gorilla Charles and his clan of eight West Lowland Gorillas can now cavort in comfort, and boy, do they love all the attention! But the zoo has dozens of highlights, making them impossible to list. A partial list has to include the Komodo dragons, Siberian tigers, African bush elephants, Great Indian rhinoceros, and the magnificent polar bears who you can watch swimming through an underwater window. But nothing beats the screams of excitement that are unleashed when my kids get their first glimpse of the towering giraffes.

133

Chapter Seven

Little ones who tire of all the travel can retire to the Children's Area near the entrance where they can ride a pony or camel, see animal shows, and frolic in the new water park, called Splash Island. Opened in summer 2002, Splash Island is an ingenious playground where kids can navigate the Canadian Waterways starting in the clouds that bring the rain, and ending with a dip in the ocean. As kids venture downstream from wetlands to lake to ocean, they encounter water slides, ground sprays, misters, and all the creatures that live there, like ducks, beavers, seals, and polar bears. There's also an adventure play ship, which depicts a Canadian Coast Guard Ship, and benches for mom and dad. The water park is perfectly situated across from a stage where kids entertainment is offered on summer weekends.

Seasonal events bring us to the zoo regularly throughout the year, with top kids performers headlining concerts in the Special Events pavilion or on the Courtyard stage. Probably the most unique event is held on Boxing Day each year, when kids can follow the zoo keepers as they present the Siberian Tigers, Polar Bears, Reindeer, and other animals with their seasonal food treats. Strolling carollers and free hot chocolate add to the festivities. Plus there's free admission for everyone, all day!

Rouge Park

Glen Rouge Campground
Kingston Road (Hwy. 2) between Sheppard Ave and Altona Rd
Scarborough, ON
(905) 713-6007; For campground reservations, (416) 667-6299.
www.rougepark.com

Here's a unique weekend camping trip that you can take a bus to get to. Glen Rouge Campground in Rouge Park is just a short walk from a TTC bus stop and offers the only legal overnight camping ground in all of Toronto. The 11,400-acre park attracts people from all over the world, yet many Torontonians have yet to discover it. Ask them if they know which Toronto park is the largest natural environment park within an urban area in North America, and they'd probably say High Park, which is big, but not Rouge Valley big. Plus you get a taste of real wilderness here, with salamanders, white-tailed deer, and great blue herons living happily in the old-growth forest only half an hour from downtown Toronto.

Rouge Park

Hours: Late May-Labour Day weekend.

Cost: Serviced site: $30/day, $189/week, $718/month; Unserviced site: $22/day, $138/week, $526/month; Backpacker site, $14.00 daily; Firewood/per bundle, $8.

Directions: Look for the sign on the north side of Kingston Rd. On public transit, take the Sheppard 85 bus to Kingston Rd and walk east on Kingston for 1 km.

The park's many trails make it a super place for families to try out camping and see if it suits them. The best way to find your way around is to get a Rouge Park map, available at the Rouge Valley Conservation Centre. From the campground, you can walk north along the 2.7 kilometre Riverside Trail to Twyn Rivers Drive; at Twyn Rivers, access the 1.5 kilometre Vista Trail, which leads to the Conservation Centre. For an alternate route,

Daytrips from Toronto

travel east on Twyn Rivers Drive and access the 1.6 kilometre Orchard Trail to reach the centre. North of Orchard Trail, discover the new 2.5 kilometre Sauriol Trail, which takes you to Meadowvale Road.

There are dozens of nature walks held throughout the year. Call the Rouge Valley Foundation at (416) 282-8265 or the Save the Rouge Valley System at (416) 282-9983 for information on upcoming walks, or check the website. Spring is delightful for the wild-flowers that bloom throughout the park, and fall brings the coho salmon spawning season.

The campground has 87 fully-serviced sites (with water and hook-ups for RVs) and 78 tent sites, all situated near the Rouge River. There are laundry facilities, bathrooms with showers, a kid's playground, firepits and barbeques. You can canoe or kayak the Lower Rouge Marshes to Lake Ontario, but stay to the main channel of the river to avoid disturbing the wildlife.

You can combine camping at Rouge with activities at Petticoat Creek Conservation Area nearby, where there's a huge (1.5 acres) outdoor swimming pool, hiking, and activities within minutes of the campground.

Bluffer's Park

7 Brimley Road South
Scarborough, ON, M1M 3W3
(416) 392-8186; Marina (416) 266-4556

My husband once appeared in a made-for-TV movie that was shot along the Scarborough Bluffs. He had to spend many blustery days down at the Bluffs, pretending to be a New England whaler, and absolutely loved the rugged shoreline, if not the weather. Lucky Scarborough has the Bluffs – the wildest most natural

> **Bluffer's Park**
>
> **Hours:** Daily, dawn - dusk. Beach bathroooms open 9 am - 9 pm.
>
> **Cost:** Free.
>
> **Directions:** Take Brimley down to the lakeshore for the marina. The only road access is from Bellamy Road at Cliffside, which leads down to Bluffers Park.

part of the lakeshore and the most romantic place for a picnic according to one of Toronto's websites for singles. But the many times I've been here, it's overwhelmingly families who are out enjoying the wild natural surroundings and picnicking on the shore.

Park in the Bluffer's parking lot and follow the path to the shoreline. You can go directly to the beach and admire the bright white sands that form the cliffs, eroding gradually despite the grasses that cling to the sides, offering some stability. If you forgot your picnic, no worries. There's a snack bar in the park, or head over to the marina where a terrific view of boats coming and going and superb seafood await you in Bluffer's Restaurant and Dogfish Bar.

Chapter Seven

Scarborough Historical Museum

1007 Brimley Road
Scarborough, ON, M1P 3E8
(416) 338-8807

Scarborough Historical Museum commemorates the site staked out by the Thomson Family, the first settlers who arrived in 1796. Children are introduced to the sights, sounds, and tastes of yesterday and can participate in a variety of hands-on activities and games. Several of Scarborough's oldest and most significant buildings were moved here, including the Cornell House, built in 1858, the McCowan log cabin, the Kennedy Gallery, and the Hough Carriage Works.

Families can spend an afternoon in the park and visit the petting zoo, wading pool, and playground or take to the numerous bike paths and trails located throughout the grounds.

> **Scarborough Historical Museum**
>
> **Hours:** July 2-Sept 1: Wed-Sun, noon - 4 pm; Sept 2-Dec 18: M-F, 10 am - 4 pm.
>
> **Cost:** Adult, $2.50; Youth, $1.50; Kids, $1.
>
> **Directions:** Located on the east side of Brimley Rd, north of Lawrence Ave.

The Guild Inn

191 Guildwood Parkway
Scarborough, ON, M1E 1P6
(416) 338-8798
www.city.toronto.on.ca/culture/the_guild

Perched on the edge of the Scarborough bluffs, the Guild Inn is a 33-room villa set in beautiful gardens and parkland. All around the house, owner Spencer Clark laid out his collection of columns, capitals, reliefs, carvings, and facade elements taken from buildings being torn down during Toronto's post-war building boom. It's a great place to play "I spy," with its myriad sculptures, fragments, and bric-a-brac lying about waiting to be discovered. You can also get a brochure with a map of the collection and try to find all of the artifacts, which is a great way for kids to learn how to use a map.

> **The Guild Inn**
>
> **Hours:** Daily, daylight hours.
>
> **Cost:** Free.
>
> **Directions:** From downtown, take Kingston Road east to Guildwood Parkway and turn right 2 kms. From Highway 401, take the Morningside exit south 5 kms to Guildwood Parkway and turn right 1km. Buses 116 and 116A from Kennedy Subway Station stop right at the Guild Inn entrance.

The Clarks were also great philanthropists and art collectors, and founded an Arts and Crafts colony here in the 1930s, where artists could experiment with wood, leather, ceramics, and other materials, and be taught by leading artists. The Inn was requisitioned by the government for use during WWII, but was returned to the Clarks soon after. The property and the architectural fragments were sold to the province to be maintained as a public park, and today many events are held here. Families enjoy the annual art show in July. But the best thing to see, in our opinion, is Cliffhanger's annual play (see below), performed outdoors on the stage of the Guild's impressive Greek theatre. Kids love leaping up on stage afterward and will gladly emote for the camera!

Daytrips from Toronto

Cliffhanger Productions

The Guild Inn (see above)
(416) 264-5869
www.cliffhangerproductions.ca

Since 1998, Alice Walter and Christine Foster have been mounting children's theatre productions in Scarborough's lovely Guild Inn Gardens. They've adapted Homer's *Odyssey*, and Romany, French Canadian, and Russian folk tales for kids, and continue to break new ground with each passing year. The plays are performed on the Guild Inn's dramatic Greek theatre stage, which makes for a truly magical evening (or afternoon) out. There's no better place to see theatre under the stars, and once a week kids can attend a theatre workshop held right after the matinee. In 2002, they were able to add a second run in Earl Bales Park in North Toronto, which might become a second venue for the company. Call for show times or check the website. Don't miss the chance to see this marvelous, talented company.

Chinese Community Centre of Greater Toronto

5183 Sheppard Avenue East
Scarborough, ON, M1B 5Z5
(416) 292-9293
www.cccgt.org

At this impressive cultural center, Canada's largest Chinese community gathers regularly for classes, presentations, and celebrations. It's a very welcoming place, which many Torontonians have discovered is the best place to take classes on different aspects of Chinese culture. It bustles on weekends in particular, when you're apt to see a group of seniors going through their tai chi postures, or kids learning the finer points of table tennis from an ex-champion.

Special events are laid on throughout the year, many of them geared especially for families. They have made a point of working with downtown Toronto cultural institutions, which has meant their presence is felt all over the city. During March Break, they hosted an opera camp for kids run by the Canadian Opera Company. For a mere $25 for the entire week, kids received training in drama, music, and stage combat from professional teachers, plus classes in set, prop, and stage design. It was definitely the best thing going last March! Throughout the year, classes are offered for children, including kung fu, table tennis, go chess, drawing, pencil sketching, and cartooning.

Recently, the federal government declared May Asian Heritage Month, so look for lots of activities at this time at the centre. Other annual events include the Chinese New Year's celebration and the Mid-Autumn Harvest Moon festival in September. Interestingly, they also have a lot of outreach activities geared to parents of children adopted from China. Well worth seeking out.

Chapter Seven

Where to Eat

By the Bluffs

3101 Kingston Road
Scarborough, ON, M1M 1P1
(416) 267-6732

Brunch here is one of the best in the city, but not fancy. But this is homestyle fare served in friendly fashion. Great for lunch or dinner too, it's handily located on Kingston Road.

Durham County

Durham is the region just east of Toronto beyond Scarborough and encompassing the major centres of Oshawa, Pickering, and Whitby. One of the main economic forces in Durham is automotive manufacturing, and attractions like the elegant Parkwood Estate reflect the impact the auto industry has brought to the region over the decades.

Lucy Maude Montgomery, who penned 22 novels including the famous *Anne of Green Gables* series, lived in Durham County for about ten years. Uxbridge was founded in 1805 by 12 Pennsylvania Quaker families, traces of whom are still evident in some of the area's historic buildings.

Pickering Museum Village

Highway 7, 3 km east of Brock Road
Greenwood, ON, L1V 6K7
(905) 683-8401

Pickering Museum Village
Hours: June-Sept, Wed-Sun, 11 am - 5 pm.
Cost: Adults, $4; Students, $3; Children, $2.50; Family, $12.
Directions: Located on Highway 7 in the village of Greenwood.

Pickering Museum Village is a grouping of 14 heritage buildings highlighting the life of early settlers to the region. Travel down a fairy-tale like winding road to a charming little village, with work sheds, a hotel, a school house, church, community hall, three homes with outhouse, and a general store. During summer months, costumed interpreters bring the museum to life offering hands-on experiences for young and old.

Two annual fall events draw Torontonians back for a visit. The History in Action event is a demonstration of skills, crafts, and steam equipment of harvest time, held in October. The spine-tingling Spirit Walk is held over two September weekends and leads groups through the village where costumed "ghosts" recount and act out episodes from their lives. Keep in mind that this can be a bit scarier than it sounds. Kids 10 and up interested in history will love it, however, as the focus is on the local Matthews family, whose paterfamilias was one of two rebels hanged in punishment for his role in the Rebellion of 1837.

Daytrips from Toronto

Petticoat Creek Conservation Area

Whites Road, south of Hwy 401
Pickering, ON
(905) 509-1534
www.trca.on.ca/parks_and_attractions/places_to_visit/petticoat_creek

I usually balk at driving any distance just for a swimming pool, but this one is worth the drive. The centrepiece of this conservation area is a giant wading pool covering one and a half acres and surrounded by A1 parkland. Not only does it have a super view of the Bluffs, but it's close to the Scarborough Historical Museum and the Guild Inn, so you can have a really full day out in Scarborough.

> **Petticoat Creek Conservation Area**
>
> **Hours:** June-Labour Day, 9 am - dusk.
>
> **Cost:** Adults, $3.50; Kids (5-12), $2.
>
> **Directions:** From Hwy 401 East, take exit #394 (Whites Road) and head south to Lake Ontario.

Archibald Orchards and Estate Winery

6275 Liberty Street
Bowmanville, ON, L1C 3K6
(905) 263-2396
www.archibalds-estatewinery.on.ca

Archibalds is a family-run farm which hosts kids events in the summer, along with producing some of Ontario's finest fruit wines. At Halloween, they mount a 'Spooktacle' which is a gentle way to introduce little kids to the chills and spills of Halloween. A great place to stop and have a bite on your way to nearby attractions like the Bowmanville Zoo or Tyrone Mill.

> **Archibald Orchards and Estate Winery**
>
> **Hours:** Jan-May: Fri-Sun, 10 am – 6 pm; June-Dec: Daily, 10 am - 6 pm.
>
> **Cost:** Free.
>
> **Directions:** From the 401 east, take the Liberty St exit north and follow it until you reach the farm.

Tyrone Mill

2656 Concession Road 7
Tyrone, ON, L1C 3K6
(905) 263-8871

We stumbled on this 1846 water-powered mill quite by accident after someone at Archibald's Orchards told us about it. Lumber is milled here

> **Tyrone Mill**
>
> **Hours:** Mon-Sat, 9 am - 6 pm; Sun, 12 - 5 pm.
>
> **Cost:** Free.
>
> **Directions:** Seven miles north of Highway 401, Liberty street exit at Bowmanville.

along with flour and other custom milling. The nutty-flavoured whole wheat flour is in huge demand among Toronto pastry chefs, and we always bring a bag or two home with us for the bread machine.

Our first visit was a revelation for Max (18 months old at the time) who immediately spotted the miniature train zipping around overhead. Then we watched the antique doughnut fryer as it efficiently dispatched a bunch of tiny cider doughnuts out of the mixing bowl and into the fat. They are super scrumptious and always seem to disappear on the drive home. If you want a bit of fresh country air, take a short walk around the mill pond and watch the mill-works in action afterwards. Upstairs you can tour an antique woodworking shop.

Best time to visit? Probably fall when the air is crisp, the apple cider doughnuts are piping hot, and the sound of the mill working is industrial music-to-our-ears.

Chapter Seven

Bowmanville Zoological Park

340 King Street East
Bowmanville, ON, L1C 3K5
(905) 623-5655
www.bowmanvillezoo.com

Bowmanville Zoological Park
Hours: May: Daily, 10 am - 5 pm; June: M-F, 10 am - 5 pm, Sat-Sun, until 6 pm; July-Aug : Daily, 10 am - 6 pm; Sept: M-F, 10 am - 4 pm, Sat-Sun, until 5 pm; Oct: Sat-Sun, 10 am - 4 pm.
Cost: Adults, $12.00; Youth (13-18), $9.00; Children (2-12), $6.00, Under 2, free.
Directions: Take Hwy 401 East, Exit at Liberty St.(432), follow North to King St. and turn right, this is also considered Highway 2.

Small kids love the Bowmanville Zoo which seems tailor-made for tiny folk with its duck-filled ponds, grazing deer, and meandering creek. Animals are easy to spot since many of them are just a few feet away from the viewing areas. Over 300 animals live on its 42 acres, many of them in training for film and television roles. In fact, that is the big difference between Bowmanville and other zoos: many of their animals have starred on stage and screen, and they enjoy showing off their talented menagerie to visitors. Bongo, a lion who won the hearts of thousands of visitors, was the zoo's biggest animal celebrity. He scaled the heights of Hollywood, starring in *George of the Jungle*, *Ghost of the Darkness*, and many other films. He died of cancer in late 2001, but not before siring four cubs who were born shortly after his death. They're already training for the big time!

My four-year-old son Max loved his ride on Caesar, the zoo's 14-year-old elephant. "It's like being on top of a monster truck!" he announced from 20 feet up in the air. Later, sitting spellbound in the Animatheatre, he watched as Bowmanville's expert trainers showed the audience how they get a jaguar to bare its teeth, a pony to add and subtract, and an elephant to lie down and play dead. You're also likely to run into an animal on the paths. During one visit, resident trainers came walking by with a ring-tailed lemur, similar to television's Zaboomafoo.

There's a restaurant, gift shop, and small amusement park with a carousel for tiny tots. The park's 42 acres can be seen in an hour easily, but you'll want to make sure to catch the Animatheatre show, included in the admission price.

Cedar Park Resort

6296 Cedar Park Road
Bowmanville, ON, L1C 3K2
(905) 263-8109

Cedar Park Resort
Hours: Mid-June - Labour Day: Daily, 10 am - 7 pm.
Cost: Adults, $4.50; Kids (3-12), $3.50; Mini-golf, $3 extra per person; Water slides, $6 extra per person. Note: Cash only.
Directions: Hwy 401 East to Exit 431 (Regional Road 57) northbound. Turn east on 6th concession and look for Cedar Park Road.

This waterpark has nothing out of the ordinary, but it pays to know it's here when you're in Durham in the heat of a soupy summer day. In fact, why not come here after a visit to the Bowmanville Zoo or Jungle Cat World?

There's a large supervised swimming pool, three water slides, and a mini-golf course. The snack bar has good burgers and milkshakes too, though there are plenty of picnic tables scattered about as well.

Daytrips from Toronto

The Robert McLaughlin Gallery

72 Queen Street
Oshawa, ON, L1H 3Z3
(905) 576-3000
www.rmg.on.ca

The Robert McLaughlin Gallery
Hours: Mon-Wed, Fri, 10 am - 5 pm; Thurs, 10 am - 9 pm; Sat-Sun, noon - 4 pm.
Cost: By donation.
Directions: Located next to Oshawa Civic Centre and City Hall.

Toronto isn't the sole source of excellent arts programming in the GTA. This gallery is among Canada's finest, and its family activities are bang-on. A recent Fun Day at the Gallery had kids creating a masterpiece based on the current exhibitions, and a Mystery Tour through the galleries. Summer camps range from mixed media to sculpture and mask-making.

The original mandate of The Robert McLaughlin Gallery included collecting and exhibiting work by the abstract painting group Painters Eleven, a group of Toronto abstractionists working in the 50s and 60s. This interest in non-representational art continues, and informs the excellent programming and interpretative material in the gallery. You'll see paintings here by artists you probably won't have heard of before; Joanne Tod, Graham Coughtry, and Doris McCarthy are among the contemporary artists represented. But you'll come away with a better understanding of what themes and concerns contemporary artists are grappling with these days.

There's a good gallery restaurant with dishes kids like, and a promised visit to the local automotive museum could round out a day in Ontario's Motor City.

Canadian Automotive Museum

99 Simcoe Street South
Oshawa, ON, L1G 4G7
(905) 576-1222.
www.city.oshawa.on.ca/tourism/can_mus

Canadian Automotive Museum
Hours: M-F, 9 am - 5 pm; Sat-Sun, 10 am - 6 pm; Holidays, 9 am - 5 pm.
Cost: Adults, $5; Seniors and students (12–18), $4.50; Children, $3.50; Under six, free; Family, $13.50.
Directions: Exit # 417 (Highway 401 Eastbound) or Exit #418 (Highway 401 Westbound) to Simcoe Street South.

While this museum won't win any awards for creative displays or interactivity, it is a swell place to bring a boy (or girl) who's mad about cars. The museum is housed in a former car dealership, which still retains that lovely oily smell that is pure ambrosia according to my son. Row upon row of vintage cars sit awaiting scrutiny: "I like that one, and that one, and that one," Max kept repeating as we went down each aisle. Many of the cars were produced by local hero, GM Canada founder Colonel Sam McLaughlin (see Parkwood Estate and Gardens, below): a 1905 carriage, a 1912 touring car, a 1914 truck that resembles a horse-drawn buggy, plus McLaughlin Buicks from 1918, 1931, and 1934. Sir John and Lady Eaton's Rolls-Royce, nicknamed Ladybird, is one of three the couple ordered in one year. Standouts include a 1931 red Alpha Romeo which had handling so precise and sensitive that it was described as "telepathic." Upstairs, oddities include a 1918 Chevy converted to a snowmobile (only in Canada) and a 1965 Amphicar, suspended overhead to reveal its underwater propellers.

Chapter Seven

Parkwood Estate and Gardens

270 Simcoe Street North
Oshawa, ON, L1G 4T5
(905) 433-4311
www.parkwoodestate.com

If Casa Loma appeals to your kids, then take them to see Parkwood – the home of the late founder of General Motors of Canada. The 55-room mansion was featured on A&E's *America's Castles* in 1996, and has starred in countless Hollywood films. When Robert Samuel McLaughlin and his wife, Adelaide, decided to construct a family home in 1915, they gathered some of the best known architects, landscape designers, artists and craftsmen to create an estate so resplendent, that even 80 years later, visitors stare in awe at its beauty, both inside and in the exotic gardens that grace the 10-acre site. Hand painted murals and rich tapestries cover many of Parkwood's walls, and unique pieces, such as the gilded Steinway piano that bears a hand-painted scene on the underside of its top, delight antique-lovers.

It's hard to know what kids like the most – guessing what some of the new-fangled conveniences are, or seeing one of the country's first indoor swimming pools and private automated bowling alleys. The guides do a great job of pointing out all the neat details (telephone switchboards, music speakers) that kids love, and ask questions that get kids thinking about what it must have been like to live then, and in this magnificent place. The McLaughlins had five daughters and evidence of them is all over. A back staircase allowed them to come up from the tennis court unseen by guests, and a large playroom kept them from underfoot. The Aelion organ was one of only eight in Canada and was the DVD of its time among rich folk at the turn of the century. Other mod cons in the house include a central clockworks, a telephone exchange with multiple phone lines (all those daughters doncha know!), and a speaker system. The mansion was left to the foundation with all its original artwork, and furniture; in fact, it feels as though the McLaughlins just moved out

The outlying gardens are, in British style, designed as distinct rooms. Retaining walls and a stone walk frame sumptuous displays of annual beds surrounding an antique European sundial in the Terrace and Sundial Garden. Enjoy Europe again in the Italian Garden, created for R.S. McLaughlin's personal enjoyment, just outside his office. An imported Italian sculpture in the lily pool is a focal point in the secluded oasis that is a coveted location for wedding portraits. The White and Rose Gardens are single-colour gardens that hark back to the turn of the century, and offer a little seen visual sensation that is worth repeating at home.

In summer, grab a bite in the Garden Teahouse restaurant, a glamorous neoclassical summer house at one end of a dramatic avenue of fountains. It's like being on the set of *The Philadelphia Story*; you half expect a bathing-suited Katherine Hepburn to walk into view. In fact, if you think Parkwood looks familiar, you may be right. The estate has become one of the most popular movie film sites in Ontario. During the past few years, dozens of feature films and tele-

Daytrips from Toronto

vision episodes have been shot at the spectacular mansion. The grounds were transformed into a giant carnival for the movie, *Billy Madison*, in 1994, and portions of *Mrs. Winterbourne* starring Shirley McLaine were filmed there in 1995. Lucky visitors in the past have caught glimpses of movie favourites, such as Ann Jillian, Kirstie Alley, Danny Aiello, Ricki Lake, William Shatner, Robert Urich, John Candy, and the like.

Come in winter and lunch is served in the Greenhouse tearoom. There are wonderful seasonal events here making grand use of the spectacular grounds, including Easter Egg Hunts, Mother's Day Teas, and a Christmas Tree Lighting celebration.

Cullen Gardens and Miniature Village

300 Taunton Road
Whitby, ON, L1N 5R5
(905) 668-6606; (905) 686-1600; 1-800-461-1821
www.cullengardens.com

A day in the country at a place kids will adore: that sums up Cullen Gardens. My son gets lost among the 160 miniature replicas of Ontario buildings, leaping for joy whenever a miniature train comes around a corner or emerges, whistle-tooting, from a tunnel. The gardens in spring are a riot of colour when over 100,000 tulip bulbs are in bloom – the best display outside of the Netherlands. For a taste of Nature reworked by talented hands, meander through the Wildflower Park and Bird Sanctuary, where over 280 specimen have been planted. Located east of

> ### Cullen Gardens and Miniature Village
>
> **Hours:** Mid-April - early January: Spring & Fall, 10 am - 5 pm; Summer, 9 am - 9 pm; Winter, 10 am - 10 pm; Closed Christmas Day.
>
> **Cost:** Adults, $12; Student, $8.50; Children 3-12, $5; Under 2, free; Family pass (two adults, three kids up to age 16), $39.99.
>
> **Directions:** Just 45 minutes east of downtown Toronto. Exit Highway 401 at Exit 410, Whitby. Travel north on Highway 12 to Taunton Road. Turn left (west) on Taunton Road. Cullen Gardens & Miniature Village is 1 km on the north side.

the main gardens, the three-acre park offers a variety of habitat from cedar woods to more open spaces with ponds and prairie plantings. Staff once spotted the Indigo Bunting, the rarest bird sighted thus far, and kids will love watching for tadpoles, frogs, turtles, dragonflies, and other insects around the ponds.

After enjoying the grounds, settle into an afternoon at the Family Fun Centre. Two splash pools, a kid's water slide, a maze, wagon rides, and pay-as-you-play mini-golf will keep kids busy for hours. Bring a picnic or dine in the Garden restaurant overlooking the grounds and enjoy daily live entertainment in summer and winter.

Cullen Gardens is well known for their full calendar of Spring, Summer, and Fall Flower Festivals along with the famous Festival of Lights. From mid-November to early January, trees, buildings, and miniatures are all adorned with thousands of sparkling lights, and a magical sequence has a Santa Claus parade going down the Main Street of a miniature Christmas Village. Now that shop windows aren't filled with the animated Christmas scenes I remember from my childhood, Cullen Gardens is the most magical place I can think to recapture that feeling of wonder with my kids.

143

Chapter Seven

Pingle's Fun Farm

1805 Taunton Road
Hampton, ON, L0B 1J0
(905) 725-6089
www.pinglesfarmmarket.com

Picking pumpkins on the fun farm!

Pingle's Fun Farm
Hours: May-December: Daily, 8 am - 8 pm; Sat-Sun, closes at 6 pm.
Cost: Free.
Directions: Half an hour east of Toronto. Take Exit 425 off the 401, go north 8 km.

Pingles is well-known in Toronto for its terrific Harvest Festival weekends in September and October and the annual opening of the mega maze, usually in late August. Its Pumpkin Fun Weekend activities are next in line with wagon rides, puppet shows, and more. Kids love the straw jump and farm animals. Come here anytime in summer to find bedding plants, pick your own strawberries, apples, and in autumn, fall raspberries and pumpkins. The market is tempting with preserves, baking and fresh produce; we always end up bringing home a bushel of whatever is in season. Finally, Pingles closes its season with a spooky haunted hayride and boo barn.

York Durham Heritage Railway

19 Railway Street
Uxbridge, ON, L9P 1E5
(905) 852-3696
www.ydhr.on.ca

York Durham Heritage Railway
Hours: Mid-May - Mid-Oct: Sat-Sun, and holiday Mondays. Uxbridge departures 11 am and 2:30 pm; Stouffville, 12:30 pm and 4 pm.
Cost: Adults, $17; Seniors and students (13-18), $13; Children (4-12), $9.
Directions: Take Hwy 404 north to Davis Dr in Newmarket, east to Uxbridge.

What kid doesn't enjoy a train ride, especially when Santa's on board? The Ride with Santa Train is just one of many special events this unique tourist train offers throughout its busy season. Riders on the York-Durham Heritage Railway are treated to a nostalgic ride on a fifty-year-old diesel train through some of the most beautiful country in the province. Passengers settle into authentic railcars from the 20s and 50s, and for the next 60 minutes enjoy the rolling landscape of the Oak Ridges Moraine, with its winding creeks, lakes, and marshes, to say nothing of the bucolic farmland this area is well-known for. The journey takes you on a 20 km (12.2 mile) ride between the historic towns of Uxbridge and Stouffville; you can board at either end of the line where there's a half-hour layover to turn the engine around for the return trip.

Kids love the restored 1904 train station in Uxbridge with its unique witch's hat cupola and museum of train lore. Special trips include Halloween Spook Trains, the Ride with Santa Train, murder mystery parties, fall colours, and both Mother's and Father's Day trains. A nice side-trip in Uxbridge is the Lucy Maude Montgomery House, where the famed children's author penned 22 of her novels.

Daytrips from Toronto

Cedar Beach Park

15014 9th Line
Stouffville, ON, L4A 7X3
(905) 642-1700

Courtesy Ontario Tourism

Cedar Beach Park
Hours: Mid-June - Sept, 8 am - nightfall.
Cost: Adults, $4; Kids (2 to 15), $2. Cash only.
Directions: Hwy 404 to exit 45 (Aurora Road) east, then south on 9th Line (Regional Road 69).

Cedar Beach on Musselman's Lake is one of the closest swimmable beaches to Toronto, with wonderful shallow water for wee ones.

It's a popular resort for campers and school groups and has a nostalgic feel that reminded me of Bala in Muskoka. But since this is just a few minutes from Stouffville, you might find quite a few teenagers here on a weekend, as parasailing, water skiing, and tubing are all offered by local firms. For our water babies, it was enough to play in the sand, build enormous castles, and watch older kids fling themselves off the giant trampoline, moored in the water about 50 feet from shore. You can rent rowboats and canoes from the trailer park office (across from the pavilion). This is a great place to spend the rest of the day after a journey on the York Durham Railway, just 15 minutes away in Uxbridge.

Pleasure Valley

2499 Brock Road
Uxbridge, ON, L9P 1R4
(905) 649-3334
www.pleasurevalley.on.ca

Pleasure Valley
Hours: Victoria Day-Labour Day: Sat-Sun and holidays, 10 am - 7 pm. Horseback riding: July-Sept, Daily, 9 am - 5 pm.
Cost: Per person, $14; Family of four, $48; Kids 3 and under, free.
Directions: From Hwy 401, take Brock Road exit (#399) northbound.

A day in the country can be hard to arrange if one kid has her heart set on trail riding, while another is more interested in water parks, mini-golf, and the like. If you ever have this dilemma, then Pleasure Valley in Uxbridge is an ideal destination. In summer, it's a favourite spot for trail rides, (reservations required, over 10 years only), while those wanting to rollerblade will find a wonderful trail through the woods. It's great for beginners as the trail is a smooth 2 km glide, and rentals and safety equipment are included. After working up a sweat on horseback or blades, it's time to jump (or slide) into the old-fashioned spring-fed pond. A giant children's playground features a 100' mountain superslide and bouncy castle, while the 18 hole mini-golf course tempts diminutive duffers. Further on, a 400' wet and wild heated waterslide sends bigger kids and adults rocketing into a splashdown area. Bring a picnic, snacks, or a full-blown cookout – free barbecues onsite. You can also just kick a ball around on the playing fields, or play volleyball or softball. Bring your own equipment.

In wintertime, it offers 26 km of trails groomed for both classic and skating styles of cross-country skiing. A heated lodge with a crackling fireplace and snackbar positively bustles all season. Ski rentals are available.

Chapter Seven

Where to Eat

South China Buffet Restaurant

1300 King Street East
Oshawa, ON, L1H 8J4
(905) 576-2922

This is no ordinary Chinese restaurant. For one thing, being a buffet, kids can always find something they like among all the dishes. Plus, kids pay 60 cents per year of age under 11 when accompanied by an adult – a good mathematic puzzle for your kids to do while munching on spring rolls. Events include a Halloween haunted house, a breakfast with Santa, and in spring, a visit from the Easter Bunny.

West of Toronto: Towards the Escarpment

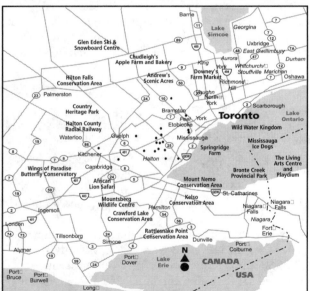

Brampton, Mississauga, and Escarpment Country

Like the Prairies, which get a bad rap for being rather featureless and flat, there isn't a lot going on when you scan the horizons of Southern Ontario. So the appearance of a long, flat ridge to the west of town is notable. For someone used to the Rocky Mountains, it seems a bit short on the vertical. But in the Niagara Escarpment, Torontonians have a pretty amazing natural resource.

The Escarpment is where two gigantic tectonic plates meet, resulting in a fault running 725 km (about 450 miles), north to south. Running along the length of it, from Georgian Bay down to Niagara, is the Bruce Trail, Canada's oldest and best-used marked trail. The Bruce has welcomed day trippers and overnight hikers to its 800 kilometre (500 mile) length for decades, and is one of Southern Ontario's most popular weekend destinations. There's a great website for the Bruce Trail (www.brucetrail.org), which is a trip in itself for hiking enthusiasts. But if you'd like to explore the Escarpment bit by bit, check out the conservation areas that I've outlined below. They all have excellent recreational facilities like picnic areas, short hiking trails, fishing spots, and even a museum and reconstructed longhouse.

As you drive toward the Escarpment, you'll pass Brampton and Mississauga. Both of these cities have attractions worth visiting. Read on, get acquainted, and start exploring west.

Daytrips from Toronto

Things to Do

Wild Water Kingdom

7855 Finch Avenue West
Brampton, ON, L6T 3Y7
(905) 794-0565
www.wildwaterkingdom.com

<table>
<tr><td colspan="2">Wild Water Kingdom</td></tr>
<tr><td>Hours: Mid-June to August, 10 am - 8 pm.</td></tr>
<tr><td>Cost: Adults, $23.50; Kids under 10, $17.50; Twilight rate after 4 pm, $13.50.</td></tr>
<tr><td>Directions: On Finch Street West just 2 km west of Highway 427.</td></tr>
</table>

I regard water parks as the kid's equivalent of a spa — though definitely not as relaxing! And just as spas have been popping up all over, so have water parks, many of them attached to amusement parks. Canada's largest water park features 100 acres of water slides, wave pools, and sports facilities. If that's what you're after, the new attractions here are worth driving to Brampton for.

The wave pool is where my kids want to be, where they can bodysurf for hours on end. But there are many more things for bigger kids, starting with The Big Tipper, two massive buckets that pour 800 gallons of water down on the crowd below. A couple of slides stand out too: the Midnight Express and the Night Rider, which both plunge riders into darkness, and send them screaming through high banktwists, freefalls, back-to-back turns, and a 360 degree loop. I warn those with a bad back, you may be feeling it for a few days afterward (just ask my husband, veteran water slider!).

Then there's the 6,000 square-foot Caribbean Cove swimming pool — definitely grown-up territory with its ornate landscaping and waterfalls, and bar serving tropical cocktails. This is particularly popular during Caribana when crowds flock here to cool down after spending days samba-ing down the streets of Toronto. (Tip: avoid both July and August holiday weekends!)

Downey's Farm Market

13682 Heart Lake Road
Inglewood, ON, L0N 1K0
(905) 838-2990
www.downeysfarm.on.ca

<table>
<tr><td colspan="2">Downey's Farm Market</td></tr>
<tr><td>Hours: M-F, 8 am - 7 pm; Sat-Sun, 8 am - 3 pm.</td></tr>
<tr><td>Cost: Much is free here, during the spring and summer pick-your-own season. During the fall and Halloween season, admission is charged to Downey's Funland, which includes most activities.</td></tr>
<tr><td>Directions: Take Highway 410 north through Brampton until you reach the farm, just south of King Street.</td></tr>
</table>

If the Kritter Corral weren't enough, this farm boasts the largest 'goat walk' in Ontario. Have any idea what that is? Well, it's a man-made contraption that goats walk along to reach a feeding dish suspended eight metres (25 feet) up in the air. Vending machines release goat feed into a dish, which you then send up to the goats using an ingenious pulley system. Kids can't get enough of this, and from the size of the goats, I'd say they feel the same way.

Chapter Seven

In fall, Downey's Pumpkinfest lets little goblins choose a pumpkin from literally thousands lying in the vast pumpkin fields. And remember to make your own scarecrow – a wonderful craft for the whole family to do together. The other major seasonal event is Christmas. Freshly-cut trees, wreaths, and garland are available from the last week in November to December 24. Stock up on all the baking you forgot to do, buy a fresh free-range turkey for Christmas dinner, and score some last-minute gift baskets for bosses, employees, and the neighbours you're always borrowing tools from.

The Living Arts Centre

4141 Living Arts Drive
Mississauga, ON, L5B 4B8
(905) 306-6000; 1-888-805-8888
www.livingarts.on.ca

> **The Living Arts Centre**
>
> **Hours:** Depends on shows.
>
> **Cost:** Varies according to performance or course.
>
> **Directions:** Take the QEW to Hurontario (Hwy 10), turn left onto Burnhamthorpe Road and right on Living Arts Drive.

Home to Mississauga's opera company and symphony orchestra, with two large performing arts halls and seven arts studios, the Living Arts Centre is also a dynamic venue for kids. It hosts a wonderful children's festival each May (see page 178) but throughout the year, see family concerts and performances, and take weekend art courses for kids from three to 14 years of age. We saw a marvelous *Nutcracker* here, and look forward to seeing well-known children's performers like Eric Nagler, Imago Mask Theatre, and Dufflebag theatre here. A family art workshop teaches how to cast glass into the imprint of a child's hand or foot in sand. It's a unique and special gift for a grandparent, and you can say, "We made it ourselves!" Also, LAC's Weekend Artclub for Kids has wonderful courses for teens 14 to 16 in photography, acting, woodblock printing, mixed media, pottery, and painting.

Playdium

99 Rathburn Road West
Mississauga, ON, L5B 4C1
(905) 273-9000; (905) 273-4810
www.playdium.com

> **Playdium**
>
> **Hours:** Sun-Thurs, 11 am - 11 pm; Fri-Sat, 10 am - 2 am.
>
> **Cost:** Most games are $1.50 to $2 to play. You can load up a PlayCard with cash or using a credit or debit card. Unused points can be spent at the Playdium downtown on John Street. Teens can come for Friday Midnight Madness after 10 pm and play for four hours for $25.
>
> **Directions:** Hwy 401 to Hwy 10 (Hurontario St), south to Rathburn Rd W. Or, take any Mississauga Transit bus going to Square One (TTC users: connect at Islington Station).

This is a virtual playground par excellence, with over 200 adrenalin-fueled games of skill and daring. The indoor section is subdivided into five theme zones: speed, simulation, extreme, adrenalin, and air. Try hang-gliding over the Grand Canyon, take the wheel in an Indy car race, or hit the powdery slopes on a snowboard – all in an afternoon. But a word of warning, if you come on a weekend afternoon, the place can be utter mayhem. In summer, the outdoor rock climbing, go-karts, and mini-golf provide a change of pace. If you plan on coming back often, consider getting a Virtual Citizenship which gives Playdium members discounts on attractions, meals, and merchandise.

Daytrips from Toronto

Mississauga Ice Dogs

Hershey Centre
5500 Rose Cherry Place
Mississauga, ON, L4Z 4B6
(905) 502-9100
www.mississaugaicedogs.com

Let's face it, going to see a Toronto Maple Leafs game can break the bank for many families. Why not head to Mississauga instead and see the Ice Dogs of the Ontario Hockey League play in their state-of-the-art Hershey Centre? It's a great chance to see the excitement of hockey up close and to meet some of tomorrow's NHL stars. Being the least expensive sports ticket in town, the Dogs get crowds of about 3,000 fans per game, who make almost as much noise as a full house at the Air Canada Centre. They play an average of five games per month, with Sunday afternoon games at 2 pm that are ideal for families. It's a very family friendly outing, with a ticket deal that gets four of you in to a Sunday game for about $50, with drinks, popcorn, and programs included. If your kids become fans, you can celebrate a birthday at the game, with Ice Dogs loot bags for the kids.

Mississauga Ice Dogs

Hours: Check the website for game schedule.

Cost: Adults, $14.95 to $19.80; Kids (12 and under), $9.95 to $15.30; Sun afternoon Family 4-Pack, $59 includes four tickets, two programs, four soft drinks, and four popcorns.

Directions: From the QEW, go north on Hurontario St (Hwy 10), to Matheson Boulevard. Turn right (east) and look for the Hershey Centre on the left just past Kennedy Road. From the 401, go south on Hurontario to Britannia Road. Turn left on Britannia and go to second set of lights and turn right on Kennedy Road. Take Kennedy to Traders Blvd, and turn left. Traders Blvd turns into Rose Cherry Place. Hershey Centre is on the right.

Wings of Paradise Butterfly Conservatory

2500 Kossuth Road
Cambridge, ON, N3H 4R7
(519) 653-1234
www.wingsofparadise.com

For toddlers and infants, nothing beats an aquarium or a butterfly conservatory, where they can get up close to creatures in a way that isn't possible at most zoos or animal parks. Since Toronto and surroundings are devoid of any decent aquariums, we've often made daytrips out to butterfly conservatories and nature parks. This conservatory in Cambridge is a delight with a spectacular display of gorgeous butterflies, and much less crowded than the one in Niagara. If you can combine a visit here with a Sunday brunch, do so – the café has wonderful healthy cuisine.

Wings of Paradise Butterfly Conservatory

Hours: 10 am - 5 pm, with last admission sold at 4 pm. Closed Dec 24-26, New Year's Day.

Cost: Adults, $8.25; Youth (13-17), $7.25; Children (3-12), $4.25, Under 3, free.

Directions: Take the 401 West to Exit 282 (Hespeler Road), travel north to Kossuth Road, then left on Kossuth Road for six km. Conservatory is on the left hand side.

Chapter Seven

African Lion Safari

Safari Road
Cambridge, ON, N1R 5S2
1-800-461-WILD
www.lionsafari.com

African Lion Safari

Hours: April - Mid-October; Spring: M-F, 10 am - 4 pm; Sat-Sun, 10 am - 5 pm. Summer: Daily, 10 am - 5:30 pm. Fall: Daily, 10 am - 4 pm.

Cost: Summer: Adults, $22.95; Kids, $16.95; Spring/Fall, $19.95, $13.95.

Directions: Follow the African Lion Safari signs after exiting Hwy 401 South at Exit 299 between Milton and Cambridge.

While we applaud the efforts of zoos that continually work to improve conditions for the animals, sometimes all that space and foliage can make viewing animals almost impossible. Thankfully, African Lion Safari offers visitors a wonderful experience by turning the idea of a zoo on its head. Instead of viewing caged animals at a distance, at African Lion Safari the visitors are put in 'cages' (cars actually) while the animals are allowed to roam free. The experience is vastly improved as everyone gets to see prides of lions, bunches of baboons, and herds of bison up close and personal, from the safety of the family car.

"Did you see that?" Max yelled, as a giraffe strode by, almost knocking the mirror off our car door. A few minutes later, the same giraffe returned to lick our front windshield with her long black tongue. Then it was off to watch the baboons, famous for their rooftop antics. Many families recount stories of a brand new station wagon that had its antenna bent or its hood scratched by an inquisitive ape. And if you have a new car or a rental, leave it in the parking lot and take the park's safari buses instead. But our family car survived the rite of passage without a scratch, and if watching a baby baboon pee on someone's windshield isn't your idea of a good time, then maybe you need to loosen up!

The park is in the business of breeding endangered species for release into the wild and maintains one of North America's most successful Asian Elephant breeding programs. They take their conservation mission very seriously and beyond the larger animals in the reserves, you can see Ring-tailed Lemurs, Ground Horn-bills, Spider Monkeys, Celebes Crested Macaques, and the endangered Angolan Colubus monkeys. Most recently the park adopted a "crash" of four endangered white rhinos from South Africa, which they'll try to breed for reintroduction into the wild at a later date.

If you go on a hot day, you'll appreciate the water park. My husband and I took turns splashing around with the kids so we could see some of the shows offered, like the Parrot Paradise Show, the Elephant Swim, and the Birds of Prey flying demonstration. Your pass also gets you a cruise on the African Queen (where more animals can be observed) and a ride on the Nature Boy scenic railway.

Cheaper than a trip to Africa and a whole lot more exciting than the zoo, our trip to African Lion Safari was an outing we'll be talking about for months – and probably for years – to come.

Daytrips from Toronto

Halton County Radial Railway

13629 Guelph Line
Milton, ON, L9T 5A2
(519) 856-9802
www.hcry.org

Max fastened his eyes on the streetcar we were about to board and asked the driver where it was going. "I'll be going up Harbord Street today. Do you know where that is?" he asked, clearly expecting his young passenger not to know. Instead Max yelled "Harbord Street — that's where we live!" to the surprise of not only the driver but everyone within earshot at this unique interactive park.

Halton County Radial Railway

Hours: May, June, Sept, and Oct: Sat–Sun and holidays only, 10 am - 5 pm; July-Aug: M-F, 10 am - 4 pm; Sat-Sun, 10 am - 5 pm.

Cost: Adults, $7.50; Seniors, $6.50; Youth, $5.50; Children under three and adults over 90, free.

Directions: Take highway 401 west to exit 312, Guelph Line. Travel north on Guelph Line until you reach the museum on east side of the road (about 15 km (10 miles).

This not-for-profit railway history museum restores old electric rail vehicles to mint condition and puts some of them back in service on a two-kilometre ride through the surrounding forest. Several trains are available for riding; you can choose from the Harbord streetcar, retired from the Toronto Transit Commission in 1963, a 1893-style open car rebuilt for the 1934 centenary of Toronto, and a 1915 interurban passenger with striking stained glass windows, which used to run between Port Stanley and London. There's an old streetcar shelter that once stood in Meadowvale that was rescued from a farmer's field, and the old Rockwood station dating from 1912, handsomely lined with wooden paneling, wood-burning stoves, and a stationmaster's clock. This is a museum that Max will gladly return to anytime, if only for another ride on his neighbourhood streetcar.

Country Heritage Park

8560 Tremaine Road
Milton, ON, L9T 2Y3
(905) 878-8151; 1-888-307-FARM
www.countryheritagepark.com

After years of driving past this collection of farm buildings on Highway 401, we finally stopped and experienced one of Toronto's best-kept daytrip secrets. Formerly the Ontario Agricultural Museum, the Country Heritage Park is a magnet for school groups who come to see what rural life was like 170 years ago. And how was it? Well, pretty primitive to start

Country Heritage Park

Hours: July-Aug: Sat-Sun, noon - 5 pm. Open year round for group and educational programs. Phone ahead for special events or check the website.

Cost: Adults, $7; Child (6-12 years), $4; Under 6, free; Family package, $20 (includes two adults and up to three children)

Directions: Off the 401 just west of Milton.

with. But as you move around the park's 80 acres, you see how modern miracles like cream separators and tractors reached rural Ontarians and changed their lives profoundly.

Chapter Seven

Kids love the old International Harvesters, the Massey Ferguson tractors, and threshing machines on display. The park lays on special events every summer weekend, so families can plan to attend on Milk and Dairy Days, Corn Fest weekend, Sheep Dog Trials, or our favourite, the All Colour Antique Tractor, Stationary Engine, and Toy Show. In August, the Garlic Is Great Festival will show visitors a stinking good time, and during Labour Day weekend, the park's famed tractor collection chugs over to the Milton Fairgrounds.

Andrew's Scenic Acres

9365 10th Sideroad
Milton, ON, L9T 2X9
(905) 878-5807
www.andrewsscenicacres.com

Andrew's Scenic Acres
Hours: May to August, Pony rides, Sat & Sun, 8 am - 8 pm.
Cost: Pony rides, $3; Fun Farm area, $1 per person in Sept-Oct; Hay rides, free.
Directions: Take Hwy 401 to Trafalgar North (Exit 328). Drive north approximately 7 km to Sideroad #10 (Ashgrove). Turn west to the farm (about 7 km).

As family fun farms go, Andrews has long been known as a great place to spend a summer or autumn afternoon. Families bring picnics or line up for Oktoberfest sausages and veggie burgers from the barbeque. Serious berry pickers come dressed for the sun and hop on the berry wagon to get out to the fields. Kids have a blast in the playground on the antique tractor, hay jump, and swings. The animal corral is an entertaining spot too, with its rabbits, turkey, goats, and chickens.

In recent years, the Andrews have added an adult attraction with their Scotch Block winery, which specializes in award-winning fruit wines (try the Regal black currant or the framboise). It's almost impossible to resist taking home a farm-baked pie or a bottle of their finest, in addition to the just-picked berries. After a day of hiking or exploring one of Milton's many conservation areas, Andrew's is a perfect pit stop before heading home.

Chudleigh's Apple Farm and Bakery

9528 Highway 25
Milton, ON, L9T 4N9
(905) 878-8781; (905) 878-2725

Chudleigh's Apple Farm and Bakery
Hours: July-Oct, 10 am - 5 pm. The retail store and bakery is open Nov-June as well.
Cost: $5 per person, for orchard and entertainment; Families, $12; Three and under, free.
Directions: Take the 401 West to Highway 25, Exit 320. (Approximately 15 minutes west of Pearson International Airport). Go north on Highway 25. Chudleigh's Apple Farm is approximately 3 km north on the left side of the road.

Chudleigh's is synonymous with apples for Torontonians, many of whom have grown up with their apple pies or picked apples fresh in their orchards on a school trip. Check their website to see exactly when picking can start for all of their 17 varieties. The season generally starts in late August with Tydemans, Wealthys, and McIntoshes, then carries on with Spartans, Galas, and Cortlands, and ending only in late October with Granny Smiths. Kids as young as two can take part, picking apples from dwarf trees, though it might be hard coaxing them away from the entertainment area, with its twin hay towers, swinging bridge, and slides. This farm also has a corn maze and pony rides too.

Daytrips from Toronto

Springridge Farm

7256 Bell School Line
Milton, ON, L9T 2Y1
(905) 878-4908
www.springridgefarm.ca

| **Springridge Farm** |
| **Hours:** April-Christmas, 9 am - 5 pm. |
| **Cost:** Pony and wagon rides, $2. |
| **Directions:** Take Derry Rd. 5 km west of Hwy. 25. Turn right on Bell School Line, and go 1 km. |

Nestled high on the side of the Niagara Escarpment in Milton, this farm is as picturesque as it gets. Seasonal offerings peak in October when the Harvest festival and Halloween are celebrated with pumpkin pie, cider, apples, and caramel apples, a Boo Barn, barbecue foods, and a giant 5-acre corn maze. The rest of the year, kids enjoy haystack jumping, running through the corn maze, plying in the giant sandbox, or visiting the farm animals. The corn maze here is spectacular – about five acres of maze that's more than 1.5 metres tall. Pumpkin picking is a favourite.

Conservation Areas near the Escarpment

Conservation Halton
(905) 336-1158
www.conservationhalton.on.ca

Torontonians are fortunate to have the six parks of Conservation Halton at their doorstep. In these nature theme parks, find everything from rock climbing, hiking, mountain biking, skiing, and snowboarding, to a 15th century Iroquoian village. The parks also host a wide range of special events that promote a better understanding and appreciation of the natural world (check the website for special events throughout the year).

The six conservation areas form part of the Niagara Escarpment World Biosphere Reserve. Of Mount Nemo, Crawford Lake, Mountsberg, Kelso, Rattlesnake Point, and Hilton Falls, the first three are best for young kids, with lots of activities and attractions to stimulate little minds. The other three are beautiful spots for hiking, paddling, and communing with Nature, but suit families with older children accustomed to hiking.

Courtesy Ontario Tourism

Chapter Seven

Crawford Lake Conservation Area and Iroquoian Village

Milton, ON
(905) 854-0234
Trail guide: www.conservationhalton.on.ca/crawmap.pdf

Plan a hike or a cultural adventure at Crawford Lake, our favourite conservation area on the Escarpment. With a Visitor Centre and cafeteria, a reconstructed 15th century Iroquoian village, 16 km of hiking trails and an elevated boardwalk around the glacial lake, Crawford Lake is a day-long adventure for everyone.

> **Crawford Lake Conservation Area and Iroquoian Village**
>
> **Hours:** Daily, 10 am - 5 pm; Closed Christmas Day.
>
> **Cost:** Adults, $4; Children (5-14), $2.75; 4 and under, free.
>
> **Directions:** Crawford Lake Conservation Area is located at Steeles Avenue and Guelph Line, 5 km. south of Highway 401 and 15 km. north of the QEW.

For someone from the Prairies like myself, the Iroquois village was a revelation. Entering the compound through the high wooden stakes of the palisade, I was awestruck by the size of the longhouses here. Used to the teepees of the Cree and Blackfoot in Alberta, these evoked a completely different way of life, which is, of course, exactly what the interpreters will tell you about. Fires are usually burning in the Turtle Clan longhouse, which is lined with beds, furs, and other accoutrements of life. It's a cozy place despite its large size, which could easily accommodate several families.

A pleasant walk takes you around the lake where you can look for the area's rare species: Jefferson salamanders, wild ginseng, and burning bush among them. Picnic tables are available near the visitor centre and adjacent to the Iroquoian village and upper parking lot.

Special events at Crawford Lake revolve around the Iroquoian village and its native species teaching garden, and celebrate the changing seasons. There's a nighttime event in midsummer, Indian summer, season of the first frost, and the opening of the "Snowsnake" season, an Indian holiday game. Check the website for the programming schedule.

Daytrips from Toronto

Mountsberg Wildlife Centre

Milton, ON
(905) 854-2276
www.conservationhalton.on.ca/mountsberg

Mountsberg Wildlife Centre
Hours: Sat-Sun and holidays, 10 am - 4 pm.
Cost: Adults, $4; Child (5-14), $2.75; 4 and under, free.
Directions: From Highway 401 go south on Guelph Line. Turn west on Campbellville Road for 4 km and then go north on Milburough Line for 1 km to park entrance.

We weren't sure what to make of the hooded bird, perched on a man's gloved hand, as we arrived at the Mountsberg Wildlife Centre one fall afternoon. We had come for a fall fair expecting apple cider and pumpkin carving, but didn't know that Mountsberg had an important raptor centre as well. Here you can stroll the 1.6 km trail and get up close and personal with hawks and owls, housed in special enclosures. The effect of gazing into the eyes of these magnificent birds is nothing short of exhilarating. The raptor centre includes a treatment facility for injured birds, a video theatre, exhibit gallery, and an outdoor amphitheatre and flyway that frequently features presentations with live birds. Mountsberg is also known for its extensive wetlands, making it a birdwatcher's paradise.

The centre's newest attraction is the Cameron PlayBarn where kids can swing on a ripline, whoosh down a slide, or zip down a fireman's pole. The barn has elevated boardwalks, climbing ropes, a spiral climber, and tonnes of straw, as any self-respecting barn must!

To plan your visit to Mountsberg, check the web site for seasonal events. Past events have included star-gazing evenings, holiday wreath-making, bird-watching, and Bat Nights in August.

Kelso Conservation Area

Milton, ON
(905) 878-5011
www.conservationhalton.on.ca/kelso

Kelso Conservation Area
Hours: Spring/Fall: Opens daily 8:30 am; Summer: 8 am. Closing time varies seasonally; call ahead.
Cost: Adults, $3.75; Children (5–14), $2.50; 4 and under, free.
Directions: From Highway 401, take Highway 25 north to Campbellville Road; go west to Tremaine Road. Go south until you reach Kelso Road. Turn right to park entrance.

The Kelso Conservation Area is a mecca for outdoor enthusiasts, its rolling landscape dotted with picnic tables, bike trails, and ski runs (see Glen Eden, page 156). Indulge in a swim at a sandy beach, fish for trout in the lake, or join the mountain bikers on marked trails on the majestic Escarpment. You may even catch one of the bike races that are held here weekly from April through August. Paddling enthusiasts will enjoy renting a kayak, paddle boat, or canoe, and can brush up on their J-stroke with lessons offered here.

If you get caught in a downpour, you can take shelter in the Halton Regional Museum where exhibits relating to regional history are mounted regularly (but don't wait for a rainstorm to check it out!).

Chapter Seven

Glen Eden Ski & Snowboard Centre

Milton, ON
(905) 878-8455
www.gleneden.on.ca

So close to Toronto, and such a great place to learn to ski or snowboard. Glen Eden offers Kinder ski classes for four- and five-year-olds, snowboarding classes for teens and adults, as well as private lessons and daycare services.

Glen Eden also offers five-day Christmas and Spring Break ski camps, which include a one-hour lesson daily as well as an all-day pass to the hills. Three cafes all have super views onto the slopes, and an outdoor patio barbeque gets fired up on sunny winter days.

Hilton Falls Conservation Area

Milton, ON
(905) 854-0262
www.conservationhalton.on.ca/hilton

Hike the beautiful trail to Hilton Falls and reward yourself with a picnic right at the 10 metre high falls. In winter, the frozen falls make for a stunning photo-op, and cross-country trails are groomed and easy for beginners. In summer, you can fish for large-mouth bass in the reservoir or brook trout in 16 Mile Creek.

Glen Eden Ski & Snowboard Centre

Hours: Dec-March: Mon-Sat, 8:30 am - 10 pm; Sun, 8:30 am - 4:30 pm.

Cost: Adults: day pass, $27, evening pass $23; Juniors (5-14): day pass, $23, evening pass, $19; Children 4 and under, $6 for day and evening passes. For beginners, a $29.50 Discover Ski and Snowboard program is available weekday evenings. It includes a one-hour lesson, ski rentals, and an evening lift ticket. Group lessons also available from $215 for eight weeks.

Directions: From Highway 401, take Highway 25 north to Campbellville Road; go west to Tremaine Road. Go south until you reach Kelso Road. Turn right to park entrance.

Hilton Falls Conservation Area

Hours: Opens daily, 8:30 am. Closing time varies seasonally; call ahead.

Cost: Adults, $3.50; Children (5-14), $2.25; 4 and under, free.

Directions: From Hwy 401, take Hwy 25 north to Campbellville Road. Go west for 6 km (3.5 miles) to park entrance.

Daytrips from Toronto

Mount Nemo Conservation Area

Milton, ON
(905) 336-1158
www.conservationhalton.on.ca/nemo

Mt. Nemo is a hiker and rock climber's paradise, with the best cliff ecosystems on Ontario's Niagara Escarpment and easy access points onto the Bruce Trail. There is an old-growth forest with ancient cedars said to be one thousand-years-old along with large fern groves, scenic look-outs, and crevice caves you can see while hiking the escarpment trail. There are north and a south loop trails that pass through forest and along cliff edges. It's advised that kids be about eight years-old before tackling these hikes, each of which are about two km in length, and take about an hour to do.

Mount Nemo Conservation Area

Hours: Opens daily, 8:30 am. Closing time varies seasonally, please call ahead.

Cost: $5.00 per vehicle/self serve fee box.

Directions: Mount Nemo Conservation Area is located north of the QEW on Guelph Line, between Highway 5 and Britannia Road.

Rattlesnake Point Conservation Area

Milton, ON
(905) 878-1147
www.conservationhalton.on.ca/rattle

Rattlesnake is very popular with experienced rock climbers, whose ropes can be seen dangling above many of the trails. If you have tweens or teens who enjoy hiking *en famille*, take advantage of the breathtaking views from the cliffs here. But for parents with small children, the experience can be nerve-wracking. I won't do it again until my kids are at least eight, and even then I'm not quite sure I could stomach them hiking without holding my hand (which I'm sure they wouldn't do at that age!).

Rattlesnake Point Conservation Area

Hours: Opens daily, 8:30. Closing time varies seasonally; call ahead.

Cost: Adults (15-64), $3.50; Children (5-14), $2.25; 4 & under, free.

Directions: From Highway 401, take Highway 25 south to Steeles Avenue, west on Steeles to Appleby Line, south on Appleby for 3 km. From the QEW, take Appleby Line north; 1 km north of Derry Road on top of the escarpment.

Chapter Seven

Bronte Creek Provincial Park

1219 Burloak Drive
Oakville, ON, L6M 4J7
(905) 827-6911
www.ontarioparks.com/bron

Bronte Creek Provincial Park is a four-season oasis blessed with the cleanest river in southern Ontario, where Coho and Chinook salmon and rainbow trout spawn. This is also Toronto's closest provincial park, and the best remaining example of tall grass prairie vegetation in the region, thanks to the many devoted volunteers who contributed to its restoration.

Bronte Creek Provincial Park

Hours: Daily, 8 am - dusk.

Cost: Adults, $4; Kids (4-17), $2.

Directions: From the QEW West take Burloak exit #109 north.

But perhaps the neatest thing about Bronte Creek is that it combines a day in a park setting with a farm, so if some in your group want to get some exercise on the fitness trail, or fish for salmon and trout, so be it. The smallest members will enjoy the 1890s farm, where they can play in a hayloft and pet the animals.

There's also a huge, outdoor pool and fully-lit tennis courts for night games. Then in winter, a full slate of outdoor sports are possible, including outdoor skating, tobogganing, and cross-country skiing.

Events here are legion, perhaps the most popular being the Easter Eggstreme with its egg hunt for kids 1 to 10 years of age. Spring continues with sheep shearing, an art festival, a heritage wedding reenactment, country dancing, an ice cream social, an archeology day, a honey festival, and many more events held throughout the year. If you want a spontaneous weekend excursion, look no farther than Bronte Creek (and the Kortright Centre) for the best place to go and see something really worthwhile. And if you're on the park website, tell your kids about the neat interactive games located in the Kids in the Park section.

Chapter Eight

Visiting Niagara Falls

The Niagara River is a short river by most standards – only 50 kilometres (30 miles) long – but when it rushes over the crest of the Horseshoe Falls and plunges 52 metres (170 feet) with a thunderous roar, it makes for the greatest show on earth.

Niagara Falls is an awesome, spectacular sight, and the most visited of the Natural Wonders of the World by a long shot, attracting 15 million visitors annually. The Falls is the main attraction here, make no mistake, but one of the charms of the area is the great diversity of activities and attractions it offers. No matter what people tell you, a daytrip to Niagara Falls isn't enough time to really "do" the Falls and see everything this region has to offer.

Starting with the Falls themselves, there are numerous ways you can take the spectacle in. If watching 100,000 cubic feet rush over the Horseshoe Falls every second isn't enough for you, you can stand right next to it, fly over it, ride a boat up to it, view it from a tower, or walk behind it. And then you can watch it all over again on a giant IMAX screen!

Many daredevils have tried to conquer the falls. Blondin the Great, perhaps the best known, first tight-roped across the gorge in 1859 and repeated the feat numerous times. And in 1901, Annie Edson Taylor was the first person to go over the falls in a barrel. She survived, but many others who followed her in all sorts of contraptions, did not.

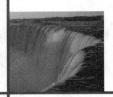

Chapter Eight

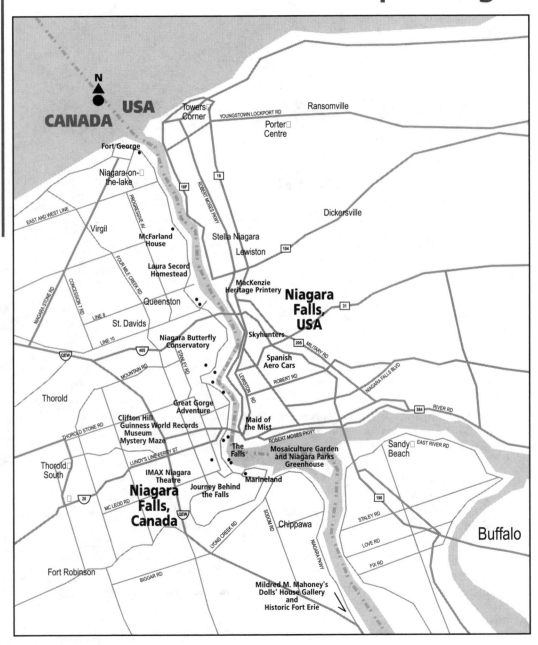

Visiting Niagara Falls

A much safer and more popular way to see the Falls is from below, on the historic *Maid of the Mist* boat tour, which has been taking visitors to the base of the Falls since 1846. Coming to Niagara Falls and not doing the *Maid of the Mist* would be like visiting Paris and not going up the Eiffel Tower. It's essential! But seeing the river up close in the downstream gorge is awesome as well. Take the Great Gorge Adventure, which runs along a boardwalk right next to the raging river, or glide high above the gorge and whirlpool in the Spanish Aero Cars. If you have a day to spend exploring, consider renting bikes and do the Niagara Parks Recreation Trail from Fort Erie at the U.S. border to Niagara-on-the-Lake, a charming village just a short drive away that hosts the annual Shaw theatre festival.

Spend at least one night here to see the illumination of the Falls and fireworks displays on Friday and Sunday nights throughout the summer. If you're lucky, you'll see the Falls capped with a rainbow as light refracts through the ever-present mist that rises from below – particularly appropriate for a town that makes so much money from its casino.

Orienting Yourself

The vast majority of the attractions can be found strung along the Niagara Parkway – a green belt that runs parallel to the Niagara River. Winston Churchill called the Parkway "the prettiest Sunday drive in the world," and on a sunny summer afternoon, it does seem the most peaceful and idyllic place on Earth.

Yet Niagara is also where some of the hardest fought battles in Canadian history took place. Memories of the War of 1812, which pitted the Americans against the British, are everywhere. This is where the very future of North America was decided, and visiting Fort Erie, perched right on the frontier, is the perfect place to time travel. Listen to a soldier dressed in period costume tell you what life was like for a soldier in the 1700s. Find out about the many battles between the British and Americans that were waged along this river. Take your pick of Historic Fort Erie or Fort George, and round out your visit with some eye-opening history.

Then, if you've always admired the scarlet coats of the dashing Canadian Mounties, make sure to "get your man" at the Falls. Look for the Mountie on photo duty near the Table Rock building at the edge of the Falls. They're happy to be in your photo (that's what they're there for, after all), and you'll have the best Niagara Falls souvenir going.

Chapter Eight

Get the Passes

To save both time and money, get either the Daytripper's pass or the two-day Niagara Falls Attractions Super Pass, which includes all of the attractions operated by the Niagara Parks Commission. Supplement it with tickets for the *Maid of the Mist*, and you'll have seen all the highlights of the region.

Super Passes include:
- Journey Behind the Falls
- Great Gorge Adventure
- Spanish Aerocars
- Butterfly Conservatory
- Niagara Glen Rim Tour
- Mosaiculture Garden
- McFarland House
- Laura Secord Homestead
- MacKenzie Printery
- Old Fort Erie
- 2 day pass on the People Mover Bus.
- Plus you get $1.00 off Coupon for Skyhunters and a free Medium Fries at Table Rock Fast Food restaurant.

The Super Pass is $39.95 for adults and $21.15 for children 6 to 12.

The daytrip package (Adults $24, Child 6 to 12 yrs. $12) includes tickets to Journey Behind the Falls, Butterfly Conservatory, Great Gorge Adventure, an all-day pass for the People Mover bus, and a $2.00 off admission coupon for the Niagara Spanish Aero Car.

Niagara Parks has livened up several of the attractions with the Park Pals – Blossom Butterfly, Buddy Bloom, Misty Yellow, and Misty Blue – sunny-faced mascots who'll take you for a walk through the park, while entertaining the kids with familiar songs. Shows take place daily throughout the summer at the Illumination Stage, just outside of the Victoria Park Restaurant across from the Falls. Shows run every Saturday and Sunday during the Spring Festival until June 30, and continue daily Wednesday through Sunday for July and August. Show times are 11:30am, and 1, 2:30, and 4 pm, and they're free.

Visiting Niagara Falls
Things to Do

Niagara River Recreational Trail
www.niagaraparks.com or
www.niagaraparks.com/index.html/DYNS/recreation_trail_area/PS/90/PN/1

If your family is at home on bikes or rollerblades, this scenic trail is unbeatable for both its scenery and the fascinating history it describes. Begun in 1986, this 56 km (35 mile) paved path runs parallel to the Niagara River from historic Fort Erie in the south to Fort George in the north, (just south of the beautiful little town of Niagara-on-the-Lake). Nine bridges close gaps over creeks, and a series of bronze markers along the way bring the history of this important corner of Canada to life. Helmets are encouraged for bikers of all ages despite the fact that there are few road crossings.

Since most people don't have a full day to devote to the trail, it can be divided into four sections, each one taking about one to two hours to pedal at a leisurely pace. From north to south they are: (1) Niagara-on-the-Lake to Queenston; (2) Queenston to the Spanish Aero Car; (3) Chippawa to Black Creek; (4) Black Creek to Fort Erie.

History buffs will enjoy traveling the same route that British regulars and local militia-men took as they hurried to protect their land from invaders. All their stories are here to be read on the monuments and plaques that dot the trail.

If you set out from Niagara-on-the-Lake, you'll meander past vineyards and bucolic farmland along one of the oldest roads in the province. Major-General Isaac Brock rode along it one cold, wet, October morning, as he galloped to his destiny. The path climbs up the steep escarpment to the Queenston Heights where a column stands marking Brock's final resting place.

Niagara Falls at sunrise

Courtesy Ontario Tourism

Chapter Eight

Maid of the Mist

5920 River Road
On Niagara Parkway, at the foot
of Clifton Hill
Niagara Falls, ON
(905) 358-5781
www.maidofthemist.com

Maid of the Mist

Hours: They change throughout the season, but boats begin departing around 9:30 am with the last boat departing as late as 8 pm in midsummer.

Cost: Adults, $12.25; Children 6-12, $7.50; Five and under, free.

Directions: You can find the elevators to the Maid of the Mist dock at the foot of Clifton Hill.

For 150 years, the *Maid of the Mist* has been Niagara's best-known attraction, and it's still the one thing that virtually all visitors plan to do. What could be more exhilarating than getting ferried up to the thundering water and coming back more than a little misty-eyed from the experience? The roar of the Falls as you approach, the sight of titanic sheets of cascading water, and the swirling waters that churn and toss around you – this is the stuff of a full-blown Hollywood epic. Seven minutes never seems long enough (the entire ride lasts about 20).

Some people think this should be called the *Maid of the Monsoon*, so wet do her passengers get. Large blue and yellow water capes are provided, but no matter how well you cover up, you're bound to get damp. But a little water doesn't deter the hundreds of thousands of people that take this ride every year. It's a celebrity magnet too; our friends claim to have been on the same boat as Tom Cruise and family, and you can see photos of the Royals, all of whom have been on it at one time or another. (Look for a photo of a distinctly sour-looking pair of royal princes on the wall).

Courtesy Ontario Tourism

Visiting Niagara Falls

Journey behind the Falls

Table Rock Complex
Km 0, Niagara Parkway
Niagara Falls, ON
1-877-NIA-PARK
www.niagaraparks.com

Journey behind the Falls

Hours: Depending on the month, this opens as early as 9:15 and shuts as late as 8 pm. Call ahead for current schedule.

Cost: Adults, $7; Children, $3.50; Five and under, free.

If your kids wonder what it's like to go behind a waterfall, then this is the best opportunity you'll ever have. The tunnels were dug in the 1940s, and have taken millions of people out to the edge of the Falls for a sight like no other. Standing beside the raging curtain of water, you get absolutely soaked – but you also get a great photo. Be sure to steal a look at the photo gallery of some of the daredevils that have braved the ferocious waters.

IMAX Niagara Theatre

6170 Fallsview Boulevard
Niagara Falls, ON, L2G 7T8
(905) 374-4629
www.imaxniagara.com

IMAX Niagara Theatre

Hours: Call for showtimes.

Cost: Adults (13 and older), $12; Kids 4-12, $6.50; Add a second feature for $5.85.

Over 10 million viewers have seen *Niagara: Miracles, Myths and Magic*, which despite all the hype in its name, really does deliver one of the more satisfying films in the entire IMAX genre. The film traces the 12,000-year-old history of the Falls, with awesome vistas stretching over the six-storey high screen, and describes how daredevils carried out their death-defying stunts. Then the film works its larger-than-life format to the max and takes you on a heart-pounding ride right over the Falls. I didn't take my four-year-old to see this (we don't need any more nightmare fodder right now!), but you're the best judge of what your kids can or cannot take.

Don't miss the Daredevil's Gallery that features Niagara's greatest collection of historical artifacts used by those who have challenged the mighty Falls. And you can do worse than to shop at the National Geographic store here for nifty science gadgets and educational games and toys.

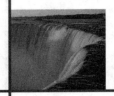

Chapter Eight

Great Gorge Adventure

Niagara Parkway
1-877-NIA-PARK
www.niagaraparks.com

> **Great Gorge Adventure**
>
> **Hours:** Dawn to dusk.
>
> **Cost:** Adults, $5.75; Child, $2.90.
>
> **Directions:** 4.1 km (2 miles) north of the Falls on the Niagara Parkway.

One way to experience the power of the mighty Niagara River rapids is to take a quick elevator trip down to this whitewater boardwalk on the river's edge. Here, downstream from the Falls, the gorge has been cut deep and narrow by millennia of rushing white water. Trillions of gallons are forced through this accelerating trough, resulting in one of the wildest stretches of whitewater in the world. A nature interpreter is on site from mid-May to September to help you discover a glimpse of the geology and natural history against the backdrop of the raging rapids. Free guided tours are offered at 11 am and 5 pm daily.

The gift shop is an attraction in itself with a downstairs "mineshaft" where you can put on a miner's hat and pan for gems.

Skyhunters

At Feather in the Glen giftshop
8 km/5 miles north of the Falls
Niagara Parkway
Niagara Falls, ON
1-877-NIA-PARK
www.niagaraparks.com

> **Skyhunters**
>
> **Hours:** Display July-Aug: Daily, 10 am - 4:30 pm. Flying Shows: 11:30, 1:30, and 3:30, weather permitting.
>
> **Cost:** Adults, $4; Children, $3; Under five, free.
>
> **Directions:** 8 km (5 miles) north of the Falls on the Niagara Parkway.

Falcons, hawks, owls, and eagles are Nature's ruthless and predatory air force. A new attraction at the Falls lets visitors get a close-up look at these turbo-charged flyers and demonstrates their power and agility in a daily show on the Parkway.

I can't do better than the brochure, which puts it this way: "They employ low-visibility camouflage, stealth technology wings, high-performance optics, and night vision. They're mission-capable of devastating ground attack as well as deadly air-to-air combat. And they've been doing it for thousands of years."

Visiting Niagara Falls

Spanish Aero Car

Niagara Parkway
5km/3 miles north of the Falls
Niagara Falls, ON
1-877-NIA-PARK
www.niagaraparks.com

> **Spanish Aero Car**
>
> **Hours:** Daily, 9 am - 5 pm.
>
> **Cost:** Adults, $6; Children, $3; Five and under, free.
>
> **Directions:** Located 5 km (3 miles) north of the Falls at People Mover stops #8 & #16.

Since 1916, the Spanish Aero Cars have been swinging their way across the Niagara Gorge with narry an incident (a sign proudly proclaims). And the day we visited, we had to wait an hour until high winds died down, before they'd let us on the ride. But we weren't arguing!

The cable car is suspended from six sturdy cables that stretch 1,800 feet across the Gorge, and offers a wonderful view of the Niagara Whirlpool, 210 feet below. Amazingly, one-third of the drainage of the North American continent passes through this area, 2,200 feet across at the Falls, churning into a 180-ft deep basin here at the whirlpool. The whirlpool is caused by an abrupt northeasterly turn in the gorge that forces the water through the gorge's narrowest channel, causing the pent-up water to churn menacingly. If you're lucky, you might see great vultures gliding on the thermals that rise up from the gorge.

The ride lasts only 10 minutes, but for anyone with an aversion to heights, that might be too long. Take my advice and do the much-tamer nature walk (otherwise known as the Great Gorge Adventure, page 166), alongside the river.

Mosaiculture Garden and Niagara Parks Greenhouse

Niagara Parkway
1/2 km south of the Falls
Niagara Falls, ON
1-877-NIA-PARK
www.niagaraparks.com

> **Mosaiculture Garden and Niagara Parks Greenhouse**
>
> **Hours:** Daily, 10 am - 5 pm; open weekend evenings during the summer.
>
> **Cost:** Adults, $4.50; Children, $2.50; 5 & under, free.
>
> **Directions:** Located next to the Niagara Parks Greenhouse, 1/2km south of the Falls.

Kids love topiary, even though they might not know what the word means. The clever people at Niagara Parks have created a new garden that celebrates topiary and teaches visitors how to make their own. Topiary are living sculptures – larger than life chia pets – made from hundreds of thousands of living plants. Kids go mad for these whimsical creations, and the Mosiaculture garden has bison, caribou and Inuit, geese, bears, a pony, and fun lollipop trees as well. It's also a delightful place to hear a concert on weekend evenings.

Chapter Eight

Kids can explore gardening at Sprout's Corner where painting flower pots, planting seeds, and face-painting is all part of the fun. While we were there, Niagara mascot Buddy Bloom showed up for a photo session with the kids. But the real stars are the topiaries themselves. Be tempted to create one of your own after watching an interactive demonstration. Wire frames are sold in the onsite horticultural giftshop.

If it rains while you're there, you can take shelter in the historic greenhouse where spring gets a colourful start with a hydrangea show, keeps it going with geraniums, annuals, and finally a begonia show in mid-September. Exotic birds fly about indoors, making merry and filling the air with the sounds of paradise. Max loved it here – in fact we were surprised and delighted by his enthusiasm for flowers. Afterwards he emptied our pockets of pennies and threw them in the fountain outside the entrance. When we asked him what he wished for, he replied, "A banana." All that touring makes a little guy hungry! Fortunately, Niagara Parks have put a million snack bars along the way, so you're never far from food at the Falls.

Niagara Butterfly Conservatory

Niagara Parkway
1-877-NIA-PARKS
www.niagaraparks.com

If your family includes infants or toddlers, make sure to visit the butterfly conservatory. Kids of all ages are enchanted by the 2,000 fluttering beauties that populate this glass structure, the largest of its kind in the world. Start your visit with the interpretive area next to the entrance.

Niagara Butterfly Conservatory

Hours: Daily, 9 am - 5 pm.

Cost: Adults, $8; Children, $4.50; 5 and under, free. Admission included in the one or two-day Niagara Parks pass.

Directions: Take the People Mover 9 km north toward the Floral Clock or drive along the Parkway.

Interactive games like 'Match the butterfly to its larvae' make learning about these graceful creatures fun. Another area debunks myths about butterflies, and describes the monarch's long migration from Canada to Mexico. A short video explains the basics about butterflies, and then it's time to see the real thing in the conservatory.

As warm and misty as a rainforest, butterflies of every shape and color alight everywhere, including on your clothes. One of the staff congratulates Max for having worn an orange t-shirt, an ideal color for attracting the delicate beauties. And it's true they seem to love landing on his shoulders – if only he'd stand still for a minute so I could take a picture!

Every morning at 9:30 am, staff open the glass doors of the nursery to let the new 'crop' of butterflies go. It's a wonderful photo opportunity, but don't worry if you miss it. The nursery is a busy place, and you're almost certain to see a butterfly emerging whenever you get here. Another spot for photos are the colourful plates covered with pieces of mango, orange, and starfruit that are placed around the conservatory. Max and I watched as a monarch unfurled its proboscis onto a thick slice of orange and had a long drink.

Visiting Niagara Falls

You can't help but walk through the gift shop as you exit, but it's a pleasure since this one is devoid of all of the tacky souvenirs found at most Falls shops. It's 'all butterflies, all the time' here, with butterfly garden seeds, ornaments for indoors and out, jewelry, t-shirts, and lovely umbrellas. We came away with butterflies to stick on our windows, which will be a great reminder of this trip when snow covers the ground and butterflies are nowhere to be seen.

You can combine a visit here with a horse-drawn carriage ride through the world-famous Niagara Parks Botanical Garden located next door. A café mainly for snacks is at the entrance.

Marineland

**7657 Portage Road
Niagara Falls
(905) 356-9565
www.marinelandcanada.com**

Marineland

Hours: May-Oct, 9 am - 6 pm. After ticket booths close, attractions stay open until nightfall. More restricted hours in spring and fall; call ahead.

Cost: Adults, $30.95; Children 5-9, $26.95; 4 and under, free.

Directions: From Toronto – Follow the QEW to Niagara and take the Mcleod Rd Exit. At the traffic lights at the end of Mcleod Rd, turn left and follow the Marineland signs.

For days after our visit to Marineland, Max couldn't stop talking about his encounter with a killer whale. Kids love the belugas, orcas, and seals that this popular Niagara Falls attraction has in abundance. Friendship Cove is the park's marine mammal petting zoo, where you line up alongside an enormous series of pools and interact with one of the beluga or killer whales. Line-ups can be very long here, and your time with the whale very short. So be sure to get the camera ready ahead of time. It's an oddly exhilarating experience, even though I imagine the novelty has worn off long ago for the whales.

Two shows are presented several times each day. An interesting indoor show in the aquarium focuses on animal behavior and features dolphins, seals, and sea lions. A madcap show at the outdoor King Waldorf Theatre features the park's killer whales in a pantomime worthy of Medieval Times. The story line is good versus evil – the evil Black Knight is out to wreak havoc and the brave orca must outwit him. Many boos, hisses, dunks, and some exciting trick riding later, the knight gives up and goes home to blow-dry his hair. Max enjoyed it so much we thought we'd see it again later (you can see the shows as many times as you'd like). In the end, we ran out of time. The park was a lot larger than we thought, and took us about five hours to cover, including seeing shows, feeding fish, and stops for snacks and lunch. Bring good walking shoes!

After the shows we wanted to try some of the rides (they're all included in the admission prices). Kids under eight will enjoy the smaller rides close to the front gates and theatres. They have names as dangerous-sounding as adult rides, such as Space Avenger, Hurricane Cove, and Sky Hawk, and in retrospect that may be what turned Max off. Because when he finally decided which one to try, he chose the leisurely pace of the Viking Boat Carousel over the rocket and ferris wheel.

Chapter Eight

Dolphins at Marineland

Courtesy Ontario Tourism

If you have older kids or teens, you'll want to head to the far reaches of the grounds after seeing the shows. That's where most of the rides (including the largest steel roller coaster in the world) spin their gears. We watched in amazement as people willingly boarded the mammoth contraption, which hurtled them around a series of artificial mountains and wooded valleys. From time to time the cars would completely disappear into the greenery and the screams would grow fainter until they re-emerged with a roar from the wilderness.

As much as my son loved patting the head of a killer whale at Friendship Cove, I have mixed feelings about this attraction. The day we visited, we saw animals in overcrowded conditions that appalled us. I also felt the animal feed sold to visitors is inappropriate. For instance, I was amazed to see that sugar corn pops are sold to feed to the bears! In the bear enclosure, we saw 16 bears in a space more suited to two or three. People threw the sugary treats down to them, and to no one's surprise, fights ensued. Fur flying and bears growling and gnashing teeth is not something my four-year-old son was prepared to deal with. We turned tail and left. But not before seeing the deer pen, a giant dirt-covered space devoid of greenery, entered via an ornate turreted gateway. About 500 deer are penned up here, bored silly most of the time, but ready to run right over you if you have food in your hands. Of course, the only way to animate these creatures is to feed them, so we did. Or tried to. For $1.50, you are given an ice cream cone full of pellets. And good luck trying to hold on to it. There was no way I was going to give Max the cone, as I barely survived getting head-butted by a couple of highly aggressive deer. In the car driving back to the hotel, Max referred to this as the 'scary deer castle' – and I couldn't agree more.

So go if you must, but stick close to the whale and dolphin shows and enjoy the rides, but please don't feed the animals!

Visiting Niagara Falls

Clifton Hill

Known for its tacky attractions and carnival sideshow vibe, Clifton Hill used to be the place to go for funhouses, haunted houses, and wax museums. Today it's undergone a facelift, and bears scant resemblance to its old tattered self, for better or worse. Some people wax nostalgic for the good old days of Clifton Hill, but having experienced a couple of the older, unimproved "attractions," I'm not sure what the appeal ever was.

First the good part: the new Clifton Hill is a great place for families to burn off a little steam, or take cover from the rain. There's a brand new indoor midway, a dinosaur mini-golf course, and a couple of decent attractions. There are also places to avoid, like the Funhouse (not fun!), Adventure Dome, and anything resembling a haunted house. Then again, we had a good time at Ripley's Believe It or Not and the Guinness World Book of Records.

Guinness World Records Museum

4943 Clifton Hill
Niagara Falls
(905) 356-2299
www.guinnessniagarafalls.com

If you hit some rainy weather while at the Falls, then a visit to this well laid-out museum is a winner, particularly if your kids are familiar with the Irish brewers' annual book of world records.

> **Guinness World Records Museum**
>
> **Hours:** Summer, 9 am - 2 am; call for hours the rest of the year.
>
> **Cost:** Adults, $9.25; Students $7.69, Children $5.59
>
> **Directions:** Midway up Clifton Hill, beside the Dinosaur mini-golf course.

This is where your kids access record-breaking facts and feats from the world of sports, music and entertainment, space, food, and the natural world. Who doesn't need to know that the oldest snowboarder is an 80-year-old Chinese immigrant to Canada? Or where the biggest pizza was made (Maine)? Or that Bulgarians eat more sugar than anyone else on the planet (6.26 lbs annually).

There are lots of things to gross kids out, like the eating contests involving baked beans, eels, kippers, raw eggs, and snails. And then there's that fellow from San Jose who holds the record for blowing bubbles (99) with a live tarantula nestled inside his mouth.

Kids love playing on the biggest pinball machine in the world and posing for photos in a chair large enough to seat Robert Wadlow, the world's tallest man. There are neat sections on weird weather facts and space. If you want to get in the Book, you got to have what it takes, and after checking out all the records, we decided our favourite record holder is Ashrita Furman of New York. He's held more than 60 records over the years, including backwards unicycling, distance pogo-sticking, brick carrying, and hopscotch.

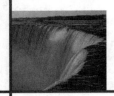

Chapter Eight

MacKenzie Heritage Printery

Off the Parkway
1 Queenston Street
Queenston, ON
(905) 262-5676
www.mackenzieprintery.ca

MacKenzie Heritage Printery

Hours: June 1-22: Daily, 10 am - 4 pm;
June 23-Labour Day: Daily, 10 am - 5 pm;
Sept 5-Oct 31: hours to be determined;
call ahead.

Cost: Adults, $2.50; Children, $1.50;
Under 6, free.

Directions: Follow Niagara Parkway
13.3 km north to Queenston.

Max my son has a hand printed poster on his bedroom wall that asserts he'll not marry, nor haunt alehouses, not play dice or cards for seven years while working for William Lyon MacKenzie. Not a problem since Max is only 4, and MacKenzie's been dead for 150 years. It's actually a copy of a document that young printing apprentices had to sign before starting their careers in Upper Canada in the early 19th century. It was printed at the MacKenzie Heritage Printery in Queenston where William Lyon MacKenzie lived prior to going to Toronto and starting his second career – that of a political reformer. After being elected mayor of Toronto, MacKenzie led a revolt against the Family Compact – a notorious group of families who controlled the colony. It's worth stopping in this charming little village to see where King began publishing his influential paper, the *Colonial Advocate*. And the history of printing in Canada is well-represented here with a collection of presses showing the evolution of the printed word in this country. We got a kick out of seeing our guide operate several of them, the most modern being a linotype machine that was used until 1976 to print the daily St.Catherine Standard. The museum's most valuable press by far is the Louis Roy, dating from 1760, of which there are only eight left in the world.

Visiting Niagara Falls

Laura Secord Homestead

29 Queenston Street
Queenston, ON
(905) 371-0254; 1-800-NIA-PARK
www.niagaraparks.com

Laura Secord Homestead
Hours: May-Oct.
Cost: Adults $2.50, Children $1.50, Under 5 years are free
Directions: Follow Niagara Parkway north 13 km to Queenston.

Courtesy Ontario Tourism

Laura Secord in front of house

We adored our visit to the charming little village of Queenston, right under the monument to 1812 hero Sir Isaac Brock. Here you'll find the restored home where Canadian heroine Laura Secord and her family lived from 1803-1835. Kids love to hear the stirring story of how Secord overheard American officers discussing plans to attack a British garrison nearby and then made a heroic 32 km (20 mile) trek to warn the British soldiers of the impending attack. The house itself has some interesting objects too. Ask one of the costumed interpreters to show you the curling iron and the beggar's bed, and have a close look at the painting of the Death of General Wolfe. It's a who's who of 19th century Upper Canadian society.

McFarland House

15927 Niagara Parkway
Niagara-on-the-Lake, ON
(905) 371-0254; 1-877-NIA-PARK
www.niagaraparks.com

McFarland House
Hours: 10 am - 5 pm daily.
Cost: Adults, $2.50; Children, $1.50.
Directions: Follow Niagara Parkway north 21.6 km.

Fresh baked scones waft out of this 1800 Georgian home, tucked amid orchards and vineyards at the southern end of Niagara-on-the-Lake. During the War of 1812, the formidable home was used as a hospital by both the British and the Americans, and a British gun emplacement, located on the property, protected the river. We love to stroll through the period herb garden, sample home baking with a glass of local wine on their patio. Light lunches and ice cream are also available for take-out to be enjoyed in the park, or along the adjacent Niagara River Recreation Trail. Tours are available through the summer months, and for a real taste of life circa 1840, combine a visit here with one to Fort George, just up the parkway from here.

Chapter Eight

Fort George

Queen's Parade
Niagara-on-the-Lake, ON
(905) 468-4257
www.niagara.com/~parkscan

Built over 200 years ago by the British Army, Fort George has a colourful past kids love to explore. As the main head-quarters of the British Army in southern Ontario, it was the command and control center for Isaac Brock during the War of 1812, a rallying point for Upper Canadian Militia and Six Nations Warriors, a depot for the Provincial Marine, and the scene of bloody battles during the War of 1812, as Canadians from diverse backgrounds banded together to defeat several American invasions.

> **Fort George**
>
> **Hours:** April 1-Oct 31: Daily, 10 am - 5 pm.
>
> **Cost:** Adults, $6; Children 6 and up, $4; Under 6, free.
>
> **Directions:** On the outskirts of Niagara-on-the-Lake, on the Niagara Parkway.

For more thrills, check out the Ghost Tours of Niagara offered at Fort George from May through September. They're at 8:30 pm Sundays in May and June, and on Sunday, Mon, Wed, and Thurs. in July and August. Tickets are $10 for adults and $5 for kids under 13.

Mildred M. Mahoney's Dolls' House Gallery

657 Niagara Blvd
Fort Erie, ON L2A 3H9
(905) 871-5833
www.mahoneydollhouse.com

Fans of antique dollhouses make pilgrimages to Fort Erie to see the amazing collection of 140 dollhouses amassed by Mildred Mahoney, said to be the largest in the world. The dollhouses date from 1780 to 1980 and include rare master-pieces from England, Europe, the U.S., and Canada, as well as a fascinating example of a Japanese palace. Housed in a historic home with its own interesting history, it's a rare

> **Mildred M. Mahoney's Dolls' House Gallery**
>
> **Hours:** May 1-Dec 31: Daily, 10 am - 4 pm; Jan 1-April 30: Call for an appointment.
>
> **Cost:** Adults, $5; Students, $3; 6 and under, free.
>
> **Directions:** 3.2 km (2 miles) north of the Peace Bridge, south of the Falls.

treat to be able to surprise young girls with eye candy like this, and enjoy the spectacle just as much yourself.

Highlights include the Marygate House, a striking five-storey English manor house with servants quarters, nursery, sewing room, and men's and ladies' drawing rooms. Another is the Japanese palace and its collection of Hina Matsuri dolls, which Japanese girls proudly display each March 3rd. Get your kids to pick a favourite dollhouse and draw a picture of it afterwards. It's grist for the mill for days afterward.

Visiting Niagara Falls

A note about Bertie House, the grand historic home that houses the collection. One of the more intriguing historical facts about Fort Erie was its role in smuggling escaped slaves into Canada as part of the Underground Railroad. Bertie House is said to have a tunnel that aided in their escape, though to this day, the tunnel has not been found. The house was built in 1835 in the Greek Revival style, boasts 12-foot ceilings and a 22-foot curving staircase, and in 1866 hosted King Edward VII when he was Prince of Wales.

Historic Fort Erie

350 Lakeshore Road
Fort Erie, ON
(905) 371-0254; 1-877-NIA-PARK
www.niagaraparks.com

Historic Fort Erie

Hours: Late-April-Oct:
Daily, 10 am - 6 pm.

Cost: Adults, $6.50; Kids, $4;
Under 5, free.

Directions: Fort Erie is about
one mile south of the
Peace Bridge. Take the
Central Avenue exit of the
Queen Elizabeth Way.

If your family likes forts and living history, you can't do much better than a visit to Fort Erie. This fort has an amazing situation, right on the banks of the Niagara River with Buffalo just across the water. It's easy to imagine the British forces rebuffing an American invasion, and today costumed interpreters do an excellent job of transporting you back in time. Step inside Fort Erie as uniformed British, Canadian, and Iroquois soldiers go about their business preparing to defend this outpost against yet another American invasion (they were nothing if not persistent!).

The original fort was built in 1763 right at the water's edge, but after winter storms and ice ravaged it repeatedly, the British decided to rebuild it on higher ground. When the United States declared war on Great Britain on June 18, 1812, the fort was still unfinished.

To this day, Fort Erie was the bloodiest battlefield in Canadian history. In August, the fort puts on a living history weekend when you can relive the thrill of an 1814 battle. Experience period camps, musket and artillery demonstrations and drills, and a glimpse of soldiers and their families on campaign.

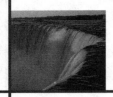

Chapter Eight

Where to Stay

Niagara Falls is jammed with hotels, from motels to luxurious suites. If this is a once-in-a-lifetime trip, I'd suggest a little splurge on a hotel along the Fallsview strip. These have unparalleled views looking right out over the Falls, and are worth the extra cost, especially in summer, when fireworks explode over the Falls on Friday and Sunday nights. Our kids needed to be in bed by the 10 o'clock start time, so it was a special treat to watch the spectacle in our pajamas from our hotel room window. Another treat is the funicular that takes visitors up and down the Fallsview hill to the Table Rock building and the Parkway. You can access the People Mover buses here to go farther afield or just walk to attractions like the Mosaiculture Garden and Journey behind the Falls.

Niagara Falls offers so many dining options, I can't really recommend one over another. We ate well the entire time we were here, at Clifton Hill fast food joints, at a Fallsview family breakfast spot, and in some of the Niagara Parks snack bars and restaurants located at the attractions. There's such variety that diners can find almost any cuisine they have a yen for. If you don't have a view from your hotel window, consider having a memorable breakfast or dinner in the Minolta Tower, also located in Fallsview. Prices are reasonable, the kids can have Shirley Temples, and you'll never tire of the view from up here!

Appendix

A Kid's Calendar of Festivals and Events

January

Cullen Gardens Festival of Lights

Runs from late November to the first week of January. (905) 686-1600 or 1-800-461-1821; www.cullengardens.com.

February

Winterfest

A festival devoted to having fun in the winter, you can catch this at either Nathan Phillips Square in Toronto or at Mel Lastman Square in North York. (416) 395-0490; www.city.toronto.on.ca/winterfest. This is a Top Ten Favourite Event; see page 32 for more.

International Automobile Show

The car show that brings thousands to see the new cars, gawk at hummers, and live out their fantasies of driving in luxury. A wonderland for boys of all ages. (905) 940-2800; www.autoshow.ca.

Chinese New Year's

Every year the Chinese Cultural Centre has a big New Year's Party, with lots of family appeal. (416) 292-9293; www.cccgt.org.

March

Sugarbush Maple Syrup Festival

In rural Ontario, Quebec and parts of Eastern Canada, sugaring off is still an important part of rural life in the springtime. Kids in Toronto have a unique opportunity to view a working sugar bush and experience both modern and historical methods of maple syrup production at two locations – either Bruce Mill or Kortright Centre. Tour the sugar bush, take a horse-drawn wagon ride (weekends), and enjoy pancakes with real maple syrup. (905) 832-2289; www.kortright.org. This is a Top Ten Favourite Event; see page 35 for more.

St. Patrick's Day parade

This annual event usually begins at U of T's Varsity Stadium, goes down Bloor Street, right on University, and past Queen's Park, ending at Queen Street and University Avenue. Thirty floats, over a dozen marching bands, leprechauns and an Irish Wolfhound parade make this event a big draw for kids. (416) 487-1566.

April

Beaches Easter Parade

Time was when everyone turned out for the parade decked out in new clothes and bonnets. Today, the Lions Club and the Beaches neighbourhood carries on the tradition, though in a more pagan and free-wheeling fashion! Come to see funny vehicles, costumed volunteers, marching bands, mini-floats, lots of balloons, and the Easter Bunny parade down Queen Street East. Easter Sunday at 2 pm, on Queen Street East between Victoria Park and Woodbine.

Easter Eggstreme at Bronte Creek Provincial Park

Spring is in the air! Chicks, lambs, bunnies, and piglets! Egg, eggs, and more eggs! Games, activities, and prizes. Visit the Easter Bunny! Egg hunt for kids 1-10. (905) 827-6911; www.ontarioparks.com/bron-events.

Sprockets Toronto International Film Festival for Children

Come see the best in family films from around the world and the festival's one-of-a-kind film-craft workshops. Held over two weekends, the fest's award-winning live-action and animated cinema will inspire, enthrall, and entertain kids and adults alike in a friendly, festive atmosphere. (416) 967-7371; www.e.bell.ca/filmfest/sprockets. This is a Top Ten Favourite Event; see page 36 for more.

Four Winds Kite Festival

Real pros compete for two days at this festival, but amateurs are welcome too, so don't shy away! Kids can build their own kites for a small fee and learn all about the art of flying a kite. Usually held the last weekend of April or the first weekend of May; check the website to find out the dates. Held at the Kortright Centre. (905) 832-2289; www.kortright.org.

May

Mother's Day

There are dozens of themed events going on this weekend at Toronto area-attractions. Check the listings for Bronte Creek Provincial Park, Kortright Centre, and Crawford Lake Conservation Area. Call and find out what they've got planned.

Living Rivers Festival

This is a relatively new family eco-festival celebrating Toronto's Don River. There are environmental art workshops, a procession and water ceremony, eco arts and crafts, theatre and a labyrinth, and four stages showcasing some of Toronto's finest music and theatre talent. Plus an eco-market featuring Toronto's green businesses. (416) 469-2977; www.festiveearth.com

Black Creek Pioneer Village

A 19th century spring fair is recreated with sheep-shearing, side-saddle riding, family fun, and entertainment. (416) 736-1733; www.trca.on.ca/bcpv.

Appendix

Milk International Children's Festival
Toronto's original kid's festival features international theatre, music and dance, with young performers, workshops, and creative crafts too. Plus a unique French program of events. (416) 973-4000; www.harbourfront.on.ca/milk. This is a Top Ten Favourite Event; see page 30 for more.

Victoria Day at Fort York
See what it was like to be a soldier before the birth of Queen Victoria. Families will enjoy tours; kids will practice musket drill and watch hearth cooking in the historic kitchen. (416) 392-6907; www.city.toronto.on.ca/culture/fortyork.htm.

Victoria Day Fireworks at Cullen Gardens
It's an Ontario tradition that is carried on across the province on Victoria Day. Those old favourites, burning schoolhouses, explode in the air to everyone's delight, reminding us all that school's out in a matter of weeks! (905) 668-6606, 1-800-461-1821; www.cullengardens.com.

June

Father's Day
There are dozens of events going on to celebrate Dear Old Dad. Check out these attractions' websites or phone to find out what's on: Bronte Creek Provincial Park, Crawford Lake Conservation Area, and Centreville Amusement Park lay on special events, as do others.

Through the Garden Gate
The Civic Garden centre's annual tour of impressive gardens allows horticultural voyeurs to enjoy seeing gardens in a different part of the city each year. A master gardener is stationed at each of the 15 locations, and drink, food, and washrooms are located in a central spot. The third weekend in June, $25 per person. (416) 397-1340; www.civicgardencentre.org.

Buskerfest
Busking is the grand old tradition of performing on the street and then passing a hat. You never know what's in store when you stop and watch one of these talented street performers juggle, do magic tricks, eat fire, dance, and generally make merry! Buskers come from as far away as Australia for this annual event in support of people living with epilepsy. www.torontobuskerfest.com. (416) 964-9095.

Mississauga International Children's Festival
This festival is a tremendous hit with kids in Mississauga, but also Toronto and other districts. It's got great performers, loads of interesting hands-on activities, and isn't half as crowded as Harbourfront's Milk Festival can be. (905) 897-8955; www.kidsfestival.org. This is a Top Ten Favourite Event; see page 33 for more.

Caravan
Be a world traveler without leaving Toronto! During the nine days of Caravan, you can pick up a passport, visit over 30 different pavilions created by many of Toronto's ethnic groups, and taste native food, enjoy native dances, or buy native crafts from that country. (416) 977-0466.

Toronto International Dragon Boat Race
One of the great draws of Toronto's dragon boat race is the location on the Toronto Islands. Pack a picnic or find great Asian food onsite, and spend a lazy summer day watching these beautiful boats zip by. (416) 598-8945; www.torontodragonboat.com.

Spadina House Strawberry Fair
Welcome summer with a great family afternoon on the lovely lawns of the Spadina estate. Enjoy children's games, musical performances, and special exhibits. Lots of tasty strawberry treats for sale. Admission $2. (416) 392-6910; www.city.toronto.on.ca/culture/spadina.

July

Kidsummer
This program of activities fro kids features daily events from the beginning of July to the end of August. Check www.todaysparent.com/kidsummer for details, or check the July issue of *Today's Parent* magazine. Concerts, factory tours, games, and activities are held in venues all over the city. This is a Top Ten Favourite Event; see page 31 for more.

Cliffhanger Productions
The company stages acclaimed children's theatre every day (except Monday) throughout the summer at The Guild Inn in Scarborough and at Earl Bales Park in North Toronto. (416) 264-5869; www.cliffhangerproductions.ca. See page 137 for more details.

Civil War Re-enactment (Black Creek Pioneer Village)
This is an exploration of Canada's involvement in the American Civil War (1861 to 1865). Visitors can watch a full-scale battle, street skirmishes, and artillery, medical and civilian talks, fashion shows, and much more. (416) 736-1733; www.trca.on.ca/bcpv.

Celebrate Toronto Street Festival
Each July, the longest street in the world comes alive with one of the greatest street festivals on the continent! Five festival sites along Yonge Street feature more than 700 performances and 500,000 square feet of fantastic entertainment. This fabulous FREE festival is one of the hottest gatherings of entertainment talent in the country! (416) 395-0490; www.city.toronto.on.ca/special_events.

Outdoor Art Exhibition
Start your art collections here! This, the largest outdoor exhibit in the world, takes place in Nathan Phillips Square. Over 500 Artists participate annually in 14 categories. Original works in photography, painting, sculpture, ceramics, glass, fibre, jewelery, watercolour, wood, and metal. (416) 408-2754; www.torontooutdoorart.org.

Ontario Renaissance Festival
This quirky and enchanting festival takes place weekends from mid-July to Labour Day. See knights jousting, meet the court of Elizabeth I, immerse yourself in an age of chivalry and romance as you explore a 16th century English village set in 20 acres of woods and meadows. Free pony rides and a children's area makes this fun for all. This is a Top Ten Favourite Event; see page 34 for more. 1-800-734-3779; www.rennfest.com.

Toronto International Carnival
The largest carnival after Rio's, and the biggest cultural celebration in North America, this event brings more people to Toronto than any other. In fact, if you're planning to come for this, make sure to book a hotel room well in advance. A giant parade with incredible costumes — some 40 feet wide — is the highlight of this festival. But there are other events around town including a harbour cruise and a cultural festival held on Olympic island. (416) 465-4884; www.toronto.com/caribana.

Calendar of Festivals and Events

Molson Indy Car Racing
Summer isn't in full swing at our house until we've heard the sounds of the Indy cars echoing up from the lakeshore. Come see what the fuss is all about on a track that runs down Lakeshore Boulevard and through Exhibition Place. (416) 872-INDY.

August

Simcoe Day at Historic Fort York
The first Monday in August is a public holiday honouring Lord Simcoe, Ontario's first Governor. Musketry and artillery demonstrations, drills for kids, historic cooking, and guided tours. 100 Garrison Road, off Strachan; (416) 392-6907. www.city.toronto.on.ca/culture/fortyork.htm.

Canadian National Exhibition
Better known as The Ex or the CNE, this ten-day fair and midway is a tradition with many Toronto families. There are kids rides, live performances by international artists, and loads of displays indoors for those rainy days. Fireworks nightly too, and a spectacular air show is all part of the fun. End of August through Labour Day weekend. (416) 393-6000; www.TheEx.com. This is a Top Ten Favourite Event; see page 28 for more.

Canadian International Air Show
This is always part of The Ex, and takes place Labour Day weekend. Start time each day is 1 pm. You can count on the Canadian aerobatic squad, the Snowbirds, plus other military aircraft like CF16's, F18's, and stunt planes to take part. (416) 263-3650; www.cias.org.

September

Word on the Street
Word on the Street is a one-day literary festival that caters to all sizes of readers, with booths and tents set up all along Queen Street West from University Avenue to Spadina. There's a great kids' area called Kidstreet, featuring popular children's authors, entertainers, and activities in three areas: the TVO Kids stage, the Canadian Heritage reading tent, and the Bell Celebrity reading tent. There'll be readings, family hands-on activities, entertainment, and free giveaways throughout the day. The Bell Celebrity Reading Tent will be visited by much loved mascots and storybook characters. The complete guide is published in the Toronto Star the day before the festival, which is held the last Sunday in September. (416) 504-7241; www.thewordonthestreet.ca/toronto.

KiteFest
KiteFest is held annually in September at Milliken Park at the corner of McCowan and Steeles in Toronto's east end. Admission is free. See all kinds of kites, all shapes and sizes, from across North American, Europe, and Asia. Lots of games, entertainment, multicultural food and performances, stunt kite demo, kite contests, children activities. (905) 305-0308. www.kites.org/tkf/indexie.htm.

Canadian Pet Expo
Speak with cat and dog breeders, find out about alternative pets (lizards or hedgehogs anyone??), check out the reptile theatre and the bird showcase. There are agility and skills competitions, a petting zoo, and a marketplace of pet products and services. A family pass gets six of you in for 22 bucks. Held in the Queen Elizabeth building at Exhibition Place. (905) 642-2422; www.canadianpetexpo.com.

Pioneer Festival
Black Creek Pioneer Village's annual event is a crowd-pleaser with its tasty foods, great crafts, farmer's market, and old-fashioned entertainment. Don't miss the Mennonite Quilt auction at 12 noon. Bidding is fast and furious. (416) 736-1733; www.trca.on.ca/bcpv.

October

York-Durham Heritage Railway
Fall Colour train rides on this lovely train trip through the Oak Ridges Moraine. www.ydhr.org. (905) 852-3696.

Brooks Farms Family Fun
Visitors to the farm can enjoy train rides, the farm's famous pumpkin cannons, farm animals, the haunted hayride, the boo barn, ziplines, the corn maze, the straw jump, pony rides and the latest craze – pig races! (905) 473-3920; www.brooksfarms.com.

Magic Hill Farms
Haunted Adventure is a Halloween fright night spectacular featuring four different attractions animated by 118 scary live monsters. The show is produced by special effects professionals and film set designers so it is very effective and will scare the pants off most people. Not for kids under 8 or pregnant women. (905) 640-2347; www.magichill.com.

South Simcoe Heritage Railway
Take a Fall Colour train ride on a (toot, toot!) steam train from Tottenham to Beeton. (905) 936-5815; www.steamtrain.com.

November

Royal Agricultural Winter Fair
Don't miss the fun at the Royal, the world's largest agricultural fair. Something for everyone, including food displays, agricultural product competition, animal auctions and sales, equestrian competitions, dog shows, showcase of animal breeds and competitions, antique display and sale, garden displays and more. (416) 263-3400; www.royalfair.org. This is a Top Ten Favourite Event; see page 29 for more.

Canadian Aboriginal Festival
Held annually the last weekend in November at the Skydome, this is a national gathering of First Nations peoples from across the country. It's also the largest multi-disciplinary aboriginal arts event in North America. Main events include a Pow-wow featuring up to 1,000 dancers, aboriginal music awards, a huge marketplace, a lacrosse skills competition and fine art show, and an education day, when elders, teachers, and traditional healers will share their knowledge with the public. 519-751-0040; www.canab.com.

Cullen Gardens Festival of Lights
Every year the miniature village is decorated with 10,000 lights and a whole pageant is displayed throughout the tiny town. (905) 686-1600; www.cullengardens.com.

A Victorian Christmas at Black Creek Pioneer Village
Step back in time to enjoy a Victorian country Christmas. Enjoy festive demonstrations, hands-on activities, and homemade decorations and tasty treats. (416) 736-1733; www.trca.on.ca/bcpv.

Appendix

Santa Claus Parade
For almost one hundred years, Torontonians have been enjoying the Santa Claus Parade. It starts at Bloor and Christie streets, and ends up on Front neat St. Lawrence Market. 416-249-7833; www.thesantaclaus-parade.org. This is a Top Ten Favourite Event; see page 31 for more.

Swedish Christmas Fair at Harborfront
This is a Christmas tradition that's just celebrated its 25th anniversary. Join St. Lucia for a colourful and tasty celebration of a Scandinavian-style Christmas. Call Harbourfront. (416) 973-3000; www.harbourfront.on.ca.

December

Toronto Christmas Market
Come down to Nathan Phillips Square for a skate, and enjoy an old world Christmas market, like those in Austria and Germany. Hot chocolate, cider, and other foods are available as well as traditional Christmas crafts from Europe. From 11 am to 8 pm from the first Advent weekend for two weeks. (416) 338-0338; www.torontochrist-masmarket.com.

Mennonite Christmas Festival at Harbourfront
A great place to get gifts that support artisans and their families in the developing world. (416) 973-3000; www.harbourfront.on.ca.

Christmas by Lamplight at Black Creek Pioneer Village
Follow the magical glow of 200 lamps and lanterns as villagers light the way to an enchanted evening of food drink and merriment, circa 1860s Ontario. But be sure to book ahead for one of the three Christmas dinners; they sell out quickly every year. (416) 736-1733; www.trca.on.ca/bcpv.

Cavalcade of Lights
An annual tradition in Toronto that kicks off the holiday season with the official lighting of the giant Christmas tree in Nathan Phillips Square. The entertainment continues through the evening with live music, a spectacular ice show featuring figure skating stars, a fireworks show, and closes with a raucous late night skating party from 9:30 to 11 pm. (416) 338-0338; www.city.toronto.on.ca/special_events/.

Kensington Market Festival of Lights
Always held on December 21st starting at dusk, the festival takes place on the streets of the market, celebrating Christian, Jewish and pagan winter festivals, with music, drama, and pageantry. Climaxes in the local park with the burning of an effigy representing the Old Year. www.kensingtonmarket.org

First Night Toronto
For an alcohol-free, family-oriented New Year's celebration, First Night is hard to beat. At Skydome. (416) 362-3692; www.firstnight-toronto.com. This is a Top Ten Favourite Event; see page 35 for more.

INDEX

Index

Index

Index

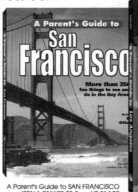
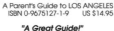

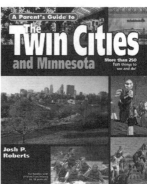